KT-368-723

A LANGUAGE-TEACHING BIBLIOGRAPHY

Second Edition

A Language-Teaching Bibliography

COMPILED AND EDITED BY
The Centre for Information on Language Teaching

AND

The English-Teaching Information Centre of the British Council

Second Edition

CAMBRIDGE · *at the University Press 1972*

Published by the Syndics of the Cambridge University Press
Bentley House, 200 Euston Road, London NW1 2DB
American Branch: 32 East 57th Street, New York, N.Y. 10022

Library of Congress Catalogue Card Number: 76–152633

ISBN: 0 521 08183 1

Printed in Great Britain
at the University Printing House, Cambridge
(Brooke Crutchley, University Printer)

Contents

CONTENTS

Introduction

This book is a completely revised and somewhat expanded version of the first (1968) edition of *A Language-Teaching Bibliography*. The aim remains the same, to provide an up-to-date guide to authoritative and useful works on the theory and practice of foreign-language teaching within a reasonable compass. The volume is designed to help language teachers, course and textbook writers, educational administrators, research workers and librarians. As in the first edition, class teaching materials have been intentionally excluded. It is not thought practicable to attempt to include them in the same volume, since six languages are involved.

The plan of the book now includes eight main divisions. *Language* (Section 1) covers aspects of linguistics which are relevant to the teaching of any language and the relationship of language to society. *Language Teaching* (Section 2) covers the complementary contributions of psychology, general educational method and teaching techniques, again relevant to the teaching of any language. Sections 3–8 cover *English for speakers of other languages*, *French*, *German*, *Italian*, *Russian* and *Spanish*. Listed under each language will be found reference and resource materials such as linguistic studies, grammars and dictionaries, and also books concerned with the methodology of teaching each particular language.

As in the first edition, this arrangement is designed to stress the community of interest among all language teachers, while enabling them to refer easily to particular languages which concern them as specialists. The languages covered are those most widely taught in English-speaking countries and English, which has been included because of its importance overseas as a second language and as a language taught to immigrants. This bibliography does not, however, cover the teaching of English as a mother tongue.

While books published in a number of different countries have been included, most of those listed are written in English. Availability was a factor in making selections, so that books out of print or difficult to obtain have normally been omitted. Periodical articles have not been listed, but detailed references and summaries of those covering the same field which have appeared in recent years will be found in *Language Teaching Abstracts*,* which also has a regular bibliographical supplement listing and annotating new books as they appear, thus keeping this bibliography up to date.

The selection of books for such a bibliography is not easy, and inevitably

* Published by Cambridge University Press, quarterly, 1967– .

informed readers will find omissions or question some inclusions. As in the first edition, selections have been made by a number of different hands; as far as possible a common policy has been followed but slightly different criteria may have been applied to the different language sections because of the nature of the published material available.

In preparing this new edition the annotations under many of the original entries have been revised and shortened. Care has also been taken to refer to the latest editions available. Altogether 288 new entries have been included and 163 old ones removed, the total number of books listed now being 837 as against 712. The problem of adequately classifying books dealing with more than one subject has been tackled by providing many cross-references. Full attention has been paid to suggestions and criticisms received from users of the first edition and a number of errors and inconsistencies have now been rectified. Comments by users of this edition will be welcomed and should be addressed to the Centre for Information on Language Teaching.

The planning, editing and bibliographical research required for this edition have been the work of Dr Rosi M. Klaar, whose services were retained by the Centre for Information on Language Teaching specially for this task.

SECTION 1

Language

LANGUAGE AND SOCIETY

1 **Balkan, Lewis**
Les effets du bilinguisme français–anglais sur les aptitudes intellectuelles. Études Linguistiques, 3. Brussels, AIMAV, 1970. 131 pp. tables, diagrs. bibliog.
Study of the relationship between educational aptitude and bilingualism carried out in Switzerland. Includes a comprehensive survey of previous work and a discussion of the nature of bilingualism and its acquisition by children.

2 **Bollnow, Otto Friedrich**
Sprache und Erziehung. Urban Bücher. Die Wissenschaftliche Taschenbuchreihe, 100. Stuttgart, W. Kohlhammer, 1966. 209 pp.
General philosophical examination of the function of speech in moulding the human being and its consequences for education. Education in language is seen as concerned not only with language training but with the whole man by developing powers of thought, discrimination and expression.

3 **Brandis, Walter, and Dorothy Henderson**
Social class, language and communication. Primary Socialisation, Language and Education, 1. London, Routledge & Kegan Paul, 1970. viii, 153 pp. tables, diagrs. bibliogs.
Contains two research reports: 1. social class differences in form-class usage among five-year-old children, which examines the different effects of parental social class (among other factors) on aspects of children's speech. 2. social class differences in communication and control, which explores the methods of control exercised by mothers over children of immediate pre-school age, with special reference to language. Based on samples of children in 'middle class' and 'working class' areas in London.

4 **Bright, William, ed.**
Sociolinguistics: proceedings of the UCLA sociolinguistics conference, 1964. Janua Linguarum. Series Maior, 20. The Hague, Mouton, 1966. 324 pp. bibliogs.
Collects fourteen papers on various aspects of sociolinguistics, some reporting research. Includes papers on language planning, multilingual societies and dialect differences.

5 **Brown, Roger**
Words and things. Glencoe, Illinois, Free Press, 1958. xvi, 398 pp. bibliog.
Popular general introduction to language, drawing on linguistics, psychology and anthropology. Because of its wide frame of reference provides considerable insight into language in relation to thought and human behaviour.

6 **Cherry, Colin**
On human communication: a review, a survey and a criticism. Studies in Communication. Cambridge, Massachusetts, and London, England, M.I.T. Press, 2nd edn. 1966. xiv, 337 pp. bibliog. First pubd. 1957.
Introduction to all aspects of communication, for non-specialist readers. Includes: communication and organisation; evolution of communication science; on signs, language and communication; on analysis of signals, especially speech; on the statistical theory of communication; on the logic of communication; on cognition and recognition. The first comprehensive survey of the various aspects of communication.

7 **Commonwealth Education Liaison Committee**
Language and communication in the Commonwealth, by G. E. Perren and Michael F. Holloway. London, HMSO, 1965. 54 pp. bibliog.
Concise survey of some major problems of language and communication in British Commonwealth countries, principally seen in terms of educational needs and policies. The position of English as a common language receives special attention.

8 **Dodson, C. J., and others**
Towards bilingualism: studies in language teaching methods. Welsh Studies in Education, 1. Cardiff, University of Wales Press, 1968. viii, 116 pp.
Includes three papers – Cycles of research: the evolution of the bilingual method of language-teaching; early bilingualism; preparing a learner's Welsh dictionary. Although primarily concerned with problems of Welsh-teaching, is of application and interest to other bilingual areas.

9 **Doob, Leonard W.**
Communication in Africa: a search for boundaries. New Haven, Connecticut; London, Yale University Press, 1961. xvi, 406 pp. bibliog.
The field of communication in Africa is outlined and commented on. The variables controlling the context of communication are stated with reference

to detailed studies of tribal life in Africa. Communication is studied not only in relation to language, but also to music, folklore and social behaviour. Valuable to those concerned with African education.

10 **Eisenson, Jon, and others**
The psychology of communication. New York, Appleton-Century-Crofts, 1963. ix, 394 pp. diagrs. bibliogs.
General survey of the field of communication through speech. Covers: the nature and origin of speech; psychological principles affecting language; the process of communication; applications to the individual and to group communication; personality and speech.

11 **Fishman, Joshua A., ed.**
Readings in the sociology of language. The Hague, Mouton, 1968. 808 pp. tables, diagrs. bibliogs.
Includes reprints of 44 influential papers and extracts (published up to 1964), collected under: perspective on the sociology of language; language in small-group interaction; language in social strata and sectors; language reflections of socio-cultural organization; multilingualism; language maintenance and language shift; social contexts and consequences of language planning.

12 **Fishman, Joshua A., and others**
Language loyalty in the United States: the maintenance and perpetuation of non-English mother-tongues by American ethnic and religious groups. Janua Linguarum. Series Maior, 21. The Hague, Mouton, 1966. 478 pp. tables, diagrs. bibliogs.
Wide survey of the sociological and linguistic factors affecting non-English-speaking groups in the United States, including suggestions for reinforcing the maintenance of such foreign language resources in the national interest.

13 **Fishman, Joshua A., and others, eds.**
Language problems of developing nations. New York and London, Wiley, 1968. xviii, 521 pp. tables, diagrs. bibliogs.
Collection of 31 essays (mostly arising from a conference held in 1966) on various sociolinguistic problems. Most are grouped under: language and national development; language planning; literature and education. Case studies of particular countries are presented.

14 **Gumperz, John J., and Dell Hymes, eds.**
The ethnography of communication. American Anthropologist, 1964, vol. 66, no. 6, part 2: Special Publication. Menasha, Wisconsin, American Anthropological Association, 1964. viii, 186 pp. diagrs. bibliogs.
Collects 13 papers on anthropological and sociological aspects of language, originally prepared in 1962 and 1963. Includes introductory survey of past work (by D. Hymes).

15 **Haugen, Einar**
Language conflict and language planning: the case of modern Norwegian. Cambridge, Massachusetts, Harvard University Press, 1966. xvi, 393 pp. illus. bibliog.
Detailed account of Norway's language reform programme since 1814 and of attempts to reach agreement on the forms of language to be taught in schools, etc. Of considerable interest in relation to language planning on a national scale in other countries where no uniformity of language exists.

16 **Haugen, Einar**
The Norwegian language in America: a study in bilingual behaviour. Vol. 1: The bilingual community. Vol. 2: The American dialects of Norwegian. Publications of the American Institute, University of Oslo *and* Indiana University Studies in the History and Theory of Linguistics. Bloomington and London, Indiana University Press, 2nd edn. 1969. xxviii, 699 pp., maps, tables. First pubd. in 2 vols. by University of Pennsylvania Press, Philadelphia, 1953.
Very comprehensive and detailed account of bilingualism of Norwegian immigrants in America. Much of the work has application to general characteristics and problems of bilingualism.

17 **Hertzler, Joyce O.**
A sociology of language. New York, Random House, 1965. xii, 559 pp. bibliog.
Attempts systematically to analyse the relationship between language and the organisation and structure of human society. Mostly refers to English in USA but includes references to many other areas.

18 **Hymes, Dell, ed.**
Language in culture and society: a reader in linguistics and anthropology. New York and London, Harper & Row, 1964. xxxv, 764 pp. bibliog.
Reprints of sixty-nine influential papers and extracts, covering particularly the relationship between language and society. Contains valuable reference

notes for further reading and introductions to the ten sections in which the book is arranged. Provides unique coverage of many anthropological and sociological aspects of linguistics.

19 **Jakobson, Roman**
Child language, aphasia and phonological universals. Janua Linguarum. Series Minor, 72. The Hague, Mouton, 1968. 101 pp. illus. bibliog.
First English translation of an influential work originally published in German in 1941. Has provided a basis for more recent work on phonology and language acquisition.

20 **Jespersen, Otto**
Mankind, nation and individual: from a linguistic point of view. London, Allen & Unwin, 1954. 198 pp. First pubd. in Great Britain 1946.
Popular exposition of the influence on language of individual, national and universal human traits. Remains fresh and stimulating, offering original views. Includes: speech and language; influence of the individual; dialect and common language; standards of correctness.

21 **Jones, W. R.**
Bilingualism in Welsh education. Cardiff, University of Wales, 1966. viii, 202 pp.
Surveys research into bilingualism undertaken in Wales, including a review of the historical background of the problem in Welsh education. Chapters on: bilingualism and intelligence; bilingualism and educational attainment; learning and teaching of a second language.

22 **Landar, Herbert**
Language and culture. New York, Oxford University Press, 1966. 274 pp. diagrs. bibliog.
Relates the study of language and linguistics to anthropological, sociological and psychological studies following the traditions of Boas, Sapir and Durkheim. An introduction for serious students.

23 **Le Page, R. B.**
The national language question: linguistic problems of newly independent states. London and New York, Oxford University Press, 1964. vi, 81 pp. map, bibliog.
Short study of problems arising from the development or adoption of national languages in former colonial territories. Examines the function of language in relation to the individual and society, and refers in detail to the problems of India and Malaysia in establishing Hindi and Malay as national languages. Pays considerable attention to the role of English.

24 **Leopold, Werner F.**
Speech development of a bilingual child: a linguist's record. Northwestern University Studies. Humanities Series, 6, 11, 18 and 19. 4 vols. Evanston, Illinois, Northwestern University Press, vol. 1, 1939; vol. 2, 1947; vol. 3, 1949; vol. 4, 1949. bibliogs.
Very detailed record of speech development (English and German) from infancy to the end of the seventh year. Intended primarily as a source book on child language, secondarily as a source book on bilingualism. Contains: vocabulary growth in the first two years (vol. 1); sound-learning in the first two years (vol. 2); grammar and general problems in the first two years (vol. 3); diary from age two (vol. 4).

25 **Lewis, M. M.**
Language and the child. Exploring Education. Slough, National Foundation for Educational Research, 1969. 127 pp. bibliog.
Although primarily concerned with the growth of mother-tongue skills in English children at school, provides an interpretation of the place of language in children's development of some relevance to foreign language teachers.

26 **Macnamara, John**
Bilingualism and primary education: a study of Irish experience. Edinburgh, Edinburgh University Press, 1966. x, 173 pp. tables, diagrs. bibliog.
Study of bilingual education in Ireland, notable for the thoroughness of the techniques employed as well as for the conclusions reached on the educational consequences of using two languages in school.

27 **Macnamara, John, ed.**
Problems of bilingualism. The Journal of Social Issues, 1967, vol. 23, no. 2 (April). 137 pp. bibliogs.
Contains nine authoritative papers dealing with bilingualism from sociological, psychological, educational and linguistic viewpoints. Past research is summarised with extensive bibliographical references.

Miller, George A.
See 259.

28 **Morris, Charles**
Signs, language and behavior. New York, Prentice-Hall, 1946. xii, 365 pp. bibliog.
Influential book which attempted to lay the foundation of semantics con-

ceived as the science of signs (whether or not the signs form a natural language). All kinds of sign-using are considered from the viewpoint of behaviouristic philosophy and psychology, and an attempt is made to ground linguistics in the general and more basic science of signs. Expanded and somewhat revised version of author's *Foundations of the theory of signs* (1938).

29 **Noss, Richard B.**
Language policy and higher education. (Vol. 3, part 2 of *Higher Education and development in South-East Asia*), Paris, UNESCO and the International Association of Universities, 1967. 216 pp. map, tables.
A detailed study of the language policies to problems, particularly in university education, of Burma, Cambodia, Indonesia, Laos, Malaysia, the Philippines, Vietnam and Thailand.

30 **Pierce, J. R.**
Symbols, signals and noise: the nature and process of communication. London, Hutchinson, 1962. xi, 305 pp. diagrs.
Review by a communications engineer of developments in theories of information and communication. Based on Shannon's theory of communication and requiring some mathematical insight by the reader, discusses implications for physics, cybernetics, psychology, music and literature.

31 **Ray, Punya Sloka**
Language standardisation: studies in prescriptive linguistics. Janua Linguarum. Series Minor, 29. The Hague, Mouton, 1963. 159 pp. bibliog.
Discusses in detail problems arising from the standardisation of a language when more widely used. Includes sections on linguistic policy, romanisation in India, the description and evaluation of writing systems (with reference to Roman and non-Roman script).

32 **Rice, Frank A., ed.**
Study of the role of second languages in Asia, Africa and Latin America. Washington, D.C., Center for Applied Linguistics of the Modern Language Association of America, 1962. vi, 123 pp. bibliog.
Collection of ten papers arising from the Survey of Second Language Teaching made by the Center 1959–61. Includes: background to second language problems; the language factor in national development; linguistic typology for describing multilingualism; lingua franca. Remains of considerable interest to those concerned with major issues of language policy in developing areas.

33 **Sebeok, Thomas A., and others**
Approaches to semiotics: cultural anthropology, education, linguistics, psychiatry, psychology. Transactions of the Indiana University Conference on Paralinguistics and Kinesics. Janua Linguarum. Series Maior, 15. The Hague, Mouton, 1964. 294 pp. tables, bibliogs.
Studies concerned with 'patterned communication in all modalities' from the standpoint of anthropology, education, linguistics, psychiatry and psychology. Includes papers on communication between patient and doctor about disease; psychological research in extralinguistic communication; paralinguistics and kinesics; emotive language.

34 **Spencer, John, ed.**
Language in Africa. Papers of the Leverhulme Conference on Universities and the Language Problems of Tropical Africa, held at University College, Ibadan. London, Cambridge University Press, 1963. vii, 167 pp.
Papers by specialists prepared for a conference held in December 1961, which provided a wide conspectus of language problems in Africa in relation to education and national development at that time.

35 **Vildomec, Věroboj**
Multilingualism. Leyden, A. W. Sythoff, 1963. 262 pp. bibliog.
Treatise on the linguistic and psychological aspects of multilingualism. Valuable particularly for its survey of previous writings on the subject, and its very extensive bibliographical references.

36 **Weinreich, Uriel**
Languages in contact: findings and problems. The Hague and Paris, Mouton, 1968. xii, 148 pp. bibliog. Reprint of 1953 edn., originally published as number 1 in the series 'Publications of the Linguistic Circle of New York', New York. Complex and influential survey of linguistic and sociological aspects of bilingualism which traces forms and causes of interference in the languages of bilinguals.

HISTORY OF LINGUISTICS

37 **Chomsky, Noam**
Cartesian linguistics: a chapter in the history of rationalist thought. Studies in Language, 1. New York and London, Harper & Row, 1966. xvi, 119 pp. bibliog. Essay which seeks to show the relevance of seventeenth, eighteenth and early nineteenth century theories of language to recent theories of generative grammar. Presented under: creative aspect of language use; deep and surface structure; description and explanation in linguistics; acquisition and use of language.

38 **Dinneen, Francis P.**
An introduction to general linguistics. New York and London, Holt, Rinehart & Winston, 1967. xi, 452 pp. tables, diagrs. bibliog.
Surveys the development of general linguistics from ancient to modern times. Seven chapters (out of thirteen) deal with the nineteenth century and after. Special attention given to de Saussure, Sapir, Bloomfield, Firth, Hjelmslev and Chomsky, whose works are described analytically. Well arranged for reference. Extensive bibliography.

39 **Fries, Charles C.**
Linguistics: the study of language: chapter two of Linguistics and reading. New York and London, Holt, Rinehart & Winston, 1964. xii, pp., pp. 35–92, 223–32. First pubd. 1962.
Reprinted from *Linguistics and reading*, succinct introductory historical description of the development of linguistics since 1820, with particular reference to work in the United States.

40 **Jacob, André**
Points de vue sur le langage: 270 textes choisis et présentés avec introduction et bibliographie. Publications de la Faculté des Lettres et Sciences Humaines de Paris – Nanterre. Points de Vue, 1. Paris, Klincksieck, 1969. 637 pp. tables, diagrs. bibliogs.
Contains 270 quotations, citations and extracts ranging from Plato to contemporary linguists on language and philosophy, language and art, language and culture, language and science and language and linguistics. Provides a comprehensive historical conspectus of attitudes to language within the framework of western thought.

Jesperson, Otto
See 103.

Kelly, Louis G.
See 300.

41 **Kukenheim, Louis**
Esquisse historique de la linguistique française et de ses rapports avec la linguistique générale. Publications Romanes de l'Université de Leyde, 8. Leiden, Universitaire Pers, 2nd edn. 1966. vi, 284 pp. bibliogs.
Detailed and thoroughly documented historical account of the development of linguistic studies of French and of general linguistic studies by French scholars, principally covering the period 1800–1960. Includes some

reference to the application of linguistics to language teaching. Valuable bibliographical references and concise statements of the work and views of numerous scholars.

42 **Langendoen, D. Terence**
The London school of linguistics: a study of the linguistic theories of B. Malinowski and J. R. Firth. Research Monograph, 46. Cambridge, Mass., M.I.T. Press, 1968. xiii, 123 pp. bibliog.
Detailed and sometimes critical study of the development of the linguistic theory of J. R. Firth and of its origins in the views of Malinowski. Includes discussion of Firth's prosodic analysis technique as exemplified by the work of some of his former students.

43 **Lehmann, Winfred P.**
Historical linguistics: an introduction. New York, Holt, Rinehart & Winston, 1962. xiii, 297 pp. maps, bibliog.
Popular introduction dealing mainly with Indo-European languages. Sections on: the classification of languages; methods employed in the gathering and analysis of material; change in language (including phonological, grammatical, analogical, and semantic change and borrowing). Selected reading lists for more advanced study.

44 **Lehmann, Winfred P., and Yakov Malkiel, eds.**
Directions for historical linguistics: a symposium. Austin and London, University of Texas Press, 1968. xiii, 119 pp. bibliog.
Includes papers on the continuing influence of Saussure, inflectional and morphophonemic changes and a larger study *Empirical foundations for a theory of language change* (Weinreich, Labov and Herzog).

45 **Lepschy, Giulio C.**
La linguistica strutturale. Piccola Biblioteca Einaudi, 79. Turin, Einaudi, 1966. 234 pp. bibliog.
Concise but comprehensive review of the development of modern structural linguistics from de Saussure to Chomsky. Summarises the distinctive contributions made by numerous European and American scholars.

46 **Leroy, Maurice**
Les grands courants de la linguistique moderne. Brussels, Presses Universitaires de Bruxelles; Paris, Presses Universitaires de France, 1963. x, 198 pp.
Outline of the development of linguistic studies from antiquity to the present day. Pays considerable attention to the contributions of compara-

tive philology in the nineteenth century, to the influence of de Saussure on the development of modern structural linguistics and to the work of European scholars throughout. An English translation by Glanville Price was published by Blackwell, Oxford, in 1967.

47 **Mounin, Georges**
Histoire de la linguistique des origines au XXe siècle. Le Linguiste, 4. Paris, Presses Universitaires de France, 1967. 226 pp.
Concise history of the development of linguistic studies from antiquity to the end of the nineteenth century. Provides a carefully integrated conspectus of the contributions of major scholars and philosophers to the foundations of linguistics as a science.

Pedersen, Holger
See 160.

Posner, Rebecca
See 161.

48 **Robins, R. H.**
A short history of linguistics. Longmans' Linguistics Library. London, Longmans, Green, 1967. viii, 248 pp. diagrs. bibliogs.
Surveys the history and development of linguistic studies in Europe from ancient Greece to the present day. Particularly valuable in showing the continuity of scholarly studies of language. The final chapter deals with linguistics in the present century.

49 **Salus, Peter H., ed.**
On language: Plato to von Humboldt. New York, Holt, Rinehart & Winston, 1969. v, 201 pp. bibliog.
An anthology of thirteen extracts from influential works illustrating the development of western European thought about language to the beginning of the nineteenth century.

50 **Schlauch, Margaret**
Language and the study of languages today. Warsaw, PWN – Polish Scientific Publishers; London, Oxford University Press, 1967. vi, 176 pp.
Popular introduction to the study of language which includes a brief review of the development of traditional philology into modern linguistics. Bibliographical notes for further reading.

51 **Sebeok, Thomas, ed.**
Portraits of linguists: a biographical source book for the history of western linguistics, 1746–1963. 2 vols. Indiana University Studies in the History and Theory of Linguistics. Bloomington and London, Indiana University Press, 1966.
Biographical sketches, written in English, of ninety influential linguists and philologists ranging from Sir William Jones to Whorf and Firth.

Vachek, Josef
See 148.

52 **Waterman, John T.**
Perspectives in linguistics. Chicago, University of Chicago Press, 1963. ix, 105 pp. tables. Paper-backed edn.: London, Phoenix, 1963.
Succinct account of the historical development of linguistic theory from ancient to modern times. Seeks to show how modern structural linguistics owes much to historical and philological studies of the nineteenth and twentieth centuries. Critical discussion of theories of de Saussure, Trubetzkoy, Hjelmslev and Bloomfield.

LINGUISTICS

Académie Tchécoslovaque des Sciences
See 174 and 175.

53 **Akhmanova, O. S., and others**
Exact methods in linguistic research. Translated from the Russian by David G. Hays and Dolores V. Mohr. Berkeley and Los Angeles, University of California Press, 1963. x, 186 pp. diagrs. bibliogs.
Collection of specialised papers by leading Soviet scholars, dealing primarily with mathematical and computational linguistics. Includes: can linguistics become an exact science? (Akhmanova); the place of semantics in modern linguistics (Akhmanova); several types of linguistic meanings (Mel'chuk); machine translation and linguistics (Mel'chuk); the application of statistical methods in linguistic research (Frumkina); information theory and the study of language (Paducheva).

Allen, Harold B., ed.
See 337.

54 **Anderson, Wallace L., and Norman C. Stageberg, eds.**
Introductory readings on language. New York, Holt, Rinehart & Winston, 2nd edn. 1966. xix, 545 pp. maps, diagrs. bibliogs. First pubd. 1962.
Selection of forty-two passages from the work of a wide range of modern linguistic scholarship, designed for use as an introductory text in first-year university courses in language to stimulate wider reading. Readings grouped under: the nature of language; language history; words, forms and meanings; semantics; language and literature; the sounds of language; usage; linguistic geography; structural and transformational grammar; clear thinking.

55 *Annual Round Table Meetings on Linguistics and Language Teaching, Georgetown University. Institute of Languages and Linguistics.* Monograph Series on Languages and Linguistics, 1– . Washington, Georgetown University Press, 1951– .
Collection of papers, delivered at annual meetings by American and other scholars, generally representative of recent research and topical problems. To date eighteen volumes have appeared which provide a continuous review of current linguistic interests in the USA over twenty years.

56 **Antal, László**
Content, meaning and understanding. Janua Linguarum, Series Minor, 31. The Hague, Mouton, 1964. 63 pp. bibliog.
Outline of a theory of linguistic semantics which dissociates semantics from traditional connections with formal logic and aims to bring it into the field of structural linguistics.

57 **Bar-Hillel, Yehoshua**
Language and information: selected essays on their theory and application. Addison-Wesley Series in Logic; Reading, Massachusetts, Addison-Wesley; Jerusalem, Israel, Jerusalem Academic Press, 1964. x, 388 pp. bibliog.
Written over a period of fifteen years, papers are grouped under: theoretical aspects of language; algebraic linguistics; machine translation; semantic information; mechanisation of information retrieval. Presupposes considerable knowledge of logic and mathematics.

58 **Barthes, Roland**
Elements of semiology. Translated from the French by Annette Lavers and Colin Smith. Cape Editions, 4. London, Cape, 1967. 112 pp. bibliog. First pubd. in French 1964.
Concise definition of the elements of Saussurean linguistics, related to more recent developments in the theory of signs and semiotics.

59 **Bazell, C. E., and others, eds.**
In memory of J. R. Firth. Longmans' Linguistics Library. London, Longmans, Green, 1966. xi, 500 pp. tables, diagrs. bibliog. of J. R. Firth's works.
Volume of twenty-seven essays by scholars associated with J. R. Firth, covering many aspects of linguistic studies. A number of these exemplify Firth's own theoretical approaches.

60 **Black, Max, ed.**
The importance of language. A Spectrum Book. Englewood Cliffs, New Jersey, Prentice-Hall, 1962. xi, 172 pp.
Collection of nine essays on aspects of language, mostly by eminent non-linguists. Includes: words and their meanings (A. Huxley); thought and language (Samuel Butler); the language of magic (Malinowski); the theory of meaning (Ryle).

61 **Bloomfield, Leonard**
Language. London, Allen & Unwin, 1935. ix, 566 pp. illus. bibliog. First pubd. 1933.
Introduction to the study of language, originally intended for the general reader or the student beginning linguistics. Approaching language and linguistics on strictly behaviourist principles, it became one of the foundations of modern structural linguistics and has had great influence on the development of linguistic theory, especially in America.

62 **Bolinger, Dwight**
Aspects of language. New York, Harcourt, Brace, 1968. viii, 326 pp. illus.
Informed introduction to the nature of language for the general reader. Refers primarily to the development of modern English in the USA.

63 **Carroll, John B.**
The study of language: a survey of linguistics and related disciplines in America. Cambridge, Massachusetts, Harvard University Press, 1953. xi, 289 pp. illus. bibliog.

Contains: linguistics and psychology; linguistics and the social sciences; language and philosophy; language and education; communication engineering and the study of speech; organisations, personnel and publications; the future of language studies. Intended primarily as a study guide and report, and still of considerable value.

64 **Caton, Charles E., ed.**
Philosophy and ordinary language. Urbana, University of Illinois Press, 1963. xii, 246 pp. bibliog.
Twelve essays on language by philosophers representative of the 'ordinary language' school, stemming from the work of Moore, Wisdom, Wittgenstein, Ryle and Austin.

65 **Chappell, V. C., ed.**
Ordinary language: essays in philosophical method. Contemporary Perspectives in Philosophy Series. Englewood Cliffs, New Jersey, Prentice-Hall, 1964. viii, 115 pp. bibliog.
Collection of five essays by Malcolm, Ryle, Austin, Mates and Cavell with a short introduction, representative of the 'ordinary language' school of philosophy.

66 **Chomsky, Noam**
Current issues in linguistic theory. Janua Linguarum. Series Minor, 38. The Hague, Mouton, 1964. 119 pp. bibliog.
Expanded version of a report originally presented at Ninth International Congress of Linguists in 1962 giving the author's account of linguistic structure under: goals of linguistic theory; on objectivity of linguistic data; the nature of structural descriptions; models of perception and acquisition.

67 **Cohen, L. Jonathan**
The diversity of meaning. London, Methuen, 2nd edn. 1966. xii, 369 pp. First pubd. 1962.
Scholarly philosophical examination of various theories of meaning. Argues that no single theory of meaning can suit the semantics of all disciplines and studies. Includes critical appraisal of the work of many recent philosophers in this field.

68 **Crystal, David**
What is linguistics? London, Edward Arnold, 1968. viii, 84 pp.
Brief and simple introduction for those who 'have perhaps heard only the

name Linguistics before, who do not know what it means...'. Includes an appendix describing the content of undergraduate courses in linguistics in five British universities.

69 **Dufrenne, Mikel**
Language and philosophy. Translated from the French by Henry B. Veatch. With a foreword by Paul Henle. Bloomington, Indiana University Press, 1963. 106 pp.
Seeks to contrast European (and particularly French) views on the philosophy of language with those associated with Anglo-American linguistic philosophy. Explores the relationships between language and logic and language and style.

70 **Eaton, Helen S.**
An English-French-German-Spanish word frequency dictionary... New York, Dover Publications; London, Constable, 1961. xx, 441 pp. First pubd. 1940, University of Chicago Press.
First published as *Semantic frequency list for English, French, German and Spanish*. Presents an attempt to correlate the first 6,000 words in these languages, using previous word counts compiled by E. L. Thorndike, G. E. Vander Beke, F. W. Kaeding and M. A. Buchanan respectively. Mainly of historic interest.

71 **Enkvist, Nils Erik, and others**
Linguistics and style. Edited by John Spencer. Language and Language Learning, 6. London, Oxford University Press, 1964. xii, 109 pp. bibliog.
Contains two essays: On defining style: an essay in applied linguistics (Enkvist), and An approach to the study of style (Spencer and Gregory). Problems of the study of style in literature are considered in relation to modern linguistic theory.

72 **Entwistle, William J.**
Aspects of language. London, Faber & Faber, 1963. ix, 370 pp. maps.
Learned account of language by a distinguished Romance philologist. Takes major structural linguistic theories into account, but maintains an independent position.

73 **Firth, J. R.**
Papers in linguistics, 1934–1951. London, Oxford University Press, 1961. xxi, 233 pp. illus, tables, bibliog. First pubd. 1957.
Gives valuable insight into Firth's work in various areas of linguistics over

thirty years. Includes: the word 'phoneme'; the principles of phonetic notation in descriptive grammar; the technique of semantics; the use and distribution of certain English sounds; the English School of phonetics; sounds and prosodies; the semantics of linguistic science; Atlantic linguistics; personality and language in society; modes of meaning; general linguistics and descriptive grammar.

74 **Firth, J. R.**
Selected papers of J. R. Firth, 1952–59; edited by F. R. Palmer. Longmans' Linguistics Library. London, Longmans, 1968. x, 209 pp. bibliog.
Collection of twelve (five hitherto unpublished) papers by J. R. Firth, mostly on general topics. Includes a complete list of Firth's own publications.

75 **Firth, J. R.**
The tongues of men and *Speech*. Language and Language Learning, 2. London, Oxford University Press, 1966. x, 211 pp. First pubd. 1937 and 1930.
Speech, first published in 1930, and *The tongues of men* (1937), for many years out of print, still provide an excellent introduction to Firth's later work in non-technical language. Many later developments in British linguistics are clearly foreshadowed in *The tongues of men*, which is valuable to those requiring a readable survey of basic linguistic concepts and problems as they were seen at the time of writing.

76 **Fodor, Jerry A., and Jerrold J. Katz, eds.**
The structure of language: readings in the philosophy of language. Englewood Cliffs, New Jersey, Prentice-Hall, 1964. xii, 612 pp. diagrs. bibliog.
Anthology of twenty-three papers by linguists, dealing with problems of language which are of concern to philosophy, grouped under: linguistic theory; grammar; extensions of grammar; semantics; psychological implications. Attempts to solve problems in the philosophy of language 'by using theories and methods drawn from empirical linguistics'.

77 **Freeman, Robert R., and others, eds.**
Information in the language sciences: proceedings of the conference held at Warrenton, Virginia, March 4–6, 1966. Mathematical Linguistics and Automatic Language Processing, 5. New York and London, Elsevier, 1968. xi, 247 pp. illus. bibliogs.
Twenty-two specialist papers covering the information needs of language

science and the principles of system design to provide for them, especially in the fields of documentation and bibliography.

78 **Garvin, Paul L.**
On linguistic method: selected papers. Janua Linguarum. Series Minor, 30. The Hague, Mouton, 1964. 158 pp.
Eleven specialised papers concerned with descriptive method in general linguistics and covering aspects of phonemics, morphology, syntax, meaning, language and culture.

79 **Gleason, Henry Allan, jr.**
An introduction to descriptive linguistics. New York, Holt, Rinehart & Winston, 2nd edn. 1965. viii, 503 pp. diagrs. bibliog. First pubd. 1955.
General introductory course dealing mainly with the analysis of (American) English and techniques of structural linguistics. Discusses: English consonants, vowels, stress and intonation; morphology and syntax; phonetics and phonemics; general aspects of language. Valuable bibliography. See also *Workbook in descriptive linguistics*, below.

80 **Gleason, Henry Allan, jr.**
Workbook in descriptive linguistics. New York, Henry Holt, 1959. 88 pp. illus. First pubd. 1955.
Book of exercises intended to accompany this author's *An introduction to descriptive linguistics.* Exercises are arranged to correspond with each chapter in that book.

81 **Greenberg, Joseph H.**
Language universals: with special reference to feature hierarchies. Janua Linguarum. Series Minor, 59. The Hague, Mouton, 1966. 89 pp. bibliog. Revised and expanded version of a paper published in vol. 3 of *Current Trends in Linguistics.* Examines the concept of universals in relation to all human languages with reference to common characteristics in phonology, grammar and lexicon.

82 **Greenberg, Joseph H., ed.**
Universals of language. Report of a conference held at Dobbs Ferry, New York, April 13–15, 1961. Cambridge, Massachusetts, M.I.T. Press, 2nd edn. 1966. xxvii, 337 pp. bibliogs. First pubd. 1963.
Collection of papers presented in 1961 by specialists seeking to examine whether generalisations about language can be universal and thus con-

tribute to a general science of human behaviour. Among other topics, the relationship of linguistics, anthropology and psychology is examined.

83 **Guiraud, Pierre**
Problèmes et méthodes de la statistique linguistique. Synthèse Library. Dordrecht, D. Reidel, 1959. 145 pp. tables, diagrs.
Critical examination of particular problems of theory arising out of the application of statistical methods to linguistics.

84 **Hall, Robert A., jr.**
An essay on language. Philadelphia and New York, Chilton Books, 1968. xiii, 160 pp. bibliog.
Introductory monograph which treats broadly the principal issues in modern linguistics from a social–historical viewpoint. Terms used are explained for the non-specialist reader.

85 **Hall, Robert A., jr.**
Pidgin and creole languages. Ithaca, N.Y., Cornell University Press, 1966. xv, 188 pp. bibliogs.
Survey of the major pidgin and creole languages, using modern techniques of linguistic analysis. Discusses their origin and distribution, their structure, both individually and in relation to their parent languages, and their linguistic, social and political significance. Includes sample texts.

86 **Halle, Morris, and others, eds.**
For Roman Jakobson: essays on the occasion of his sixtieth birthday, 11 October, 1956. The Hague, Mouton, 1956. xii, 681 pp. illus. bibliogs.
Ninety-three scholarly articles (including some parodies) on many aspects of literature and linguistics, contributed by eminent authors. Includes articles on machine translation and structural linguistics; 'distinctive features' as normal co-ordinates of language; accent and juncture; perception and recognition of speech elements.

87 **Hamp, Eric P., and others, eds.**
Readings in linguistics, 2. Chicago and London, University of Chicago Press, 1966. x, 395 pp. diagrs.
Collection of reprints of thirty-nine articles originally published between 1929 and 1961. Represents mostly European viewpoints and is therefore complementary to *Readings in linguistics, 1*, edited by Martin Joos.

88 **Harris, Zellig S.**
Structural linguistics. Phoenix Books. Chicago, University of Chicago Press; Toronto, University of Toronto Press, 4th impression, 1960. xvi, 384 pp. First pubd. 1951 as *Methods in structural linguistics.*
Comprehensive attempt to expound a unified approach to the structural analysis of languages. Each operation in the successive stages of analysis and its relation to the operations and results at other stages is explained. There is no change in the text of the 1960 impression, but later developments in linguistics are mentioned in the new preface.

89 **Hayakawa, S. I.**
Language in thought and action. In consultation with Leo Hamalian and Geoffrey Wagner. London, Allen & Unwin, 2nd edn. 1965. xviii, 350 pp. bibliog. First pubd. by Harcourt, Brace, New York, 1939.
Expanded and revised version of the same author's *Language in action.* Popular and influential introduction to semantics and an attempt to indicate its importance for all kinds of verbal communication in contemporary society.

90 **Herdan, Gustav**
Language as choice and chance. Groningen, Noordhoff, 1956. xiii, 356 pp. tables, diagrs. bibliogs.
Comprehensive attempt to show that the statistical study of languages is an integral part of linguistics. The thesis is advanced that the complete picture of language embraces both the casual nexus and probability description.

91 **Herdan, Gustav**
Quantitative linguistics. London, Butterworth, 1964. xvi, 284 pp. tables, diagrs. bibliogs.
Thorough and sophisticated application of the laws and methods of statistics to the study of linguistic structure and development.

92 **Hill, Archibald A.**
Introduction to linguistic structures: from sound to sentence in English. New York, Harcourt, Brace, 1958. xi, 496 pp.
An introduction to linguistics, intended for use at university level by both students of English and students of linguistics. Proceeds from analysis of contrasting features of sounds in English, through morphology, to sentence structures.

93 **Hill, Archibald A.**
The promises and limitations of the newest type of grammatical analysis: 1. Mainly promises; 2. Mainly limitations. Lectures in memory of Louise Taft Semple. Published with the help of the Charles Phelps Taft Memorial Fund, Cincinnati, University of Cincinnati, 1966. 38 pp.
Succinct critical appraisal of transformational grammar in the context of modern linguistic analysis.

94 **Hill, Archibald A., ed.**
Linguistics today. New York and London, Basic Books, 1969. xii, 291 pp.
Twenty-five short chapters by experts provide an overview of the present state of language science in the United States. Although these treat numerous technical aspects of the theory and application of linguistics, the style and presentation is suitable for the non-specialist.

95 **Hjelmslev, Louis**
Prolegomena to a theory of language. Translated by Francis J. Whitfield. Madison, University of Wisconsin Press, 2nd edn. 1961. 144 pp. First pubd. 1953.
Celebrated attempt to break with traditional and some modern linguistic theory by laying the foundations of a new study of language (glossematics). Language is defined so as to include non-natural as well as natural languages, and there is an attempt to state the general principles governing their formation. Glossematics studies how these principles are manifested in particular languages.

96 **Hockett, Charles F.**
A course in modern linguistics. New York, Macmillan, 1958. xi, 621 pp. illus. bibliog.
Introductory college course in linguistics, intended not to popularise, but to present the subject as simply and concretely as possible. Comprehensive and detailed explanations of the basic principles and procedures of structural linguistics.

97 **Hockett, Charles F.**
Language, mathematics, and linguistics. Janua Linguarum. Series Minor, 60. The Hague, Mouton, 1967. 243 pp. diagrs. bibliog.
Separately published version of a paper in *Current Trends in Linguistics*, vol. 3. First part provides an introduction to certain mathematical con-

cepts relevant to linguists, the second (and larger) explores the properties of certain grammatical systems, mainly generative, which can be expressed in algebraic forms.

98 **Hughes, John P.**

The science of language: an introduction to linguistics. New York, Random House, 1962. xiv, 305 pp. diagrs. bibliog.

Clearly written general introduction to linguistic studies. Part 1 deals with basic definitions and concepts, the historical development of linguistics and the characteristics of the world's major languages. Part 2 describes techniques of linguistic description and analysis. Suitable for the non-specialist and general reader as well as for the beginning student.

99–101 **International Congress of Linguists**

Proceedings of the Seventh International Congress of Linguists, London, 1–6 September 1952. Distributed by International University Booksellers, London, 1956. lxxii, 575 pp.

Proceedings of the Eighth International Congress of Linguists, Oslo, 4–9 August 1957. Oslo University Press, 1958. xxxi, 885 pp.

Proceedings of the Ninth International Congress of Linguists, Cambridge, Massachusetts, 27–31 August 1962. Janua Linguarum. Series Maior, 12. The Hague, Mouton, 1964. xxii, 1174 pp.

The *Proceedings* of these conferences reproduce the texts of papers offered by a world-wide range of linguistic scholarship every four years. Many provide preliminary reports of recent researches, others survey past development. They give a general view of contemporary linguistic scholarship in nearly all fields. Discussions of papers are often included. Important for general reference as well as for unique coverage of many specialist activities.

102 **Jakobson, Roman, and Morris Halle**

Fundamentals of language. Janua Linguarum, 1. The Hague, Mouton, 1956. ix, 87 pp. bibliog.

Authoritative and detailed exposition of the author's views on phonology and phonetics (part 1); and a shorter, more general account of Jakobson's view of language as a twofold activity, in relation to the problems of aphasia (part 2). Influential contribution to modern linguistic theory.

103 **Jesperson, Otto**

Language: its nature, development and origin. London, Allen & Unwin, 1968. 448 pp. bibliog. First pubd. 1922.

Considers language in its historical perspective and concentrates on the causes of linguistic change and their contribution towards efficiency in communication by language. Summarises nineteenth-century progress in philology. In four parts: history of linguistic science; the child; the individual and the world; development of language.

104 **Jespersen, Otto**
Selected writings of Otto Jespersen. Tokyo, Senjo, [ca 1961]. vi, 849 pp.
Planned to commemorate the hundredth anniversary of Jespersen's birth, this volume collects together reprints of thirty-four of his papers (dating from 1894 to 1933) on a variety of linguistic topics, many of which are not otherwise readily available. All are in English.

105 **Joos, Martin, ed.**
Readings in linguistics, 1. The developments of descriptive linguistics in America 1925–56. Chicago and London, University of Chicago Press, 4th edn. 1966. vi, 421 pp. mimeographed. First pubd. 1957.
Includes reprints of forty-three articles by American linguists, representing mainly the development of Bloomfield's principles. See also *Readings in linguistics, 2*, edited by Eric P. Hamp and others.

106 **Katz, Jerrold J.**
The philosophy of language. Studies in Language. New York and London, Harper & Row, 1966. xvii, 326 pp. bibliog.
Considers the approaches to language inherent in logical empiricism and 'ordinary language' philosophy and seeks to apply the knowledge gained by empirical linguistics to philosophical problems. Applies modern linguistic theories to the problems of understanding conceptual knowledge.

107 **Lamb, Sydney M.**
Outline of stratificational grammar. With an appendix by Leonard E. Newell. Washington, Georgetown University Press, 1966. v, 109 pp. diagrs. First pubd. 1962 in multilithed edn.
Presentation of a system of descriptive grammar derived partly from glossematics and partly from American structural linguistics.

108 **Lane, Harlan L., and Guy C. Capelle**
The world's research in language learning. Part 1: Europe. Ann Arbor, Michigan, Center for Research on Language and Language Behavior, 1969. xii, 146 pp.
Survey, made in 1968, of the principal centres in European countries

engaged on programmes of research and development in linguistics and language studies. Includes addresses, names of principal investigators, heads of institutions and brief descriptions of current projects and interests. Although necessarily selective and subject to regular up-dating and amendment, provides a valuable conspectus of 1968 research interests.

109 **Langacker, Ronald W.**
Language and its structure: some fundamental linguistic concepts. New York, Harcourt, Brace, 1968. ix, 260 pp. bibliog.
Introduction to the nature and structure of language, informed by recent linguistic theory, but presented simply as information rather than as argument.

110 **Lenneberg, Eric H.**
Biological foundations of language. With appendices by Noam Chomsky and Otto Marx. New York and London, John Wiley, 1967. xviii, 489 pp. tables, diagrs. bibliogs.
Discusses language in relation to human biology. Considers the development of language in children in relation to physical development, and language in society in relation to genetics and evolution. Coordinates evidence provided by recent work in linguistics, psychology, anatomy, physiology and neurology to support the thesis that man's language capacity is biologically determined.

111 **Lenneberg, Eric H., ed.**
New directions in the study of language. Cambridge, Massachusetts, M.I.T. Press, 1964. ix, 194 pp. illus. tables, bibliogs.
Collection of seven papers discussing problems of the origin and nature of language. Includes: the early growth of language capacity in the individual; anthropological aspects of language: animal categories, and verbal abuse; a biological perspective of language; language and psychology; three processes in the child's acquisition of syntax; imitation and structural change in children's language.

112 **Lyons, John**
Chomsky. Fontana Modern Masters. London, Fontana/Collins, 1970. 120 pp. bibliog.
Succinct introduction to the linguistic and philosophical theories of Chomsky. For the general reader rather than the linguist, the book emphasises the interdisciplinary importance of Chomsky's work.

113 **Lyons, John**
Introduction to theoretical linguistics. Cambridge, Cambridge University Press, 1968. x, 519 pp. tables, diagrs. bibliog.
Intended as a comprehensive introduction to modern linguistic theory, primarily for students of linguistics, but also for those in other associated fields. Covers the structure of language, in terms of sounds, grammar and semantics. Shows the links between traditional grammatical description and modern transformational theory. Examples drawn primarily from English, but refers to other languages, especially Latin and ancient Greek.

114 **McIntosh, Angus, and M. A. K. Halliday**
Patterns of language: papers in general, descriptive and applied linguistics. Longmans' Linguistics Library. London, Longmans, Green, 1966. xi, 199 pp.
Collection of eleven essays (some previously unpublished) originally produced between 1959 and 1963, six by McIntosh, five by Halliday. A number are of particular relevance to the teaching of English as a second language.

115 **Malmberg, Bertil**
New trends in linguistics: an orientation. Translated from the Swedish by Edward Carney. Bibliotheca Linguistica, 1. Stockholm, Naturmetodens Språkinstitut, and University of Lund, Institute of Phonetics, 1964. 226 pp. diagrs. First pubd. 1959.
Attempts to provide 'objective statements about the various schools and theories' of modern linguistics. Relates American and European developments and identifies the contributions of particular scholars and groups. Bibliographical references are given in text and not collected except under authors' names in index.

116 **Malmberg, Bertil**
Structural linguistics and human communication: an introduction into the mechanism of language and the methodology of linguistics. Kommunikation und Kybernetik in Einzeldarstellungen, 2. Berlin, Springer, 2nd edn. 1967. viii, 213 pp. diagrs. bibliog. First pubd. 1963.
Review of modern linguistics, with many references to recent work, both European and American. Structural linguistics is considered in relation to information, communication, physiological and acoustic phonetics, problems of perception and the statistical analysis of language. Valuable survey of the contributions of many studies both for the advanced linguist and for the student.

117 **Martinet, André**
Elements of general linguistics. Translated from the French by Elizabeth Palmer. London, Faber & Faber, 1964. 205 pp. bibliog. First pubd. 1960.
Concise introduction to descriptive and structural linguistics as they have developed since de Saussure. (A revised edition of the French original has now been published by Armand Colin, Paris.)

118 **Martinet, André, and others, eds.**
La linguistique: guide alphabétique. Collection Guides Alphabétiques Médiations, Paris, Denoël, 1969, 490 pp. diagrs. bibliog.
Fifty-one articles, arranged alphabetically, cover the principal topics and fields of modern linguistics, providing concise definitions and explanations. Supported by very extensive bibliographical references, provides a comprehensive reference book which covers recent work in both Europe and the USA.

119 **Mohrmann, Christine, and others, eds.**
Trends in European and American linguistics, 1930–1960. Edited on the occasion of the Ninth International Congress of Linguists, Cambridge, Massachusetts, 27 August–1 September 1962, for the Permanent International Committee of Linguists. Utrecht and Antwerp, Spectrum, 1961. 299 pp. bibliogs.
Contains twelve important essays on the development of the main schools of general linguistics over the past thirty years. Includes: linguistic prospects in the United States; mathematical linguistics; comparative and historical linguistics in America 1930–60; linguistics and language teaching in the United States 1940–60; anthropological linguistics; glossematics; general linguistics – the United States in the fifties; the Bloomfield 'School'; der Stand der indogermanischen Sprachwissenschaft; orientamenti generali della linguistica in Italia 1930–60; the French school of linguistics; l'école Saussurienne de Genève.

120 **Mohrmann, Christine, and others, eds.**
Trends in modern linguistics. Edited on the occasion of the Ninth International Congress of Linguists, Cambridge, Massachusetts, 27 August–1 September 1962, for the Permanent International Committee of Linguists. Utrecht and Antwerp, Spectrum, 1963. 118 pp. bibliogs.
Important essay (Robins) on general linguistics in Great Britain, 1930–60, discusses the theories and influence of Malinowski, Firth and Daniel Jones. Other papers deal with Japanese linguistics, African languages, Oceanic linguistics, Mycenaean Greek, efforts towards a means–end model of language and Celtic languages.

121 **Mounin, Georges**
Saussure ou le structuraliste sans le savoir: présentation, choix de textes, bibliographie. Philosophes de Tous les Temps, 43. Paris, Seghers, 1968. 191 pp. illus. bibliogs.
Includes a critical study of Saussure's life and theory, followed by a collection of extracts from his works to illustrate his major contribution to linguistic thought. Bibliography includes all original works by Saussure as well as studies of his work by others.

122 **Ogden, Charles K., and I. A. Richards**
The meaning of meaning: a study of the influence of language upon thought and of the science of symbolism. Supplementary essays by B. Malinowski and F. G. Crookshank. International Library of Psychology, Philosophy and Scientific Method. London, Routledge & Kegan Paul, 10th edn. 1949. xxii, 363 pp. First pubd. 1923.
Comprehensive study of linguistic meaning in English, which stimulated much work in semantics in Britain and America. It adopts a broadly behaviouristic attitude to meaning. The long supplementary essay by Malinowski on meaning in tribal languages, in which the importance of context is stressed, remains especially illuminating.

123 **Osgood, Charles E., and others**
The measurement of meaning. Urbana, Illinois, University of Illinois Press, 1957. 342 pp. illus. tables, bibliog.
Attempt, by means of a theory of 'semantic differential', to subject contrastive meaning to quantitative measurement. The first part discusses the working out and assessment of the theory; in the rest of the book possible applications to the measurement of attitudes to personality and psychotherapy research and to communications research are considered in detail.

124 **Papp, Ferenc**
Mathematical linguistics in the Soviet Union. Janua Linguarum. Series Minor, 40. The Hague, Mouton, 1966. 165 pp. bibliog.
Traces the development of new structural and statistical techniques in the Soviet Union and its application (to, e.g., machine translation). Extensive bibliography of Russian sources.

125 **Pei, Mario A.**
Voices of men: the meaning and function of language. World Perspectives. London, Allen & Unwin, 1964. xv, 138 pp. First pubd. 1962.
Popular but documented treatment of some major issues in the study of

language. Arranged as a discussion of fifteen 'unsolved problems, many of which, by their very nature, may never be solved', ranging from the origin of language to the place of linguistics and the possibility of an international language.

126 **Philological Society**
Studies in linguistic analysis. Special volume of the Philological Society. Oxford, Blackwell, 1957. vii, 205 pp. illus.
First three papers (by Firth, Haas, Halliday) of this collection relate to general and specific points of theory in descriptive linguistics. There are five papers about various Asian and African languages and one concerned with phonology and phonetics (by Mitchell).

127 **Pike, Kenneth L.**
Language in relation to a unified theory of the structure of human behaviour. The Hague, Mouton, 2nd edn. 1967. 762 pp. illus. bibliog. First pubd. 1954–9.
Extended attempt to revise the conceptual framework for language study in the light of the function of language in the wider context of non-language behaviour; also attempts to reveal analogies between linguistic structure, the structure of society and the structure of non-language behaviour. Impressive attempt to link linguistics to social anthropology.

128 **Robins, R. H.**
General linguistics: an introductory survey. Longmans' Linguistics Library. London, Longmans, Green, 1966. xxii, 390 pp. diagrs. bibliogs. First pubd. 1964.
Survey of the field of general linguistics including semantics, phonetics and phonology, grammatical analysis, comparative studies and the relation of linguistics to other disciplines. Includes valuable historical account of the development of linguistic studies, with examples drawn from many languages, classical and modern. Provides clear definitions, examples and explanations of the terminology and taxonomy of the subject. Primarily designed for university students beginning linguistics but will be found a valuable reference work for non-specialists.

129 **Rycenga, John A., and Joseph Schwartz, eds.**
Perspectives on language: an anthology. New York, Ronald Press, 1963. iv, 356 pp.
Collection of thirty-one essays representative of modern linguistic scholarship under the following headings: language by way of definition; history:

the matrix of language; grammar and linguistics; usage: the employment of language; metalinguistics: language in its relations. Designed to provide students with a general view of linguistic studies as a background to more specialised work. Of value to the non-specialist as well as to those beginning linguistic studies.

130 **Samarin, William J.**
Field linguistics: a guide to linguistic field work. New York, Holt, Rinehart & Winston, 1967. x, 246 pp. illus. bibliog.
Comprehensive and authoritative guide to techniques of collecting field data from native speakers of languages (particularly of those not widely known). Includes guidance on selection and training of informants, the use of recording equipment and the organisation and presentation of results.

131 **Sapir, Edward**
Language: an introduction to the study of speech. Harvest Books, 7. London, Hart Davies, 1963. ix, 242 pp. table. First pubd. 1921.
General discussion of the nature of language, its variability in place and time, its relation to thought, history, race, culture and arts. Written before the influence of de Saussure and his followers had been deeply felt, the book remains one of the classic introductions to the study of language. First published in U.S.A.

132 **Sapir, Edward**
Selected writings of Edward Sapir in language, culture and personality. Edited by David G. Mandelbaum. Berkeley and Los Angeles, University of California Press; London, Cambridge University Press, 1949, xv, 617 pp. tables, bibliog.
Brings together many of Sapir's papers in various fields, including anthropology and linguistics. Contains articles dealing with language and linguistics which are still suggestive and stimulating after thirty years.

133 **Saussure, Ferdinand de**
Cours de linguistique générale. Bibliothèque Scientifique. Edited by Charles Bally and others. Paris, Payot, 3rd edn. 1960. 331 pp. illus. First pubd. 1916.
For annotation see 135.

134 **Saussure, Ferdinand de**
Cours de linguistique générale: édition critique par Rudolf Engler. 4 vols. Wiesbaden, Otto Harrassowitz, 1967– . In progress.
The published (reconstructed) text of de Saussure's *Cours de linguistique*

générale (see above) is presented together with the original notes by eight of his students who attended his lectures. For the specialist this adds considerable information about, and insight into, de Saussure's original lectures. Vols. 1–3 have so far been published.

135 **Saussure, Ferdinand de**
Course in general linguistics. Edited by Charles Bally and others. Translated by Wade Baskin from the French, 3rd edn. London, Peter Owen, 1960. xvi, 240 pp. illus. First pubd. 1916. (3rd edn. first pubd. 1931.)
Collected from students' and associates' notebooks, the book represents the substance of de Saussure's linguistic theories, which provided foundations for modern linguistics, both in America and Europe. Remains essential for the understanding of contemporary linguistic studies and their origins. English translation produces some obscurity of expression not in the original French.
See 133 and 134 for French original.

136 **Schmidt, Wilhelm**
Lexikalische und aktuelle Bedeutung: ein Beitrag zur Theorie der Wortbedeutung. Schriften zur Phonetik, Sprachwissenschaft und Kommunikationsforschung, 7. Berlin, Akademie-Verlag, 3rd edn. 1966. 130 pp. diagrs. bibliog. First pubd. 1963.
Treats the dual aspect of meaning: lexical and actual. The writer, a Marxist, feels that Western linguistic science is unnaturally isolating the study of language (*Sprache/langue*) from that of speech (*Rede/parole*), may have split the dialectic unity of content and form and obscured the central problem of semasiological research through its formalistic preoccupations. This study of the respective roles of lexical content and syntactic context in the formation of lexical and semantic variants of the verb is intended to be a contribution to the problem of the nature of verbal meaning. Bibliography contains many references to works published in the Soviet Union and East Germany.

137 **Sebeok, Thomas A., ed.**
Style in language. New York and London, The Technology Press of Massachusetts Institute of Technology, and Wiley, 1960. xvii. 470 pp. tables, diagrs. bibliog.
Proceedings of a conference on literary style held in 1958 to which critics, linguists, psychologists, philosophers and anthropologists made contributions. First attempt to consider literary style from an interdisciplinary

point of view. Sections on literary analysis; style in folk narrative; linguistic, phonological, metrical, grammatical, semantic and psychological aspects of style.

138 **Sebeok, Thomas A., and others, eds.**
Current trends in linguistics. Vol. 2: Linguistics in East Asia and South East Asia. The Hague, Mouton, 1967. xix, 979 pp. bibliogs.
Sections on China, Japan, Korea, Mongolia and Tibet by specialist authors review linguistic studies, problems of language development and script reform, etc. Under South East Asia are contributions referring to Burma, Thailand, Vietnam, Indonesia, Malaya and Cambodia. Bibliographies are particularly valuable to students of the languages covered.

139 **Sebeok, Thomas A., and others, eds.**
Current trends in linguistics. Vol. 3: Theoretical foundations. The Hague, Mouton, 1966, xi, 537 pp. diagrs. bibliogs.
Includes sections on: generative grammar (Chomsky); language universals (Greenberg); historical linguistics (Mary R. Haas); language, mathematics and linguistics (Hockett); word formation (Malkiel); tagmemic theory (Pike); semantic theory (Weinreich).

140 **Sebeok, Thomas A., and others, eds.**
Current trends in linguistics. Vol. 4: Ibero-American and Caribbean linguistics. The Hague, Mouton, 1968. xix, 659 pp. tables, bibliogs.
Includes sections by numerous specialists under general and Ibero-American linguistics, linguistics of non-Ibero-American languages, and applied linguistics. Much is of importance to students of Spanish and Portuguese.

141 **Sebeok, Thomas A., and others, eds.**
Current trends in linguistics. Vol. 5: Linguistics in South Asia. The Hague, Mouton, 1969. xviii, 814 pp. illus. maps, tables, bibliogs.
Presents thirty-four specialised studies under four headings: Indo-Aryan languages; Dravidian languages; three other language families; linguistics and related fields in South Asia. Particularly valuable for its survey of recent scholarship and very detailed bibliographical references.

Sebeok, Thomas A., and others, eds.
See 706.

142 **Siertsema, B.**
A study of glossematics: critical survey of its fundamental concepts. The Hague, Martinus Nijhoff, 2nd edn. 1965. xv, 288 pp. bibliog. First pubd. 1955.
Full-length review of the subject, in which the author concludes that although there are considerable defects in glossematic theory it is important for linguistics because of the insights it offers into the nature of language.

143 **Sommerfelt, Alf**
Diachronic and synchronic aspects of language: selected articles. Janua Linguarum. Series Maior, 7. The Hague, Mouton, 1962. 421 pp. maps, tables.
A collection of fifty essays in English and French, written from the twenties onwards. They illustrate the author's development towards structuralism, via the French and Prague schools of linguistic thought, his work on phonemics and phonetics and on the interrelation of language, society and culture.

Strevens, Peter
See 234.

144 *To honor Roman Jakobson: essays on the occasion of his seventieth birthday...* 3 vols. Janua Linguarum. Series Maior, 31. The Hague, Paris, Mouton, 1967. diagrs. bibliogs.
Contains a bibliography of the works of Roman Jakobson and 211 essays on an extensive range of linguistic topics, historical, descriptive and literary, written by numerous scholars from many countries.

145 **Uldall, H. J.**
Outline of glossematics: a study in the methodology of the humanities with special reference to linguistics. Part 1: General theory. Travaux du Cercle Linguistique de Copenhague, 10.1. Copenhagen, Nordisk Sprog- og Kulturforlag, 1957. vi, 87 pp.
Written later than Hjelmslev's own introduction to glossematics (*Prolegomena to the theory of language*), this book explains the philosophical basis and general principles of the theory in terms more easily understandable to the general reader or linguist.

146 **Ullmann, Stephen**
Language and style: collected papers. Language and Style Series, 1. Oxford, Blackwell, 1964. ix, 270 pp.
Contains eleven papers collected under: problems of meaning; problems of style; language and thought. These deal with major questions of semantics and stylistics with specialist insight, but are presented with a lucidity which may be helpful to the non-specialist.

147 **Ullman, Stephen**
The principles of semantics. Oxford, Blackwell; Glasgow, Jackson, 2nd edn. 1959. xii, 348 pp. diagrs. bibliog. First pubd. 1951.
Comprehensive account of the development of semantics and of controversies in this field. The psychological approach to meaning is contrasted with the structural approach and an attempt is made to show how the two sides can be drawn together.

148 **Vachek, Josef**
The linguistic school of Prague: an introduction to its theory and practice. Indiana University Studies in the History and Theory of Linguistics. Bloomington and London, Indiana University Press, 1966. 184 pp. illus. bibliog.
Traces history and development of theories associated with the Prague Linguistic Circle from 1926 onwards. Includes biographical and extensive bibliographical information about its past and present members as well as a review of its current interests, principally in phonology and morphology.

149 **Vachek, Josef, ed.**
A Prague school reader in linguistics. Indiana University Studies in the History and Theory of Linguistics. Bloomington, Indiana, Indiana University Press, 1964. vi, 485 pp. mimeographed.
An anthology of forty influential papers, written by members of the Prague linguistic group, mostly between 1928 and 1948, and not generally available elsewhere. Many represent important contributions to the development of modern linguistics. Authors include Trnka, Trubetzkoy, Mathesius, Vachek and Jakobson.

150 **Wallwork, J. F.**
Language and linguistics: an introduction to the study of language. London, Heinemann, Educational Books, 1969. viii, 184 pp. bibliog.
Clear introductory presentation of those elements of linguistics of interest to language teachers, based mostly on English. Presupposes no previous knowledge of the subject.

151 **Whatmough, Joshua**
Language: a modern synthesis. London, Secker & Warburg; New York, St Martin's Press, 1956. ix, 270 pp. plates, map, diagrs. bibliog. Paperbacked edn.: Menton Books, New York, New American Library, 1957. 240 pp. map, diagrs. bibliog.
Attempts to synthesise views about language developed in linguistics, communication theory, physiology of speech and statistical theories. Notable exposition of the author's own views: for example, the characterisation of meaning as goal-directed activity, and the use of the principle of selective variation to explain types of linguistic change.

152 **Whorf, Benjamin Lee**
Language, thought and reality. Selected writings by B. L. Whorf, edited by John B. Carroll. New York, Wiley and M.I.T. Press; London, Chapman & Hall, 1956. xi, 278 pp. illus. diagrs. bibliog.
Contains the most important of Whorf's writings on specific and general linguistic questions. The most significant papers are those dealing with the hypothesis that the structure of a language inevitably influences the attitudes and thoughts of those who speak it and that our conceptions of the world are therefore partly formed by linguistic structures from which we cannot entirely escape.

153 **Wilson, Graham, ed.**
A linguistic reader. New York, Harper & Row, 1967. xxxii, 341 pp. illus.
Collection of thirty-six reprinted papers by American and some British scholars, on various aspects of language with lucid introductions to each. Designed for the non-specialist but interested reader. Material is chosen to stimulate further reading.

154 **Wittwer, J.**
Contribution à une psycho-pédagogie de l'analyse grammaticale. Actualités Pédagogiques et Psychologiques. Neuchâtel, Switzerland, Delachaux & Niestlé, 1964. 126 pp. bibliog.
Based on modern linguistic theory and symbolic logic, and refers primarily to children learning their mother tongue.

155 **Ziff, Paul**
Semantic analysis. Ithaca, New York, Cornell University Press, 1960. xiv, 255 pp. bibliog.
Inquiry into the meaning of the word 'good', which leads into general philosophical consideration of meaning. Sketches a theory of language

which owes much to contemporary structural linguistics, especially the work of Chomsky. Difficult for those not already aware of contemporary philosophical as well as linguistic theories.

COMPARATIVE LINGUISTICS

156 **Delattre, Pierre**
Comparing the phonetic features of English, French, German and Spanish: an interim report. London, Harrap; Heidelberg, Julius Groos, 1965. 118 pp. illus. tables.
Reprints four articles on: research techniques for phonetic comparison of languages; comparing the prosodic features; comparing the vocalic features; comparing the consonantal features – all in relation to English, French, German and Spanish.

157 **Hammer, John H., and Frank A. Rice**
A bibliography of contrastive linguistics. Washington, D.C., Center for Applied Linguistics, 1965. v, 41 pp.
Lists 484 systematic comparisons between languages, mostly made for teaching purposes. Most studies involve English on one side, although some are between two foreign languages. Includes studies of French, German, Italian, Russian and Spanish in relation to English.

158 **Hoenigswald, Henry M.**
Language change and linguistic reconstruction. Phoenix Books. Chicago, University of Chicago Press, 1960. viii, 168 pp. diagrs. bibliog.
Attempts to set up procedures for the study of linguistic changes in time, based on the semantic, grammatical and phonemic systems established by contemporary linguistics.

159 **Jespersen, Otto**
Efficiency in linguistic change. Det Kgl. Danske Videnskabernes Selskab, Historisk-Filologiske Meddelelser, xxvii/4. Copenhagen, Munksgaard, 2nd edn. 1949. 90 pp. First pubd. 1941.
Discusses specific linguistic changes, their causes, and their effects upon efficiency in communication by means of speech. Best read as a supplement to this author's *Language, its nature, development and origin,* this book examines in more detail some points of the thesis that linguistic change is usually progressive.

160 **Pedersen, Holger**
The discovery of language: linguistic science in the nineteenth century. Translated by John Webster Spargo. Midland Books, 40. Bloomington, Indiana University Press, 1962. 360 pp. illus. First pubd. 1931.
Detailed history of traditional linguistic studies, often in terms of individual scholar's work, with special reference to the development of Indo-European comparative philology. Valuable for reference.

161 **Posner, Rebecca**
The Romance languages: a linguistic introduction. Anchor Books. New York, Doubleday, 1966. xix, 336 pp. maps, bibliog.
Introduction to the historical development of French, Italian, Spanish, Portuguese and Rumanian and to the comparative study of these languages.

GRAMMAR

162 **Bach, Emmon**
An introduction to transformational grammars. New York, Holt, Rinehart & Winston, 1964. x, 205 pp. bibliog.
Detailed exposition of the influential theory and procedures of transformational grammar developed from the principles of Chomsky's *Syntactic structures*. Presupposes a knowledge of modern descriptive linguistics and is written primarily for specialists.

163 **Chomsky, Noam**
Aspects of the theory of syntax. Cambridge, Massachusetts, M.I.T. Press, 1965. x, 251 pp. diagrs. bibliog.
Reviews and reforms the theory of transformational grammar as presented by the author in earlier works. Emphasises the syntactical aspects of language. Includes a chapter on problems which have so far resisted 'systematic and revealing grammatical description'.

164 **Chomsky, Noam**
Syntactic structures. Janua Linguarum, 4. The Hague, Mouton, 1957. 116 pp. bibliog.
Three models of syntactic structure are investigated and a transformational generative model is claimed to yield the most fruitful interpretation of the grammer of English. First comprehensive account of transformational generative procedures as a method of analysing grammatical structures.

165 **Chomsky, Noam**
Topics in the theory of generative grammar. Janua Linguarum. Series Minor, 56. The Hague, Mouton, 1966. 95 pp. bibliog.
Texts of four lectures originally delivered in 1964: assumptions and goals; discussion of criticisms; the theory of transformational generative grammar; some problems in phonology.

166 **Harris, Zellig S.**
String analysis of sentence structure. Papers on Formal Linguistics, 1. The Hague, Mouton, 1962. 70 pp.
Specialist monograph on an approach to syntactic description intermediate between constituent analysis and transformational analysis.

167 **Jespersen, Otto**
The philosophy of grammar. London, Allen & Unwin, 1958. 359 pp. First pubd. 1924.
Early attempt to state a comprehensive theory of grammar, based on direct observation of speech, with examples mainly from English. Although written before the development of modern linguistic theory, insists on the primacy of speech and rejects the use of classical literature in establishing grammatical categories.

168 **Koutsoudas, Andreas**
Writing transformational grammars: an introduction. New York and London, McGraw-Hill, 1966. xiii, 368 pp. bibliog.
Written primarily to provide an introductory academic course on syntax, provides a thorough description of the procedures involved in constructing a transformational grammar of any language. Sections include problems (drawn from many languages) and exercises by which the student may apply the procedures described.

169 **Ruwet, Nicolas**
Introduction à la grammaire générative. Recherches en Sciences Humaines, 22. Paris, Plon, 1967. 447 pp. diagrs. bibliog.
Deals primarily with the syntactic aspects of generative grammar bringing together the views of recent scholarship. Application primarily to the French language.

170 **Tesnière, Lucien**
Eléments de syntaxe structurale. Paris, Klincksiek, 2nd edn., 1966. xxvi, 670 pp. map, tables, diagrs. First pubd. 1959.

Considers languages as linear projections of meaningful discourse, compares and contrasts French structures with those of other languages and sets up descriptions of syntactic elements and transformations.

PHONOLOGY

171 **Abercrombie, David**
Elements of general phonetics. Edinburgh, Edinburgh University Press, 1967. 203 pp. illus. bibliog.
Concise and authoritative presentation of phonetics as part of general linguistics, for non-specialists. Examples drawn mostly from English.

172 **Abercrombie, David**
Studies in phonetics and linguistics. Language and Language Learning, 10. London, Oxford University Press, 1965. vi, 151 pp. bibliog.
Reprints of fifteen articles originally published between 1937 and 1964, covering various aspects of the subjects.

173 **Abercrombie, David, and others, eds.**
In honour of Daniel Jones. Papers contributed on the occasion of his 80th birthday, 12th September, 1961. London, Longmans, Green, 1964. xxi, 474 pp. tables, diagrs. bibliog.
Collection of fifty-one papers, many by eminent phoneticians, presented under the following headings: general phonetics; the phonetics of English; the phonetics of European languages; the phonetics of non-European languages.
Full bibliography of the writings of Daniel Jones. Many of the papers include valuable contributions to phonetic theory. Presents a unique overall view of past and current work in phonetics.

174–175 **Académie Tchécoslovaque des Sciences**
L'école de Prague d'aujourd'hui. Travaux Linguistiques de Prague, 1. Prague, The Academy, 1964. 300 pp. tables, diagrs.
Les problèmes du centre et de la périphérie du système de la langue. Travaux Linguistiques de Prague, 2. Prague, The Academy, and Paris, Klincksieck, 1966. 287 pp. tables, diagrs.
Each volume contains twenty-six papers dealing with various aspects of linguistics and phonology from the standpoint of the Prague school. Papers written in English, French, German and Russian.

176 **Brain, Walter Russell, 1st Baron Brain**
Speech disorders: aphasia, apraxia and agnosia. London, Butterworth, 2nd

edn. 1965. viii, 201 pp. illus. bibliogs. First pubd. 1961.
Includes discussion of theories of the origin of speech and its development in children, as well as a technical treatment of aphasia.

177 **Brosnahan, L. F.**
The sounds of language: an inquiry into the role of genetic factors in the development of sound systems. Cambridge, Heffer, 1961. vi, 250 pp. maps, tables, bibliog.
Explores the biological basis of speech. Seeks to answer the question of why the phonemes of any language should have the particular phonetic form they have. Recent work by biologists on the influence of genetic factors on speech sounds is considered.

Delattre, Pierre
See 156.

178 **Fairbanks, Grant**
Experimental phonetics: selected articles. Urbana and London, University of Illinois Press, 1966. vi, 274 pp. illus. tables, bibliogs.
Collection of twenty-eight papers on instrumental and acoustic phonetics, many reporting original research, mostly first published after 1950.

179 **Gray, Giles Wilkeson, and Claude Merton Wise**
The bases of speech. New York, Harper, 3rd edn. 1959. xiii, 562 pp. illus. bibliog. First pubd. 1934.
Synthesis of current views in various sciences, intended to provide basic information of the nature and function of spoken language from the points of view of sociology, physics, physiology, neurology, phonetics, linguistics, psychology, biology and semantics. Aimed at the advanced student.

180 **Harms, Robert T.**
Introduction to phonological theory. Englewood Cliffs, New Jersey, Prentice-Hall, 1968. xiv, 142 pp. diagrs. bibliog.
Compressed treatment of the conventions of generative phonology (or the aspects of generative grammar which provide for the phonetic representations of utterances). Relies on distinctive features as fundamental units of phonological description and draws on many languages for examples. Includes practical exercises in the application of procedures described.

181 **Jakobson, Roman**
Selected writings. Vol. 1.: Phonological studies. The Hague, Mouton, 1962. x, 678 pp. illus. tables, bibliogs.

Reprints of thirty-eight essays in English, French, German and Russian (1928–62), including phoneme and phonology; sur la théorie des affinités phonologiques entre les langues; Kindersprache, Aphasie und allgemeine Lautgesetze; on the identification of phonemic entities; toward the logical description of languages in their phonemic aspect (with Cherry and Halle); phonology and phonetics (with Halle).
A final Retrospect traces the course of the authors' inquiries into the relations between the two conjugate sides – sound and meaning – of any semiotic unit.

Jakobson, Roman, and Morris Halle
See 102.

182 **Jakobson, Roman, and others**
Preliminaries to speech analysis: the distinctive features and their correlates. Cambridge, Massachusetts, M.I.T. Press, 2nd edn. 1963. viii, 64 pp. illus. bibliog. First pubd. 1952.
Reprint of an influential work which first set forth in detail the theory of distinctive features for the classification of linguistic discriminations in speech sounds. Much of the material examined is taken from English, although it is proposed that twelve fundamental binary oppositions may underlie all phonemic discriminations required by the world's languages. A major contribution to phonetic theory is closely integrated with scientific laboratory analysis of speech material.

183 **Jones, Daniel**
The phoneme: its nature and use. Cambridge, Heffer, 3rd edn. 1967. xviii, 284 pp. diagrs. bibliog. First pubd. 1950.
Exposition in terms of practical phonetics of Jones' development of the theory of phonemes originated by Baudouin de Courtenay. Refers to the phonology of numerous European and non-European languages in establishing physical criteria of the identity of phonemes. With an appendix on the history and meaning of the term 'phoneme'.

184 **Ladefoged, Peter**
Elements of acoustic phonetics. Edinburgh, Oliver & Boyd, 1962. vii, 118 pp. diagrs. bibliog.
Introduction to particular aspects of acoustics of concern to linguists and phoneticians. Includes clear expositions of: sound waves; loudness and pitch; wave analysis; resonance; and their application to acoustic phonetics.

185 **Ladefoged, Peter**
Three areas of experimental phonetics: stress and respiratory activity; the nature of vowel quality; units in the perception and production of speech. Language and Language Learning, 15. London, Oxford University Press, 1967. v, 180 pp. diagrs. bibliog.
Reports findings of experimental work in collaboration with physiologists, communication engineers and a psychologist, which are of considerable importance to the teacher of spoken language.

186 **Lehiste, Ilse, ed.**
Readings in acoustic phonetics. Cambridge, Massachusetts, and London, England, M.I.T. Press, 1967. ix, 358 pp. tables, illus. bibliogs.
Collection of thirty-two reprints of articles by specialists intended to describe fundamental work in acoustic phonetics for those already specialising in other branches of phonetics or linguistics, and to provide a basic reference collection of influential research reports. Arranged in three parts: acoustic theory and methods of analysis; acoustic structure of speech; synthesis and perception. Some of the articles have hitherto been difficult of access.

187 **Lieberman, Philip**
Intonation, perception and language. Research Monograph, 38. Cambridge, Massachusetts, M.I.T. Press, 1967. xiii, 210 pp. illus. bibliog.
Detailed description of research into the production and perception of intonation. Includes analysis of data and articulatory, acoustic, perceptual, phonetic and syntactic dimensions of English, with references to Russian, Finnish, Japanese and Swedish.

188 **Malmberg, Bertil**
Phonetics. New York, Dover Publications; London, Constable, 1963. iv, 123 pp. diagrs. bibliog.
Concise introduction to the elements of acoustic, physiological, experimental and functional phonetics (phonemics).

189 **Malmberg, Bertil, ed.**
Manual of phonetics. Amsterdam, North Holland Publishing Comp., 1968. xiii, 568 pp. tables, illus. bibliogs.
Completely revised and extended version of Kaiser's *Manual of phonetics* (1957) of which only two chapters are retained unaltered. Provides a comprehensive general survey of recent developments in phonetics in eighteen chapters by specialists. Extensive bibliographies cover the development of experimental work in recent years.

Mangold, Max, and others
See 630.

190 **Moles, A., and others**
Phonétique et phonation. Paris, Masson, 1966. 258 pp. illus. bibliogs.
Contributions by thirteen specialists dealing with the physiology and psychology of the production and perception of speech sounds.

191 **Potter, Ralph K., and others**
Visible speech. New York, Dover Publications, 1966. xiv, 439 pp. illus. First pubd. 1947.
Unaltered republication of the 1947 edition of an influential book which explained techniques of analysis of speech sounds by use of the sound spectrograph. The techniques first described here underlie many later developments in acoustic phonetics.

192 **Pulgram, Ernst**
Introduction to the spectrography of speech. Janua Linguarum, 7. The Hague, Mouton, 1959. 174 pp. tables, diagrs. bibliog.
Expounds the theory and practice of speech spectrography and emphasises its importance for phoneticians and linguists. Also introduces linguistics to acousticians and communication engineers. In four parts: acoustics; phonetics, phonemics; spectrophonetics; spectrophonemics. Valuable bibliography.

Troubetzkoy, N. S.
See Trubetzkoy, N. S.

193 **Trubetzkoy, N. S.**
Introduction to the principles of phonological descriptions. Translated by L. A. Murray, edited by H. Bluhme. The Hague, Nijhoff, 1968. viii, 46 pp.
First English translation of a work originally published in 1935, summarising the author's phonological theory. Of considerable historical importance in the development of the Prague school of linguistics.

194 **Trubetzkoy, N. S.**
Principes de phonologie. Translated by J. Cantineau. Paris, Klincksieck, 1949. xxxiv, 396 pp. bibliog. First pubd. 1939.
Although one of the earlier comprehensive treatments of phonology in a structural–functional framework, this book remains an authoritative introduction to the subject and has been the basis of much subsequent work in Europe and America.

195 **Zinkin, N. I.**
Mechanisms of speech. Translated from Russian by A. F. Gove and R. Abernathy. Janua Linguarum. Series Maior, 13. The Hague, Mouton, 1968. 461 pp. illus.
Originally published in Russian 1958. Complex analysis of the processes of speech largely through using experimental cineradiographic methods. Based on previous work by Russian psychologists and speech analysts.

TRANSLATION

196 **Brower, Reuben A., ed.**
On translation. Harvard Studies in Comparative Literature, 23. Cambridge, Massachusetts, Harvard University Press, 1959. xi, 297 pp. diagrs. bibliog.
Essays by linguists, translators, a logician and an investigator in the field of machine translation. Embraces literary, scholarly and technical aspects of translation. Includes a critical bibliography of works on translation.

197 **Catford, J. C.**
A linguistic theory of translation: an essay in applied linguistics. Language and Language Learning, 8. London, Oxford University Press, 1965. viii, 103 pp. diagrs.
Detailed treatment of theoretical problems of translation from the point of view of modern linguistics. Examples drawn from many languages (in relation to English).

198 **Citroen, I. J., ed.**
Ten years of translation: proceedings of the Fourth Congress of the International Federation of Translators (FIT), Dubrovnik, 1963. Oxford and London, Pergamon Press, 1967. xxi, 398 pp.
Apart from the record of the statutory Congress, contains a number of short papers grouped under: literary translation; technical and scientific translation; linguistic aspects of translation. Contains a list of societies of translators, affiliated to FIT.

199 **Hoof, Henri van**
Théorie et pratique de l'interprétation: avec application particulière à l'anglais et au français. Munich, Max Hueber, 1962. 191 pp. illus. bibliog.
Handbook on theory and practice of interpreting with special reference to international conferences and meetings. Describes techniques and equipment, lists professional associations and schools of interpretership.

200 **Mounin, Georges**
Les problèmes théoriques de la traduction. Bibliothèque des Idées. Paris, Gallimard, 1963. xii, 297 pp. bibliog.
Sophisticated treatment of the major problems of translation in the context of modern linguistics. In six sections, the work covers the relationship of translation to linguistic theory and examines in detail cultural, lexical and syntactical aspects. Extensive bibliography.

201 **Nida, Eugene A., and Charles R. Taber**
The theory and practice of translation. Helps for Translators, 8. Leiden, E. J. Brill for United Bible Societies, 1969. viii, 220 pp. diagrs. bibliogs.
Detailed study of problems of translating in terms of linguistic structures, semantic analysis and information theory. Examples are drawn mostly from Bible translating. Includes an appendix on the organisation of translation programmes, a valuable bibliography and a glossary of technical terms.

202 **Savory, Theodore**
The art of translation. London, Cape, 2nd edn. 1968. 191 pp. First pubd. 1957.
Concise popular introduction to problems of translation, written for the general reader by a practising and teaching zoologist. Includes chapters on the principles of translation; translating the classics; the translation of poetry; translating modern languages; translating the Bible; translation in action; educational translation; science in translation; translation in industry.

Vinay, J. P., and J. Darbelnet
See 573.

GLOSSARIES OF TERMS

203 **Engler, Rudolf**
Lexique de la terminologie saussurienne. Publication de la Commission de Terminologie. Comité International Permanent des Linguistes (C.I.P.L.). Utrecht and Antwerp, Spectrum, 1968. 57 pp. table.
Covers the linguistic terminology employed by de Saussure in his published and reported works. Entries arranged alphabetically and defined by detailed references to their original use in the source texts. Table gives established translations used for the more important terms in Italian, Spanish, German, English, Polish and Russian.

204 **Hamp, Eric P.**
A glossary of American technical linguistic usage, 1925–1950. Publication of the Committee for Terminology. Permanent International Committee of Linguists (C.I.P.L.). Utrecht and Antwerp, Spectrum, 2nd edn. 1963. 67 pp. First pubd. 1957.
Comprehensive glossary of terms used in modern American linguistics. Excerpts are provided from relevant works to illustrate the meaning of each term, with detailed references to first known use and notes on variant uses by different scholars.

205 **Marouzeau, J.**
Lexique de la terminologie linguistique: français, allemand, anglais, italien. Collection Georges Ort-Geuthner. Paris, Geuthner, 3rd edn. 1951. xii, 267 pp. First pubd. 1933.
Embraces philological, stylistic and structural linguistic terminology. Each term is given with its German, English and Italian equivalent and a short explanation, often with examples, in French. Does not cover all the terms used by structural linguists but is more comprehensive than most such glossaries and provides useful survey of related fields of linguistic study.

206 **Nash, Rose**
Multilingual lexicon of linguistics and philology: English, Russian, German, French. Miami Linguistics Series, 3. Coral Gables, Florida, University of Miami Press, 1968. xxvi, 390 pp. bibliog.
Equivalents of over 5000 English terms used in linguistics and philology are given in three other languages. Designed to assist the English-speaker who wishes to read works by foreign scholars.

207 **Pei, Mario A.**
Glossary of linguistic terminology. New York and London, Columbia University Press, 1966. xviii, 299 pp.
Covers in alphabetical form definitions of terms used in descriptive and historical linguistics. Cross-references link connected terms and where possible references to their original use are given.

208 **Pei, Mario A., and Frank Gaynor**
A dictionary of linguistics. London, Peter Owen, 1958. 238 pp. bibliog.
Simplified elementary definitions, sometimes accompanied by specific examples, of the principal terms used in modern linguistics. The languages most frequently cited in linguistic discussion are also listed alphabetically, with short descriptions of them.

209 **Vachek, Josef, and Josef Dubský**
Dictionnaire de linguistique de l'école de Prague. Publication de la Commission de Terminologie, Comité International Permanent des Linguistes (C.I.P.L.). Utrecht and Antwerp, Spectrum, 2nd edn. 1966. 104 pp.
Comprehensive glossary of terms used by the Prague Circle of Linguists. Excerpts are provided from relevant works to illustrate the meaning of each term. German, Czech and English equivalents are given in parentheses.

BIBLIOGRAPHIES

210 **Dale, Edgar, and Taher Razik**
Bibliography of vocabulary studies. A Payne Fund Communication Project. Columbus, Ohio. The Ohio State University, Bureau of Educational Research and Service, 2nd edn. 1963. vii, 257 pp. mimeographed. First pubd. 1957.
Comprehensive work, containing 3,125 titles. Most of the 542 new titles are works completed since 1957.

211 **Gipper, Helmut, and Hans Schwarz**
Bibliographisches Handbuch zur Sprachinhaltsforschung. Wissenschaftliche Abhandlungen der Arbeitsgemeinschaft für Forschung des Landes Nordrhein - Westfalen, 16a. Cologne and Opladen, Westdeutscher Verlag. Part 1, vol. 1: A–G, 1962–1966. ccvii, 773 pp. vol. 2: H– , 1966– . In progress.
Extensive bibliography of works relevant to research on the semantic content of language; an introductory essay on language-content research appears in the first volume. Covers a wide range of books and periodicals both descriptive and analytical, arranged under the name of the author or editor. Many entries are annotated, some in detail. Dictionaries and reference books are included together with some written for schools.

Hammer, John H., and Frank A. Rice
See 157.

212 **Modern Language Association of America**
MLA international bibliography of books and articles on the modern languages and literatures, 1921– . In progress. Publications of the Modern Language Association of America, Menasha, Wisconsin, The Association.
The international coverage of the bibliography started with the year 1956. The previous volumes were American bibliographies only.

213 **Permanent International Committee of Linguists**
Linguistic bibliography for the years 1948– . In progress. Utrecht and Antwerp, Spectrum.
Major reference work which covers scholarly work in all languages. Each volume covers material published in the course of a single year, normally about two years before. A bibliography covering the years 1939–47 was published in 1950 in 2 volumes.

214 **Robinson, Janet O., comp.**
An annotated bibliography of modern language teaching: books and articles 1946–1967. Language and Language Learning, 23. London, Oxford University Press, 1969. xiv, 231 pp.
Intended as a guide to teachers and covers French, German, Italian, Russian, Spanish and English. Teaching materials and research reports are not included. Comprehensive coverage of periodical articles up to June 1967.

215 **U.S. Department of Health, Education and Welfare. Office of Education**
Completed research, studies and instructional materials for language development under the National Defense Education Act of 1958, title vi, section 602. A bibliography (list no. 6) compiled by Julia A. Petrov. Publication OE-12016-69. Washington, Superintendent of Documents, 1969. iii, 144 pp.
Lists 518 reports and instructional materials arising from contracts, awarded during nine years by the U.S. government under the NDEA, for research, studies, surveys and teaching materials development in modern languages (including uncommonly taught languages). Many such projects have yielded materials now extensively used in schools and colleges.

216 **Walford, A. J., ed.**
A guide to foreign language grammars and dictionaries. London, Library Association, 2nd edn. 1967. 240 pp. First pubd. 1964.
Annotated list of grammars, dictionaries and aids to language-learning covering French, Italian, Portuguese, German, Dutch, Scandinavian languages, Russian, Finnish and Chinese. Particularly valuable for its coverage of dictionaries for all purposes; includes bilingual dictionaries.

SECTION II

Language Teaching

GENERAL WORKS ON LANGUAGE TEACHING

Annual Round Table Meetings on Linguistics and Language Teaching
See 55.

217 **Bennett, W. A.**
Aspects of language and language teaching. Cambridge, Cambridge University Press, 1968. viii, 175 pp. illus. bibliog.
An introduction for language teachers to certain aspects of linguistics, theories of language learning, the construction of teaching materials and use of equipment (especially for audio-visual methods).

218 **Bruner, Jerome S.**
Toward a theory of instruction. Cambridge, Massachusetts, Belknap Press, 1966. xiii, 176 pp.
Collection of eight essays characterised by the central importance ascribed to language in the overall learning process.

219 **Council of Europe. Council for Cultural Co-operation**
Linguistic theories and their application. Modern Languages in Europe, 1. London, AIDELA in association with Harrap, 1967. 190 pp. diagrs.
Reprints four papers originally presented at the first international congress of applied linguistics held by AILA in Nancy 1964. Coseriu: lexical structures and the teaching of vocabulary. Isačenko: basic syntactic structures in teaching. Catford: translation and language teaching. Rivenc: the present state of a number of investigations into spoken languages and scientific and technical languages.

220 **Donoghue, Mildred R.**
Foreign languages and the elementary school child. Dubuque, Iowa, Brown 1968. xii, 403 pp. bibliogs.
Covers in detail the problems, methods and materials of foreign language teaching in U.S. primary schools. Refers mostly to Spanish and French, with some German.

Grève, Marcel de, and Frans van Passell
See 291.

221 **Halliday, M. A. K., and others**
The linguistic sciences and language teaching. Longmans' Linguistics Library. London, Longmans, Green, 1964. xix, 322 pp. bibliog.

Study of the application of modern linguistics to problems of language teaching. The linguistic theory embodied is mostly derived and developed from the work of Firth. The applications cited are largely directed towards the teaching of English as a second language. Provides valuable insights into the nature and structure of English.

222 **Harding, David H.**
The new pattern of language teaching. Education today. Language Teaching. London, Longmans, Green, 1967. x, 212 pp. bibliog.
Reviews the present position and estimates the future of foreign language teaching in Britain against its historical perspective. In three parts, describing the historical background, the current developments in techniques, and the present and future implications for primary, secondary and further education (including teacher-training).

223 **Incorporated Association of Assistant Masters in Secondary Schools**
The teaching of modern languages. London, University of London Press, 4th edn. 1967. xiv, 466 pp. bibliog. First pubd. 1949.
Comprehensive and now fully revised review of problems and methods of foreign language teaching in British schools. Pays particular attention to the needs of the curriculum, examinations and current methods of administration. Refers mainly to French but also to the teaching of German, Spanish, Italian, Russian and Esperanto. Section on new methods and equipment. Valuable as reference book. Useful bibliographies.

224 **Incorporated Association of Head Masters**
Modern languages in the grammar school. Revised edition of the Report of a Working Party of Division xii (Lancashire and Cheshire) of I.A.H.M. published with the assistance of the Nuffield Foundation. [London,] The Association, 1966. 93 pp. First pubd. 1963.
Study of the problems of language teaching and the curriculum in English grammar schools. Considers aims, choice of languages, methods and equipment, preparation of teachers, examinations. Appendices include list of reference works for teachers and of reading materials for pupils.

225 **Kadler, Eric H.**
Linguistics and teaching foreign languages. New York, London etc., Van Nostrand Reinhold, 1970. xviii, 187 pp. illus. tables, bibliogs.
Details the practical applications of recent linguistic theory to the teaching of foreign languages, with examples drawn mostly from French, German, Russian and Spanish. Designed primarily as a text-book for teachers in training, it includes review questions and bibliographies for further study.

226 **Lado, Robert**
Linguistics across cultures: applied linguistics for language teachers. Ann Arbor, Michigan, University of Michigan Press, 1963. viii, 141 pp. bibliog. First pubd. 1957.
Argues that all foreign language teaching should be preceded by, and based upon, a systematic comparison of the learner's native language with the language to be learned. In this way attention can be focused on the difficulties of a particular language for a particular learner in another culture. Methods of comparison at different linguistic levels are described and explained.

227 **Libbish, B., ed.**
Advances in the teaching of modern language. Vol. 1. Oxford and London, Pergamon Press, 1962. xi, 175 pp.
Symposium of eighteen short articles covering aspects of language teaching in several countries at various levels, many by experienced practising teachers.

228 **Mathieu, G., ed.**
Advances in the teaching of modern languages. Vol. 2. Oxford and London, Pergamon Press, 1966. ix, 214 pp.
Collection of twelve papers by influential language teachers on practical applications of recent theoretical work, mostly in American education. Particularly emphasises techniques and technology applicable to teaching any foreign language.

229 **Michel, Joseph, ed.**
Foreign language teaching: an anthology. London, Collier–Macmillan; New York, Macmillan, 1967. x, 404 pp. bibliog.
Reprints of nineteen extracts and articles, grouped under: some theoretical aspects of language; the foreign language teacher; practical aspects of language teaching. Related to work and developments chiefly in the United States, but of wide general interest to all concerned with language teaching. Gives some prominence to the contributions of psychology and linguistics.

230 **Moulton, William G.**
A linguistic guide to language learning. New York, Modern Language Association of America, 1966. xii, 140 pp. bibliog.
Very clear introduction to principles of contrastive linguistics, particularly for the benefit of the educated adult who wishes to learn a language on his own, but of value to all language teachers.

231 **Postman, Neil, and Charles Weingartner**
Linguistics: a revolution in teaching. A Delta Book. New York, Dell, 1966. x, 209 pp. bibliog.
Introductory description of the general field of linguistics, followed by more detailed treatment of recent work on grammar, usage, semantics, lexicography, etc. of relevance to teaching English in U.S. schools.

232 **Stern, H. H.**
Foreign languages in primary education: the teaching of foreign or second languages to younger children. Language and Language Learning, 14. London, Oxford University Press, 2nd edn. 1967. xii, 148 pp. bibliog. First pubd. 1963.
Originally published by UNESCO as a report on an international meeting of experts (Hamburg, 1962). Now revised. Includes contributions on: arguments for early second language learning; experiences and experiments; recommendations for practice and research. Summarises current situation in many parts of the world. Extensive bibliography.

233 **Stern, H. H., ed.**
Languages and the young school child. With a *Research guide* by John B. Carroll. Language and Language Learning, 24. London, Oxford University Press, 1969. vii, 270 pp. illus. bibliog.
An international collection of studies based on the documentation and findings of a conference held in 1966. Includes sixteen papers grouped under: general trends; some projects; materials; linguistic and educational research. Covers the theory and practice of teaching foreign languages to younger children in all parts of the world.

234 **Strevens, Peter**
Papers in language and language teaching. Language and Language Learning, 9. London, Oxford University Press, 1965. viii, 152 pp. table, diagrs.
Collection of twelve papers originally published between 1955 and 1964 covering aspects of linguistics, phonetics and language teaching.

235 **UNESCO**
The teaching of modern languages: a volume of studies deriving from the International Seminar organised by the Secretariat of UNESCO at Nuwara Eliya, Ceylon, in August 1953. Problems in Education, 10. Paris, UNESCO, 1955. 295 pp.
Symposium arising from consideration of aims and methods by representatives of many countries. Includes sections on: the humanistic aspect of

the teaching of modern languages; the teaching of modern languages as a key to the understanding of other civilizations and peoples; the methodology of language teaching; the psychological aspects of language teaching; the training of modern language teachers; textbooks; the teaching of modern languages by radio and television; modern language teaching in primary schools.

236 **Valdman, Albert, ed.**
Trends in language teaching. New York, McGraw-Hill, 1966. xxii, 298 pp. illus. bibliog.
Collection of fourteen papers by specialists, covering recent developments in theory and practice of language teaching. Includes contributions on psychology and educational research, psycholinguistics, programmed instruction and testing. Pays full attention to recent research findings.

237 **Verlée, Léon**
Enseignement des langues et information culturelle. Langues et Culture, 4. Brussels, Labor; Paris, Nathan, 1969. vi, 145 pp.
Examines the relationship between language teaching (at primary and secondary levels) and the cultural content of the background information. Pays particular attention to dialogue.

PSYCHOLOGY OF LANGUAGE ACQUISITION, LEARNING AND TEACHING

238 **Association de Psychologie Scientifique de Langue Française**
Problèmes de psycho-linguistique: symposium de l'Association de psychologie scientifique de langue française, Neuchâtel, 1962, by J. de Ajuriaguerra and others. Bibliothèque Scientifique Internationale. Sciences Humaines. Section Psychologie. Paris, Presses Universitaires de France, 1963. 220 pp. illus. bibliogs.
Includes papers and reports by a number of experts on the relationship of language to cognition, perception and habit. Contributors include Piaget, Bresson, Oléron, Inhelder, Fraisse, Jodelet.

239 **Belyayev, B. V.**
The psychology of teaching foreign languages. Translated by R. F. Hingley. Pergamon Oxford Russian Series. Teaching Method, 1. Oxford and London, Pergamon Press, 1963. ix, 230 pp. tables, diagrs.
Collection of essays stressing the importance of the psychological bases of language teaching. Advocates a 'conscious-practical method' and emphasises initial oral work. Examples drawn from Soviet education.

240 **Borger, R., and A. E. M. Seaborne**
The psychology of learning. A Pelican Original. Harmondsworth, Penguin, 1966. 249 pp. illus. bibliog.
Introductory but comprehensive review of the contribution of psychology to learning theory. Pays full attention to recent views and includes a short chapter on concepts and the use of language.

241 **Bresson, François, and others**
Langage, communication et décision. Traité de Psychologie Expérimentale, 8. Paris, Presses Universitaires de France, 1965. iv, 308 pp. tables, illus. bibliogs.
Includes chapters on language and communication (Bresson); verbal association (Jodelet); experimental psychology of reading, writing and drawing (Mialaret); recent research and experimental work in Europe and America is thoroughly and critically examined. Very full bibliographical references. Mostly relates to the acquisition and use of the mother tongue.

242 **Broadbent, D. E.**
Behaviour. London, Eyre & Spottiswoode, 1961. 215 pp. bibliog.
Describes and discusses developments in behaviourism. Some critical appraisal of behaviourist theories of learning. Useful to the non-specialist requiring an introduction to work in this field.

243 **Burt, Sir Cyril**
A psychological study of typography. London, Cambridge University Press, 1959. xix, 68 pp. illus. tables, bibliog.
A study of the legibility and aesthetic merits of a variety of type faces, based on tests used with both adults and children. Factorial analysis is employed to produce a classification of type faces in terms of legibility and preferences. Of value to textbook writers for young children.

244 **Carroll, John B.**
Language and thought. Foundations of Modern Psychology Series. Englewood Cliffs, New Jersey, Prentice Hall, 1964. x, 118 pp. illus. tables, bibliog.
Condensed presentation, primarily for psychologists, of modern theories of the psychology of language. Includes chapters on the learning of language, and on language and cognition, of special interest to language teachers.

245 **Church, Joseph**
Language and the discovery of reality: a developmental psychology of cognition. New York, Random House, 1961. xviii, 245 pp. bibliog.
Study of child development with special reference to the acquisition of language and its effect on cognition. Provides a psychological approach to problems of meaning and the relationship of language and thinking. Although primarily concerned with acquisition of the mother tongue, may provide some insight into the learning of second languages by young children.

246 **De Cecco, John P.**
The psychology of language, thought and instruction: readings. New York, Holt, Rinehart & Winston, 1967. xvi, 446 pp. tables, diagrs. bibliogs.
Brings together reprints of forty-three papers, many reporting research, in the fields of psycholinguistics, sociolinguistics, cognitive and developmental psychology and language behaviour. Presented in ten chapters, each with an introduction. The whole is presented with a view to its relationship to problems of instruction in 'language and thought'.

247 **Deese, James**
The structure of associations in language and thought. Baltimore, Johns Hopkins Press, 1965. xv, 216 pp. tables, diagrs. bibliog.
Applies rigorous psychological procedures of structural analysis to the study of the stream of thought or language in order to develop a new theory of association.

248 **Dixon, Theodore R., and David L. Horton, eds.**
Verbal behavior and general behavior theory. Englewood Cliffs, New Jersey, Prentice-Hall, 1968. ix, 596 pp. tables, diagrs. bibliogs.
Papers by twenty-five specialists on psychological aspects of verbal behaviour, including five on psycholinguistics. Raises a number of issues of importance in relation to S-R theory.

249 **Flavell, John H.**
The developmental psychology of Jean Piaget. University Series in Psychology. Princeton, New Jersey, and London, Van Nostrand, 1963. xvi, 472 pp. bibliog.
Detailed summary of the theoretical and experimental work of Piaget. Attempts to present an integrated picture of the development of children's thinking and cognition. Insight into linguistic development and use may

be found of special value to those concerned with teaching language to young children. A valuable guide among the complexities of Piagetian theory.

250 **Hebb, D. O.**
The organization of behaviour: a neuropsychological theory. New York, Wiley; London, Chapman & Hall, 1949. xix, 335 pp. diagrs. bibliog.
Much of this influential book deals with the processes of learning, although it is mainly directed towards the clinical psychologist or neurologist.

251 **Jakobovits, Leon A., and Murray S. Miron, eds.**
Readings in the psychology of language. Prentice-Hall Psychology Series. Englewood Cliffs, New Jersey, Prentice-Hall, 1967. xiii, 636 pp. tables, diagrs. bibliogs.
Collection of thirty-five reprinted papers on psycholinguistic topics, mostly written within the past ten years. Arranged in three parts: some major theoretical formulations; experimental approaches to language; the problem of meaning – each with a short introduction. Brings together, sometimes contrastively, the views of psychologists and linguists on areas of common interest.

252 **Kainz, Friedrich**
Die Sprachentwicklung im Kindes- und Jugendalter. Studienhefte der Pädagogischen Hochschule: Psychologie. Munich, Ernst Reinhardt, 1964. 104 pp. tables, bibliog.
Short popular account of the development of speech in the young child. Starting with the new-born baby's first use of sound as a reaction to internal and external stimuli, it describes how the child begins to acquire the simplest forms of real speech, becomes aware of symbols, thinks conceptually and masters the basic structures of everyday language.

253 **Kausler, Donald H., ed.**
Readings in verbal learning: contemporary theory and research. New York and London, Wiley, 1966. xiv, 578 pp. tables, diagrs. bibliogs.
Over fifty specialist papers (originally published 1951–65) are reprinted under the headings: acquisition; transfer; retention; with an introduction to each section. Provides a general survey of recent research into verbal learning.

Leopold, Werner F.
See 333.

254 **Lewis, M. M.**
Language, thought and personality in infancy and childhood. London, Harrap, 1963. 256 pp. bibliog.
Aims to give 'a systematic account of the growth of language in relation to general development in infancy and childhood'. Includes chapters on: the growth of meaning; language and thinking; language and personal and social development; language and exploration; the growth of reasoning; general and linguistic characteristics; language and concrete thinking; social and ethical development.

255 **Liebrucks, Bruno**
Sprache und Bewusstsein. Frankfurt am Main, Akademische Verlagsgesellschaft, 1964– . In progress.
Vol. 1: *Einleitung: Spannweite des Problems.*
Vol. 2: *Sprache: "Wilhelm von Humboldt".*
Vol. 3: *Wege zum Bewusstsein im Raum von Kant, Hegel und Marx.*
Vol. 4: *Die erste Revolution der Denkungsart; Kant: Kritik der reinen Vernunft.*
Historical account of the development of ideas on language and consciousness, principally in the thought of German philosophers of the late eighteenth and nineteenth centuries from Herder to Marx.

256 **Luria, A. R.**
The role of speech in the regulation of normal and abnormal behaviour. Edited by J. Tizard. Oxford and London, Pergamon Press, 1961. ix, 100 pp. diagrs. bibliog. Mimeographed.
Reports important research in the USSR on the dynamics of the mental development of children. Describes the acquisition of speech in stages.

257 **Luria, A. R., and F. Ia. Yudovich**
Speech and the development of mental processes in the child: an experimental investigation. Edited by Joan Simon. Translated by O. Kovasc and J. Simon. London, Staples Press, 1959. 126 pp. First pubd. in the USSR, 1956.
Report of the development of speech in a pair of identical twins in USSR. Valuable illustration of the part played by language in social communication, the development of understanding and concepts. References to previous Soviet work.

258 **Lyons, J., and R. J. Wales, eds.**
Psycholinguistics papers: the proceedings of the 1966 Edinburgh Conference. Edinburgh, Edinburgh University Press, 1966. ix, 243 pp. diagrs. bibliog.
Includes the following papers: on hearing sentences; the organisation of linguistic performance; the creation of language by children; some reflections on competence and performance; syntactic regularities in the speech of children. Discussion and extensive bibliography.

259 **Miller, George A.**
Language and communication. New York and London, McGraw-Hill, 1951. xiii, 298 pp. tables, diagrs. bibliog.
Presents the results of scientific studies of language and communication relevant to psychology at the time of publication. Intended chiefly for students of psychology. Includes chapters on: the phonetic approach; the perception of speech; the statistical approach; rules for using symbols; individual differences; the verbal behaviour of children; the role of learning; verbal habits; some effects of verbal habits; words, sets and thought; the social approach.

260 **Miller, George A.**
The psychology of communication: seven essays. London, Allen Lane. The Penguin Press, 1968. ix, 197 pp. diagrs. bibliogs.
Collection of papers on various aspects of the cognitive mechanisms of language and communication in man.

261 **Oldfield, R. C., and J. C. Marshall, eds.**
Language: selected readings. Penguin Modern Psychology, UPS 10. London, Penguin, 1968. 392 pp. illus. tables, bibliogs.
A collection of twenty-five articles by influential specialists (all originally published since 1959) on language, stressing the interests of psychologists. Contents are grouped under: acquisition and development; perception and production; psychological aspects of linguistics; quantitative and mathematical aspects; pathology and brain function. Contains valuable bibliographical references and editorial introductions to each section.

262 **Osgood, Charles E., and Thomas A. Sebeok, eds.**
Psycholinguistics: a survey of theory and research problems. With *A survey of psycholinguistic research 1954–1964*, by A. Richard Diebold, and *The Psycholinguists*, by George A. Miller. Indiana University Studies in the History and Theory of Linguistics. Bloomington, Indiana University Press, 1965. xii, 307 pp. tables, diagrs. bibliogs.

Contains three sections: the original survey, produced in 1954; the second survey, 1954–64; the appendix, *The psycholinguists: on the new scientists of language*, written in 1964. Valuable in showing the origins and bases of psycholinguistics as an area of work. Extensive bibliographic references.

263 **Penfield, Wilder, and Lamar Roberts**

Speech and brain-mechanisms. Princeton, N.J., Princeton University Press; London, Oxford University Press, 1959. xiii, 286 pp. illus. tables, bibliog.
Specialist study, based on neurosurgical evidence, of brain dominance, aphasia and other speech disturbances. Covers cerebral mechanisms of speech and the learning of language. Contains much of interest and importance to students of the psychology of language learning.

264 **Piaget, Jean**

The language and thought of the child. Translated from the French by Marjorie Gabain. London, Routledge & Kegan Paul, 3rd edn. 1959. xxiv, 288 pp. tables. Paper-backed edn. 1960. First pubd. in French, 1923.
Influential work which examines the functions of language, types and stages in conversation, understanding and verbal explanation, questions, and ego-centric language as revealed by exchanges between children from ages four to eight years. Based on careful observation and transcription of utterances. Provides valuable insight into children's thought as shown by their verbal behaviour.

265 **Rivers, Wilga M.**

The psychologist and the foreign-language teacher. Chicago and London, University of Chicago Press, 1964. viii, 212 pp. bibliog.
Critical survey of the contributions of psychology to the methodology of language learning and teaching. An appendix provides useful comparative analysis of recent psychological theories of learning.

266 **Rosenberg, Sheldon, ed.**

Directions in psycholinguistics. New York, Macmillan; London, Collier–Macmillan, 1965. x, 260 pp. tables, diagrs. bibliogs.
Edition of papers presented at an institute held in 1963 grouped under: psychology of grammar; psycholinguistics and verbal learning; the modification of verbal behaviour; individual differences in verbal behaviour; psycholinguistics and language pathology.

267 **Saporta, Sol, and Jarvis R. Bastian, eds.**
Psycholinguistics: a book of readings. New York, Holt, Rinehart & Winston, 1961. xvii, 551 pp. tables, diagrs. bibliogs.
A volume of reprints covering the wide field where behavioural psychology and structural linguistics meet. Contains sections on: the nature and function of language; approaches to the study of language; speech perception; the sequential organisation of linguistic events; the semantic aspects of linguistic events; language acquisition, bilingualism, and language change; pathologies of linguistic behaviour; linguistic relativity and the relation of linguistic processes to perception and cognition. Contains material otherwise difficult of access. Authors include Bloomfield, Jakobson, Leopold, Weinreich, Haugen, Whorf and Vygotsky.

268 **Skinner, B. F.**
Verbal behaviour. The Centenary Psychology Series. London, Methuen; New York, Appleton-Century-Crofts, 1957. xi, 478 pp. diagrs.
Comprehensive and thorough attempt to account for language in terms of behaviouristic psychology. Aspects of language in use are noted and explained within the framework of stimulus–response situations, and general conclusions are drawn about all aspects of linguistic behaviour. Many programmed instruction techniques have been based on the theory of language learning contained in this book.

269 **Social Science Research Council. Committee on Intellective Processes Research**
The acquisition of language. Report of the Fourth Conference sponsored by the Committee on Intellective Processes Research of the Social Science Research Council. Edited by Ursula Bellugi and Roger Brown. Monographs of the Society for Research in Child Development, 92. Lafayette, Indiana, Purdue University, Child Development Publications, 1964. 191 pp. bibliogs.
Papers and discussions of a conference held in October 1961. Subjects covered: the development of grammar in child language; the acquisition of syntax; the development from vocal to verbal behaviour in children; speech as a motor skill with special reference to nonaphasic disorders; mediation processes and the acquisition of linguistic structures.

270 **Spearritt, Donald**
Listening comprehension – a factorial analysis. A.C.E.R. Research Series, 76. [Melbourne,] Australian Council for Educational Research, 1962. x, 149 pp. tables, bibliog.

Detailed research report of an investigation into the factors involved in the skill of understanding spoken language, with reference to the mother tongue. Using a battery of thirty-four tests administered to a sample of school-children, the project sought to determine the relationship of the various factors which could be identified. Description of the rigorous techniques employed will be of interest to specialists concerned with language-test construction.

271 **Templin, Mildred C.**
Certain language skills in children: their development and inter-relationships. Monograph Series, 26. Minneapolis, University of Minnesota Press, 1957. xviii, 183 pp. tables, bibliog.
Describes the growth in a group of 480 American children, from three to eight years, of articulation of speech sounds, sound discrimination, sentence structure and vocabulary. Careful controls and experimental techniques were used in order to establish norms of development. Of interest to teachers of a second language to young children, since it provides some criteria of achievement based on mother-tongue learning.

Thorndike, Robert L., and Elizabeth Hagen
See 329.

272 **Titone, Renzo**
La psicolinguistica oggi. Zurich, Pas-Verlag, 1964. 313 pp. tables, diagrs. bibliog.
General treatment of psycholinguistics in relation to language acquisition and learning. Stresses that teaching methodology depends not only on adequate linguistic analysis but on a clear understanding of the psychology of language learning.

273 **Titone, Renzo**
Studies in the psychology of second language learning. Istituto Superiore di Pedagogia del Pontificio Ateneo Salesiano (Roma). Quaderni di Orientamenti Pedagogici, 8. Zurich, Pas-Verlag, 1964. 181 pp. tables.
A collection of six papers, three of which deal with the psychological factors involved in teaching young children and adolescents, one with the learning of grammar and two with experimental studies of phonetic problems. Previous work is extensively reviewed and collated.

274 **Vygotsky, L. S.**
Thought and language. Edited and translated by Eugenia Hanfmann and Gertrude Vakar. Studies in Communication. Cambridge Massachusetts, M.I.T. Press; New York, Wiley, 1962. xxi, 168 pp. bibliog.
First published in Russian in 1934 and reprinted in 1956. Introduction to first English translation by Jerome S. Bruner. Refers to earlier work of Piaget, Buehler and Stern and covers intellectual and linguistic development and concept formation in children, including the development of scientific concepts. Illuminating study of the development of child language and thinking.

Walters, Theodore W.
See 336.

275 **Weir, Ruth Hirsch**
Language in the crib. Janua Linguarum. Series Maior, 14. The Hague, Mouton, 1962. 216 pp. diagrs. bibliog.
The pre-sleep soliloquies of a two-and-a-half-year-old English-speaking boy were tape-recorded. Presents a detailed analysis of this language in terms of phonology, morphology, syntax and vocabulary. The study of sentence patterns is further elaborated into a consideration of paradigmatic and sequential selection.

276 **Weisgerber, Bernhard**
Beiträge zur Neubegründung der Sprachdidaktik. Weinheim, Julius Beltz, 1964. 274 pp. table, bibliog.
Consideration of recent advances in educational and linguistic theory in relation to ideas of how the child learns language, and the implications of this for the teaching of language at all stages. Mostly concerned with the mother tongue but also takes into account the effect of learning a second language on the concept one has of the mother tongue. Concludes with a long schematic table showing the stages of the acquisition of speech and the corresponding development of concept formation, powers of analysis and expression in the child, and the implications at each stage for the educationalist.

277 **Weisgerber, Leo**
Das Menschheitsgesetz der Sprache als Grundlage der Sprachwissenschaft. Hochschulwissen in Einzeldarstellungen. Heidelberg, Quelle & Meyer,

2nd edn. 1964. 202 pp. diagrs. bibliog. First pubd. 1950. Title of first edition: *Das Gesetz der Sprache*.
Theoretical and philosophical four-part discussion of the role of language in human existence. Language as the major conditioning factor in man's existence; the effect on man as a social animal of belonging to the speech community of his mother tongue; the psychological implication of knowing one's native tongue and other languages; the philosophical aspects of language and the value of the study of language.

TEACHING METHODS

278 **Adam, J. B., and A. J. Shawcross**
The language laboratory. London, Pitman, 2nd edn. 1965. viii, 72 pp. illus. First pubd. 1963.
Short practical description of the equipment and uses of a language laboratory, based on experience up to 1963, mostly in a London college.

279 **Billows, F. L.**
The techniques of language teaching. London, Longmans, Green, 1961. xi, 259 pp.
Imaginative yet practical advice primarily, but not exclusively, for teachers of younger children. Includes chapters on situational language-teaching, unsupervised work and group work, visual aids and the teaching of composition, prose literature and poetry. Language-learning is viewed as part of a pattern of self-expression and of social and educational development. Examples mostly from the teaching of English as a second language.

280 **Birkmaier, Emma Maria, ed.**
Britannica review of foreign language education, volume 1, 1968. Chicago, Encyclopaedia Britannica, 1969. xii, 450 pp. bibliogs.
Sponsored by the American Council on the Teaching of Foreign Languages, presents a review of foreign language teaching based on an analysis of the ACTFL bibliographies. Fourteen contributions are arranged under 1. Context and organisation of foreign language learning; 2. Theory and practice of foreign language teaching and learning. Provides a comprehensive analytical review of recent research philosophy and practice in foreign language teaching. This review is the first volume in an annual series.

281 **Bohlen, Adolf**
Bild und Ton im neusprachlichen Unterricht. Der Neusprachliche Unterricht in Wissenschaft und Praxis, 7. Dortmund, Lambert Lensing, 1962. 134 pp. illus. Survey of the uses of audio-visual aids in foreign language teaching, primarily for teachers in German schools. The emphasis is on methodology rather than on technical data.

282 **Brooks, Nelson**
Language and language learning: theory and practice. New York and Burlingame, Harcourt, Brace and World, 2nd edn. 1964. xv, 300 pp. bibliogs. First pubd. 1960.
Comprehensive treatment of most aspects of foreign language teaching based on older as well as newer principles. Pays full attention to underlying theory but provides many examples of practical classroom situations. Valuable to the experienced as well as the inexperienced teacher.

283 **Bung, Klaus, ed.**
Programmed learning and the language laboratory, 2: collected papers. London, Longmac, 1967. 280 pp. tables, bibliogs.
Six papers covering the use of language laboratories in relation to self-instructional programmed materials. Suggests principles and methods on which a programmed language learning centre can be based.

284 **Bung, Klaus, ed.**
Programmed learning and the language laboratory, 1: collected papers. London, Longmac, 1968. 243 pp. tables, diagrs. bibliogs.
Eleven papers presented in two sections, the first dealing with programmed learning in general and the second with its application to language teaching, especially through language laboratories.

285 **Corder, S. Pit**
The visual element in language teaching. Education Today: Language Teaching. London, Longmans, Green, 1966. xi, 96 pp. illus.
Concise introductory study, for teachers and teachers in training, of the place of visual materials in language teaching with examples drawn from films, audio-visual courses and television. Includes a chapter on the special problems of teaching meaning.

286 **Council of Europe. Council for Cultural Co-operation**
Modern language teaching by television: a survey based on the principal experiments carried out in Western Europe, by Raymond Hickel. Translated from the French by W. Horsfall Carter. Education in Europe, Section 4: General, 4. Strasbourg, The Council, 1965. 185 pp. bibliog.
Report of recent research in W. Europe in modern language teaching, (*a*) in general pedagogics and adult education, (*b*) in use of TV as medium of instruction – based on questionnaires sent to authorities concerned in nineteen countries. Surveys problems in schools and adult TV broadcasts, technical, financial and practical considerations, advantages and disadvantages of TV language teaching.

287 **Dodson, C. J.**
Language teaching and the bilingual method. London, Pitman, 1967. vii, 182 pp. tables, diagrs.
Exposition of a method, based largely on experiment and experience in Welsh schools, which exploits the controlled use of the mother tongue in teaching foreign languages. Many practical examples and much detailed suggestion for the beginning teacher.

Dorry, Gertrude Nye, comp.
See 450.

288 **Dutton, Brian, ed.**
A guide to modern language teaching methods. Audio-Visual Language Association Publications, 1. London, Cassell, 1965. viii, 206 pp. illus.
Contains sections by three contributors on audio-visual methods, audio-lingual methods, linguistics and programmed instruction. Written for the practical teacher but critically reviews techniques and underlying theories. Numerous practical examples.

Eriksson, Marguerite, and others
See 582.

289 **Finocchiaro, Mary**
Teaching children foreign languages. New York and London, McGraw-Hill, 1964. xi, 210 pp. bibliog.
Written for those concerned with foreign language teaching in elementary schools in the United States, this book pays special attention to relevant problems of administration and curriculum planning. Modern methods of

language teaching applicable to younger children are described and illustrated in terms of classroom procedures, while considerable attention is given to the construction of suitable syllabuses. Examples of materials to teach French, Spanish, German, Hebrew and Italian are provided.

290 **Great Britain. Department of Education and Science**
Language laboratories. Education Survey, 3. London, H.M.S.O., 1968. vi, 32 pp.
Introductory guide to language laboratory use and organisation for teachers and administrators in Britain.

291 **Grève, Marcel de, and Frans van Passel**
Linguistique et enseignement des langues étrangères. Langue et Culture, 1. Brussels, Labor; Paris, Fernand Nathan, 1968. iii, 192 pp. diagrs. bibliog.
Describes the practical applications of linguistics to language teaching, with special reference to the needs of a country such as Belgium. Includes an examination of the problems of bilingualism in education.

292 **Hall, Robert A., jr.**
New ways to learn a foreign language. The Bantam Languages Library, 1019. New York, Bantam Books, 1966. 180 pp. bibliog.
Popular exposition of techniques of language learning. Includes description of language in modern terms, problems of interference and elementary descriptions of eight major languages in relation to English.

293 **Hayes, A. S.**
Language laboratory facilities: technical guide for their selection, purchase, use and maintenance. Language and Language Learning, 16. London, Oxford University Press, 1968. xii, 138 pp. illus. bibliog.
Revision of American edition of 1963.

294 **Hilton, J. B.**
The language laboratory in school. London, Methuen, 1966. 145 pp. illus. bibliog.
Practical and non-technical description of the uses of a language laboratory in an English grammar school. Contains useful suggestions for organisation and maintenance of equipment.

295 Hocking, Elton
Language laboratory and language learning. Monograph, 2. Washington, D.C., National Education Association of the United States, Department of Audio-visual Instruction, 1964. 210 pp. illus. bibliog.
Non-technical in content and language, this book is addressed to audio-visual specialists as well as to teachers of foreign languages. Summarises the history of the language laboratory, reviews current research and looks forward to future developments.

296 Howatt, Anthony P. R.
Programmed learning and the language teacher: some implications and suggestions for the use of programmes in the teaching of a foreign language. London, Longmans, Green, 1969. x, 244 pp. illus.
Summarises the theory of programming and examines its application to language teaching. Suggests suitable programming techniques and provides a selection of sample programmes (mainly in teaching English) including some suitable for use in language laboratories.

297 Huebener, Theodore
Audio-visual techniques in teaching foreign languages: a practical handbook. New York, New York University Press, 2nd edn. 1967. xv, 179 pp. illus. bibliogs. First pubd. 1960.
Concise survey of the use of all kinds of visual and audio aids, simple as well as complex, in relation to teaching modern languages. Many examples closely related to actual lesson material in Spanish, French, German, etc. Emphasises the needs of the practical teacher.

298 Huebener, Theodore
How to teach foreign languages effectively. New York, New York University Press, 2nd edn. 1965. xii, 240 pp. bibliog. First pubd. 1959.
Practical guide for the foreign language teacher based on experience in New York schools. Includes sections on audio-lingual, audio-visual and language laboratory techniques. Illustrated by examples of over forty complete lessons in French, German, Italian and Spanish.

299 Jespersen, Otto
How to teach a foreign language. Translated from the Danish by Sophia Yhlen-Olsen Bertelsen. London, Allen & Unwin, 1904. 194 pp. bibliog.
Although written over half a century ago, this book advocates many of the language-teaching methods still applicable. Recommends grading of voc-

abulary, idiom, grammar and sounds. Visual aids are discussed with emphasis on proper cultural content. The scientific use of phonetics is demonstrated and phonetic transcription is recommended in the initial stages.

300 **Kelly, Louis G.**
25 centuries of language teaching: an inquiry into the science, art, and development of language teaching methodology, 500 B.C.–1969. Rowley, Massachusetts, Newbury House, 1969. xii, 474 pp. illus. maps, tables, bibliog.
Presents a discussion of modern theory and practice in language teaching within a detailed historical framework. Valuable for its copious references to hitherto largely unknown or unrecognised historical sources, and examination of their influence on the development of language teaching techniques.

301 **Lado, Robert**
Language teaching: a scientific approach. New York and London, McGraw-Hill, 1964. xv, 239 pp. illus. bibliog.
Concise and comprehensive introduction to the theory and practice of language teaching, which gives full consideration to developments in psychology, linguistics and technological aids. Examples chosen from English, French, Spanish and German illustrate the procedures recommended. Contains much practical advice to the classroom teacher on the conduct of lessons and the preparation of teaching material. Includes sections on language testing, the language laboratory, visual aids and programmed learning.

Lee, W. R., and Helen Coppen
See 476.

302 **Leisinger, Fritz**
Der elementare Fremdsprachenunterricht: Grundfragen seiner Methodik. Erziehungswissenschaftliche Bücherei, Reihe 3: Unterrichtslehre. Stuttgart, Klett, 1967. 176 pp. bibliog. First pubd. 1949.
Handbook for the teaching of foreign languages in German primary and senior elementary schools, mainly of interest as a statement of an enlightened approach characteristic of the 1940s and early 1950s before the arrival of the audio-visual course.

303 **Leisinger, Fritz**
Elemente des neusprachlichen Unterrichts. Stuttgart, Ernst Klett, 1966. 352 pp. bibliog.
Account in uncomplicated language of the relationship of the findings of modern linguistic science to current practice in modern language teaching. The first part of the book deals with the linguistic basis and gives an account of language as communication. Later sections explain most of the basic concepts in contemporary linguistics. The second part deals with language teaching practice and examines current views on aims and methods, attempts to evaluate newer approaches made possible by the application of technology to teaching, discusses the acquisition of the different language skills and deals with the role of translation, grammar, written work and reading in the learning of a language.

304 **Léon, Pierre R.**
Laboratoire de langues et correction phonétique: essai méthodologique. Publications du Centre de Linguistique Appliquée de l'Université de Besançon. Paris, Didier, 1962. 274 pp. illus. bibliog.
Comprehensive study of the methodology of using language laboratories. Includes chapters on historical development of methods and equipment; modern linguistics and technical equipment; the functions of a modern language laboratory (including the use of film); research and special equipment. Refers extensively to French and American experience. Technical descriptions related to linguistic theory. Very full bibliography.

305 **Levenson, Stanley, and William Kendrick, eds.**
Readings in foreign languages for the elementary school. A Blaisdell Book in the Modern Languages. Waltham, Massachusetts, and London, Blaisdell, 1967. xix, 556 pp. illus. tables, bibliog.
Collection of sixty-one articles by a wide range of experts on foreign language teaching at the primary school level in the U.S. Part 1 covers the rationale – philosophical, psychological and administrative. Part 2 covers methods and materials, aids and evaluation. Examples from French, Spanish and German.

306 **Mackey, William Francis**
Language teaching analysis. London, Longmans, Green, 1965. xiii, 554 pp. tables, diagrs. bibliog.
Comprehensive and detailed analysis of the problems and factors involved in second-language learning, with numerous examples from English and other European languages. Part 1 – language – deals with language theories

and descriptions, language differences and language learning; Part 2 – method – outlines different methods and discusses selection, gradation and presentation; Part 3 – teaching – covers lesson analysis in terms of language, plan and techniques, with chapters on automated language teaching and on testing. Includes appendices on language drills and games and an extensive classified bibliography including periodical references.

307 **Malandain, Claude**
Utilisation des films fixes pour l'enseignement des langues vivantes aux enfants: problèmes psychologiques liés à l'utilisation d'images et films fixes chez l'enfant. Linguistique Appliquée. Paris, Didier, 1966. 152 pp. illus. tables, bibliog.
Scholarly study of the theory of use of film-strips in audio-visual courses associated with Centre de Recherche et d'Etude pour la Diffusion du Français. Describes psychological bases as well as experimental findings of the methods employed.

308 **Marty, Fernand L.**
Language laboratory learning. Wellesley, Massachusetts, Audio-Visual Publications, 1960. xi, 256 pp. illus.
Collection of papers dealing with various aspects of language laboratory materials and techniques. Includes description of a basic French course; special courses (literary, phonetics, comprehension of scientific material, etc.); principles of sound recording; operating a language laboratory; equipment and installation. Includes much technical information simply presented.

309 **Nida, Eugene A.**
Learning a foreign language: a handbook prepared especially for missionaries. New York, Friendship Press, rev. edn. 1957. vii, 212 pp. illus.
Describes principles and procedures in language study for those concerned with learning from native-speaking tutors or informants. Includes a treatment of principles of linguistics from the point of view of the learner of a spoken (and probably unwritten) language, with especial emphasis on phonology. Based on a sophisticated application of modern linguistics.

310 **Palmer, Harold E.**
The principles of language-study. Language and Language Learning, 5. London, Oxford University Press, 1965. ix, 142 pp. First pubd. 1922.

An influential work in which many principles and techniques now generally accepted were first advocated. Important background reading for those who wish to understand the bases of later techniques of oral practice and grading of material. Contains much forceful practical advice to teachers which remains valid today.

311 **Rivers, Wilga M.**
Teaching foreign-language skills. Chicago, University of Chicago Press, 1968. xi, 403 pp. bibliogs.
Examines linguistic and pedagogical principles underlying current methods of foreign language teaching. Although related to United States school system, discussion applies to teaching foreign languages generally at most levels in other countries. Written for serving teachers and those in training. Much practical advice on techniques.

312 **Schröter, Günter, and Hans Ladwein**
Der neusprachliche Unterricht. Erziehung und Unterricht in den Mittelschulen, 6. Frankfurt am Main, Diesterweg, 2nd edn. 1962. 147 pp. diagrs. bibliog.
Guide for the modern language teacher, divided into three major sections. The first deals with the basic, general principles governing language teaching at secondary level, the second with the methodology and specific problems of teaching English as a foreign language in Germany and the third with the teaching of French there.

313 **Stack, Edward M.**
The language laboratory and modern language teaching. New York, Oxford University Press, 2nd edn. 1966. xiv, 234 pp. illus. tables, bibliog. First pubd. 1960.
Practical handbook for language teachers and teachers in training, dealing with the techniques and procedures of language laboratory teaching. Includes much valuable data and advice on equipment, organisation and administration of language laboratories as well as a critical assessment of their range of usefulness in teaching various skills. Clearly arranged for reference.

314 **Sweet, Henry**
The practical study of languages: a guide for teachers and learners. Language and Language Learning, 1. London, Oxford University Press, 1964. xv, 276 pp. First pubd. 1899.
A classic work advocating reformed methods of language teaching. Although much of this book is now principally of historical interest, its influence on later developments in methodology has been very great, especially in its insistence on speech, the selection and grading of material and the application of linguistic scholarship to language teaching.

315 **Titone, Renzo**
Teaching foreign languages: an historical sketch. Washington, D.C., Georgetown University Press, 1968. 124 pp. bibliog.
Historical survey of methods of teaching foreign languages from ancient times to the present. Gives prominence to the work of nineteenth and twentieth century 'reformers' and ends with a summary of current methods in a number of countries.

316 **Titone, Renzo, and John B. Carroll**
Le lingue estere: metodologia didattica. Zurich, Pas-Verlag, 1966. 618 pp. bibliogs.
Comprehensive treatise on foreign language teaching including sections on the contributions of linguistics, psychology and technological research. Extensive references and bibliographies.

317 **Turner, John D.**
Introduction to the language laboratory. London, University of London Press, 1965. 110 pp. illus. bibliog.
Describes basic equipment of a language laboratory, its use and administration. Includes section in methods and materials. Based on requirements of schools, etc., in Britain.

318 **Turner, John D., ed.**
Programming for the language laboratory. London, University of London Press, 1968. vii, 263 pp. illus. tables, bibliogs.
Six contributors deal with the design of language drills and their application to teaching English, French, German, Russian and Spanish.

319 **Turner, John D., ed.**
Using the language laboratory. London, University of London Press, 1968. xiii, 156 pp. illus.
Five contributors discuss the use of the language laboratories in primary and secondary schools, universities, technical colleges and industry.

320 **West, Michael**
Learning to read a foreign language and other essays on language-teaching. London, Longmans, Green, 1955. vii, 100 pp. tables, diagrs.
Collection of practical articles (referring mostly to English as a foreign language) containing the title essay (first issued in 1926); the selection and counting of words and items in the teaching of speech; catenising (chaining words together); 'simplified and abridged' [on the technique of the Supplementary Reader]; reading aloud and silent reading; how much English grammar?; examinations in a foreign language.

TESTING AND EXAMINATIONS

321 **Anastasi, Anne**
Psychological testing. New York, Macmillan, 2nd edn. 1961. xiii, 657 pp. illus. tables, bibliogs. First pubd. 1954.
Provides a comprehensive introduction to the principles of psychological testing and a description of the major types of tests in use. Previous knowledge of statistics is not required, although statistical concepts and procedures are described. Based principally on American work, but pays attention to work in other countries. Valuable for reference by those professionally concerned with all types of objective testing.

322 **Anstey, Edgar**
Psychological tests. London, Nelson, 1966. xix, 300 pp. tables, diagrs. bibliog.
Handbook for test constructors, concerned with the principles and scientific procedures underlying the design of objective tests of all kinds, with the practical problems of test construction and with the validation and use of test results. Includes many examples and tables for statistical analysis.

323 **Brown, James**
Objective tests: their construction and analysis: a practical handbook for teachers. London, Longmans, Green, 1966. vi, 57 pp. tables, diagrs. bibliog.
Concise introduction to the design, construction and use of objective tests, originally written for use in West Africa. Includes sections on elementary item analysis and basic statistics.

324 **Buros, Oscar Krisen, ed.**
The sixth mental measurements yearbook. Highland Park, New Jersey, Gryphon Press, 1965. xxxvii, 1714 pp. tables, bibliogs.
Latest edition of a standard reference book listing and reviewing published test material; contains sections on tests of foreign languages including English.

325 **Davies, Alan, ed.**
Language testing symposium: a psycholinguistic approach. Language and Language Learning, 21. London, Oxford University Press, 1968. viii, 214 pp. tables, bibliog.
A collection of ten papers written by specialists in language testing which reviews current principles and problems over a wide field. Incorporates primarily British and American experience, and includes special references to testing English as a second language.

326 **Lado, Robert**
Language testing: the construction and use of foreign language tests: a teacher's book. London, Longmans, Green, 1961. xxiii, 389 pp. illus.
General survey of techniques of language testing. Includes sections on theory of language testing, techniques to test specific skills, testing cross-cultural understanding. Many practical examples and suggestions for construction and use of new tests.

327 **Lindquist, E. F., ed.**
Educational measurement. Washington, D.C., American Council on Education, 1951. xix, 819 pp. illus. tables, bibliog.
Comprehensive reference work and handbook in which eighteen chapters by specialists cover the whole field of educational measurement. Numerous detailed illustrations of materials and techniques; extensive bibliographical references. Remains an essential reference book for those concerned with the construction or use of objective tests of all kinds.

National Foundation for Educational Research in England and Wales
See 588.

328 **Otter, H. S.**
A functional language examination: the Modern Language Association ex-examination project. Language and Language Learning, 19. London, Oxford University Press, 1968. ix, 136 pp. tables, diagrs.

Report of the British Modern Language Association examinations project of 1963–6. Deals with the structure and content of C.G.E. 'O' level examinations in modern languages and makes recommendations for their reform and for alternative syllabuses.

Savard, Jean-Guy
See 335.

Spearitt, Donald
See 270.

329 **Thorndike, Robert L., and Elizabeth Hagen**
Measurement and evaluation in psychology and education. New York and London, Wiley, 3rd edn. 1969. ix, 705 pp. illus. tables, bibliog. First pubd. 1955.
Comprehensive handbook on the principles and techniques of psychological and educational testing, including design and construction of tests; administration and scoring; validity and reliability; underlying statistical principles and practical application. Many examples of standard materials. The 3rd edition contains much new material in a revised presentation.

330 **Upshur, John A., and Julia Fata, eds.**
Problems in foreign language testing. Proceedings of a conference held at the University of Michigan, September, 1967. Language Learning: a Journal of Applied Linguistics, Special Issue, 3, August 1968. Ann Arbor, Michigan, University of Michigan, North University Building, 1968. xii, 183 pp.
Collection of fifteen papers by specialists on particular aspects and problems of language testing. Contains proposals for further research.

331 **Valette, Rebecca M.**
Modern language testing: a handbook. New York, Harcourt, Brace & World, 1967. xviii, 200 pp. illus. bibliog.
Designed primarily for use by the classroom teacher who wishes to make and use objective tests. Includes instructions on making tests, using them and evaluating their results. Provides many practical examples drawn from French, German, Spanish, Italian, etc. Well arranged for quick reference.

BIBLIOGRAPHIES

332 **Goodger, B. C.**
Modern languages. The Master Catalogue Series. London, Morgan–Grampian Educational, 1967. xii, 350 pp.

Bibliography of all modern language textbooks produced by British publishers and available in print in August 1967 (includes audio-visual and audio-lingual courses). Wherever possible the date of first publication of each book is indicated. Languages covered: French, German, Spanish, Russian, Italian and other (=uncommonly taught) languages. About 2000 books issued by forty-six publishers are listed.

Hammer, John H., and Frank A. Rice
See 157.

333 **Leopold, Werner F.**
Bibliography of child language. Humanities Series, 28. Evanston, Illinois, North-Western University Press, 1952. vi, 115 pp.
Does not claim to be a complete bibliography of the material available. Includes only Western European and American publications. Covers most fully the language learning of the pre-school-age child.

334 **Nostrand, Howard Lee, and others**
Research on language teaching: an annotated international bibliography, 1945–64. Seattle, University of Washington Press, 2nd edn. 1965. xxiv, 373 pp. First pubd. 1962.
Comprehensive collection of references to reported research in methodology, materials, psychology of language learning, linguistics etc., including books, periodical articles, unpublished papers and theses. While most sources referred to are American, important work elsewhere is also covered. Author and subject indexes are provided.

Permanent International Committee of Linguists
See 213.

Robinson, Janet O.
See 214.

335 **Savard, Jean-Guy**
Bibliographie analytique de tests de langue – Analytical bibliography of language tests. Quebec, Les Presses de l'Université Laval, 1969. xviii, 372 pp. bibliog.
Lists a great variety of tests (including a number which are unpublished): in second languages (French, English, Spanish, German, Italian, Latin and Russian); in mother-tongues (Afrikaans, English, Spanish, French and

Dutch); of aptitude; some language-based psychological tests (French and English). Provides a descriptive analysis of each test.

336 **Walters, Theodore W.**
The Georgetown bibliography of studies contributing to the psycholinguistics of language learning. Washington, D.C., Georgetown University Press, 1965. x, 125 pp.
Covers an interdisciplinary field.

SECTION III

English for speakers of other languages

GENERAL

337 **Allen, Harold B., ed.**
Readings in applied English linguistics. New York, Appleton-Century-Crofts, 2nd edn. 1964. xii, 535 pp. illus. maps, tables. First pubd. 1958.
Primarily intended for American teachers of English as a source book on current linguistic thought and its application. The second edition takes into account developments after 1958: twenty-four of the original articles have been retained; thirty-eight are new. The impact of transformational grammar on teaching theory and practice is given due recognition.

338 **Barnes, Douglas, and others**
Language, the learner and the school. A research report by Douglas Barnes, with a contribution from James Britton, and a discussion document prepared by the London Association for the Teaching of English, introduced by Harold Rosen. Penguin Papers in Education. Harmondsworth, Middlesex, Penguin, 1969. 128 pp. tables, diagrs. bibliog.
The main section describes a detailed study of language interaction in twelve lessons in the first term of secondary education in a British school. Provides valuable insight into the modes of language use characteristic of teachers of general subjects as well as the predominance of spoken language (and its terms) in lessons in all subjects. The second section discusses the language used by pupils themselves in unsupervised classroom discussion. Of particular interest to those concerned with the use of English as a medium of instruction.

339 **Bolton, W. F., and D. Crystal, eds.**
The English language, volume 2: essays by linguists and men of letters, 1858–1964. London, Cambridge University Press, 1969. xiii, 325 pp. tables, diagrs.
Second volume of statements by eminent scholars and writers on the nature and use of language, the first having covered the period 1490–1839. Records the rise of modern linguistics with excerpts from the writings of e.g. Sweet, Bloomfield, Sapir, Richards, Fries; reflects the changing nature of English language study in the light of the growth of linguistic science, and indicates the development of concern with particular aspects such as 'standard' English, spelling reform, American English, the social aspects of language. The Men of Letters are represented by Dickens, Whitman, Shaw, Orwell and others. Useful introduction and questions for study.

340 **Crystal, David, and Derek Davy**
Investigating English style. English Language Series. London and Harlow, Longmans, Green, 1969. xiii, 264 pp.
Describes the distinctive stylistic features of varieties of English using linguistic techniques. First section discusses the theoretical procedures and part 2 gives a detailed descriptive analysis of the language of conversation, unscripted commentary, religious writings, newspaper reports and legal documents. An exploratory work in the field of 'stylistics' of interest to teachers.

341 **Dakin, Julian, and others**
Language in education: the problem in Commonwealth Africa and the Indo-Pakistan subcontinent. Language and Language Learning, 20. London, Oxford University Press, 1968. xii, 177 pp. map.
Papers on English teaching in India, Commonwealth Africa, and on the teaching of English through science. Glossary of technical terms used in the book.

342 **Darbyshire, A. E.**
A description of English. London, Edward Arnold, 1967. x, 182 pp. tables, diagrs. bibliog.
Clear and concise description of English in linguistic terms, intended as an introduction for British students but of use to teachers and advanced students overseas. Introductory chapters on language in general and the techniques of linguistic analysis; section on phonology, grammar and lexis. Useful explanations of linguistic terms.

343 **Fowler, Roger, ed.**
Essays in style and language: linguistic and critical approaches to literary style. London, Routledge & Kegan Paul, 1966. ix, 188 pp. tables, diagr.
Ten essays by British linguists and literary critics, discussing the contribution of linguistics to the study of English literature and illustrating the application of linguistic analysis to, e.g., the characterisation of a period style, the interaction of grammar and metre in different types of verse, figures of rhetoric. The emphasis is mainly on works in verse, from mediaeval to modern writing; one study of French writing is included.

344 **Francis, W. Nelson**
The English language: an introduction. London, English Universities Press, new edn. 1967. xi, 273 pp. tables, diagrs. bibliogs. First pubd. 1963.
Introductory study of the language, designed primarily for native-speaking

university students, to provide a background for literary studies or for teaching. Reflects modern trends, and combines historical and contemporary material. General introduction on language study, chapters on English grammar, the history of English, the vocabulary, English speech and writing (including phonology and the history of writing), usage and variety in English.

345 **Joos, Martin**
The five clocks: a linguistic excursion into the five styles of English usage. Introduction by Albert H. Marckwardt. Harbinger Book. New York, Harcourt, Brace, 1967. xvii. 108 pp. First pubd. as part 5 of International Journal of American Linguistics, 1962, vol. 28, no. 2 (April).
Entertainingly written and stimulating discussion by an American linguist of the different types of English used in different situations. Five styles are identified, from 'intimate' to 'frozen'; the relevant situations are carefully defined and the linguistic characteristics of each style are indicated. The clock is taken as a symbol of language.

346 **Leech, Geoffrey N.**
English in advertising: a linguistic study in advertising in Great Britain. English Language Series. London, Longmans, Green, 1966. xiv, 210 pp. bibliog.
Analysis by a linguist of the English used in advertising through various media (press, television, etc.), considered in relation to its purpose and audience and to other varieties of English. Of interest for the techniques used and for the insight given into the relation between the structure and vocabulary of language and the social role it has to perform.

347 **Leech, Geoffrey N.**
A linguistic guide to English poetry. English Language Series. London and Harlow, Longmans, Green, 1969. xvi, 237 pp. illus. bibliog.
Introductory course in stylistics, designed to illustrate the relevance of modern linguistic studies to traditional critical approaches to poetry. Emphasises the relation between poetic language and other uses of English, and offers a detailed analysis of the features of poetic language with as little reference as possible to specialised linguistic knowledge. Examples for further practical work at the end of each chapter.

348 **Leech, Geoffrey N.**
Towards a semantic description of English. Longmans' Linguistics Library. London, Longmans, 1969. xiii, 277 pp. bibliog.

Aims to provide the foundation for a unified theory of English semantics. Part 1 discusses the theoretical principles, with chapters on the semantics of system and structure, formators, and the limits of semantics. Part 2 applies the theoretical standpoint of the first part to the semantics of time, place and modality in English. An advanced work in linguistic theory involving discussion of logical, philosophical and psychological problems.

McIntosh, Angus, and M. A. K. Halliday
See 114.

349 **Quirk, Randolph**
The use of English. With supplements by A. C. Gimson and Jeremy Warburg. London, Longmans, Green, 2nd edn. 1968. ix, 370 pp. bibliog.
Survey for the general reader covering many aspects of the uses of English – in daily communication, formal writing and as an international language. Supplements deal with the transmission of language (including the mechanism of speech) and notions of correctness. The second edition has been thoroughly revised and extended to incorporate recent findings, particularly in the field of grammar. Provides a very readable introduction to the linguistics of English.

Wilson, Graham, ed.
See 153.

350 **Wrenn, C. L.**
Word and symbol: studies in English language. English Language Series. London, Longmans, 1968. xiii, 197 pp.
Ten essays on the bearing that other disciplines – linguistics, history and comparative studies – have on the study of English language and literature. All relate to the use of English as a literary language and include: word and symbol; on the continuity of English poetry; the language of Milton; T. S. Eliot and the language of poetry. Useful for literary students, particularly in demonstrating the relevance of linguistics to the study of literature.

HISTORY

351 **Barber, Charles**
Linguistic change in present-day English. Edinburgh and London, Oliver & Boyd, 1964. ix, 154 pp. bibliog.
Based on lectures given to students and teachers of English as a foreign

language; simply written. Chapters on linguistic change generally and on standard English and dialect are followed by discussion of the changes of the last few decades in the field of pronunciation, vocabulary, meaning and grammar.

352 **Barber, Charles L.**
The story of language. A Pan Original. London, Pan Books, 1964. viii, 286 pp. illus. bibliog.
Popular yet comprehensive introduction to the history of language, leading to a description of the historical development of English to modern times. Concerned primarily with written language. An American edition, entitled *The story of speech and language*, was published in New York by Crowell in 1965; a nine-page index has been added.

353 **Bloomfield, Morton W., and Leonard Newmark**
A linguistic introduction to the history of English. New York, Knopf, 1963. xviii, 376, xx pp. maps, tables, diagrs. bibliog.
An introduction to the history of the English language in which the findings and techniques of linguistics are extensively applied. Includes chapters on: phonology and modern English; comparative linguistics and the Indo-European family of languages; the morphology of Old English; the dialects of Middle English; grammar and Early Modern English; the problem of correctness and good usage: 1600–1850; the English vocabulary and English word formation.

354 **Foster, Brian**
The changing English language. London, Macmillan; New York, St Martin's Press, 1968. 263 pp.
Account of the changes in modern English and an examination of some of the causes of them. Contains chapters on: the impact of America, foreign influence, the new society, word structure, sentence structure, and pronunciation. Detailed references in support of statements are mostly taken from books, newspapers and periodicals.

355 **Holmberg, Börje**
On the concept of standard English and the history of modern English pronunciation. Lunds Universitets Årsskrift, N.F. Avd. 1, Bd. 56, Nr. 3. Lund, Gleerup, 1964. 88 pp. bibliog.
Scholarly and well-documented survey of British attitudes towards the pronunciation of English from the fifteenth century to the present day.

Traces the development of ideas of uniformity and correctness up to its standardisation. Short note on more recent trends.

356 **Jespersen, Otto**
Growth and structure of the English language. Oxford, Blackwell, 9th edn. 1962. iv, 244 pp. First pubd. 1905.
Modern English characterised and the development of its most important features traced. Includes: the beginnings; Old English; the Scandinavians; the French; Latin and Greek; various sources; native resources; grammar; Shakespeare and the language of poetry. Classical introduction to the historical study of English.

357 **Nist, John**
A structural history of English. New York, St Martin's Press, 1966. xviii, 426 pp. map, diagrs. bibliogs.
Describes the historical development of English in terms of modern linguistic theory, noting the main features of the language at each stage. Includes chapters on the status and structure of English today, on the evolution and present characteristics of American English, and possible future trends.

358 **Potter, Simeon**
Changing English. The Language Library. London, Deutsch, 1969. 192 pp. bibliog.
Discussion, for the general reader, of recent changes in English usage and attitudes to English, covering pronunciation, spelling and spelling reform, vocabulary, including scientific vocabulary, grammatical structure and functional shift.

359 **Pyles, Thomas**
The origins and development of the English language. New York, Harcourt, Brace & World, 1964. x, 388 pp. bibliog.
An introduction to historical linguistics, designed for students but of interest to the general reader. Traces the development of the English language from prehistoric times to the present day. Chapter 9 considers in detail differences between British and American English.

Vallins, G. H.
See 407.

GRAMMAR AND STRUCTURE

360 **Boadi, L. A., and others**
Grammatical structure and its teaching... Lagos, African University Press, 1968. viii, 280 pp. tables, bibliog.
Designed principally for teachers of English as a second language, particularly in West Africa, but contains much of relevance to teachers elsewhere. Presents, as an alternative to traditional grammar, an outline of English structure, showing how a set of basic sentence patterns can be developed by transformations. Stresses the importance in teaching of the recognition of regularly recurring patterns in language, and discusses the selection and presentation of material in class.

361 **Branford, William**
The elements of English: an introduction to the principles of the study of language. London, Routledge & Kegan Paul, 1967. ix, 198 pp. tables, diagrs. bibliog.
Introduction to an analysis of English on contemporary lines; intended originally for English-speaking university students and teacher-trainees in South Africa. Draws mainly on American descriptions, particularly when dealing with grammar. Includes some comparisons of English with other languages, particularly African languages and Afrikaans.

362 **Cattell, N. R.**
The design of English. Melbourne and London, Heinemann, 1966. ix, 116 pp. tables, diagrs. bibliog.
Introductory account of English, designed for native speakers, in terms of generative transformational grammar. The first sections deal with the traditional approach and with the structural method of Fries. Appendix for teachers and glossary.

363 **Christophersen, Paul, and Arthur O. Sandved**
An advanced English grammar. London, Macmillan, 1969. ix, 278 pp.
Manual for advanced students of English as a foreign language; suitable also for teachers. Part 1 provides the theoretical framework; the phoneme, the morpheme, classification of words and word-groups. Part 2, intended mainly for reference, deals in detail with nominals, adjectivals, verbals, adverbials, determiners, auxiliaries. Chapters on sentence structure and immediate constituent analysis. Illustrations from contemporary spoken and written English.

364 **Close, R. A.**
English as a foreign language: grammar and syntax for teachers and advanced students. London, Allen & Unwin, 1962. 177 pp. diagrs.
Aims to explain special problems of English grammar which appear to be widespread among foreign learners in a variety of countries. Includes detailed treatment of: aspects of quantity; articles; tenses; auxiliary and modal verbs; prepositions and adverbial particles. Refers throughout to contemporary English usage; numerous examples. Presupposes a fairly advanced level of English ability on the part of the reader.

Darbyshire, A. E.
See 342.

Francis, W. Nelson
See 344.

365 **Fries, Charles Carpenter**
American English grammar: the grammatical structures of present-day American English with especial reference to social differences of class dialects. National Council of Teachers of English: English Monograph, 10. New York, Appleton-Century-Crofts, 1940. ix, 313 pp. tables, diagrs.
Primarily a historical–social linguistic study of American English, based on a study of non-literary written materials. It is valuable to the non-American teacher or reader for its descriptive method and classification of grammatical material (excluding vocabulary). Deals with forms of words under the headings of major and minor inflections and function words as used with substantives, verbs, adjectives and word groups. Finally, the uses of word order are discussed.

366 **Fries, Charles Carpenter**
The structure of English: an introduction to the construction of English sentences. London, Longmans, Green, 1957. xi, 304 pp. First pubd. in USA, 1952.
Influential work, one of the first to offer a constructive alternative to conventional grammatical analysis; based on an extensive survey of oral patterns in English. Proposes, in place of the traditional categories, four word classes of substitutable items and fifteen groups of function words. Describes the structural pattern of sentences in terms of this classification and discusses structural meaning.

367 **Gleason, Henry Allan, jr.**
Linguistics and English grammar. New York, Holt, Rinehart & Winston, 1965. xv, 519 pp. diagrs. bibliog. First pubd. 1963.
Designed for American teachers of English as a mother tongue but of value to second language teachers. Discusses, with examples, different linguistic approaches in relation to each other and to traditional grammar. Part 1, historical background; Part 2, topics in English syntax, including sections on generative grammar; Part 3 includes language variation, language comparison and literary style.

368 **Greenbaum, Sidney**
Studies in English adverbial usage. Longmans' Linguistics Library. London and Harlow, Longmans, Green, 1969. xvi, 262 pp. tables, bibliog.
Detailed analysis of adverbs in contemporary English, particularly those functioning as so-called sentence modifiers. Based on the corpus of spoken and written English of the *Survey of English Usage*, University College London, supplemented by citations from the British press and material elicited from informants. Two types of adverb are isolated, 'conjuncts' and 'disjuncts', and their syntactic and semantic features are analysed. Of interest also for the description and exemplification provided of the methods of research used.

Gurrey, P.
See 468.

369 **Halliday, M. A. K.**
Grammar, society and noun: an inaugural lecture, delivered at University College London, 24 November 1966. London, H. K. Lewis for the College, 1967. 32 pp bibliog.
Discusses the role of nominalizations in English, examining first the relationship of the nominal to the verb and to clause structure and secondly the noun in the language of social relations. Illustrates the link between linguistics and other disciplines, in this case sociology.

370 **Hornby, A. S.**
A guide to patterns and usage in English. London, Oxford University Press, 2nd edn. 1962. xviii, 261 pp. tables. First pubd. 1954.
Influential description of the syntax of English designed especially to aid the teaching of English as a foreign language. Provides an analysis in terms of verb-patterns, adjective-patterns and noun-patterns with sections on time and tense, adverbials, etc. Of particular value to those concerned with

the preparation of course-material and for use as a reference book, both by students and teachers. Concise, authoritative and very well indexed.

371 **Jacobs, Roderick A., and Peter S. Rosenbaum**
English transformational grammar. With an epilogue by Paul M. Postal. A Blaisdell Book in the Humanities. Waltham, Massachusetts, and London, Blaisdell, 1968. x, 294 pp. diagrs.
Outline description of the structure of sentences according to transformational framework of linguistic universals. Discusses embedded sentences and transformational rules of substitution, deletion, and adjunction. Presents the main findings of American linguists in the attempt to describe and classify intuitive knowledge of language.

372 **Jespersen, Otto**
Essentials of English grammar. London, Allen & Unwin, 1933. 387 pp.
Based on the author's *Philosophy of grammar* and *Modern English grammar*. Descriptive, explanatory and appreciative, with historical explanations where necessary. Stresses importance of spoken English; four chapters devoted to the sound-system. Standard work based on traditional categories and terminology.

373 **Jespersen, Otto**
A modern English grammar on historical principles. 7 vols. London, Allen & Unwin; Copenhagen, Munksgaard, 1965.
Part 1. Sounds and spellings. First pubd. 1909.
Part 2. Syntax: vol. 1. First pubd. 1914.
Part 3. Syntax: vol. 2. First pubd. 1927.
Part 4. Syntax: vol. 3. First pubd. 1931.
Part 5. Syntax: vol. 4. First pubd. 1940.
Part 6. Morphology. (With Paul Christophersen and others.) First pubd. 1942.
Part 7. Syntax. (Completed and edited by Niels Haislund.) First pubd. 1950.
Based on very extensive quotations from a very wide historical range of English literature, standard comprehensive description of English grammar as it developed. Avoids prescriptive dogmatism; remains a most valuable reference book.

374 **Joos, Martin**
The English verb: form and meanings. Madison and Milwaukee, University of Wisconsin Press, 1964. x, 251 pp.

Using the methods of modern descriptive linguistics, aims to give a thorough description of the constituent systems of the English verb. Embraces non-finite verbs; the finite schema; basic meanings and voice; aspect, tense and phase; and assertion. Based on modern usage.

375 **Juilland, Alphonse, and James Macris**
The English verb system. Janua Linguarum, 24. The Hague, Mouton, 1962. 81 pp. tables.
Monograph for specialists, which analyses in detail the thematic and inflectional systems of the English verb and the consonantal and vocalic aspects of the latter system. It then hierarchises the criteria exploited in the two aspects of the analysis, examining its consequences in the grammar and the lexicon.

376 **Lees, Robert B.**
The grammar of English nominalizations. The Hague, Mouton, 1963. xxviii, 205 pp. bibliog. mimeographed. First pubd. 1960.
Specialised monograph applying the principles of transformational grammar to the structure and syntactical functions of English nominalizations.

377 **Long, Ralph B.**
The sentence and its parts: a grammar of contemporary English. Chicago, University of Chicago Press, 1961. vi, 528 pp. bibliog.
Description of standard American English, paying attention to both spoken and written forms. Primarily concerned with syntax, also includes word-formation, phonology and spelling. Traditional in choice of categories, yet aware of developments in American and European linguistic studies. Illustrative material drawn from contemporary usage. For reference by teachers and as text for university students.

378 **Nida, Eugene A.**
A synopsis of English syntax. Janua Linguarum. Series Practica, 19. The Hague, Mouton, 2nd edn. 1966. 174 pp. bibliog. First pubd. 1960.
Doctoral thesis of 1943, in some respects superseded by later work in structural linguistics, of value for its method of immediate constituent syntactic analysis and for its comprehensiveness. Provides a synchronic view and describes the various morphological, syntactical and lexical levels within a total functional pattern. For specialists.

379 **Palmer, F. R.**
A linguistic study of the English verb. Longmans' Linguistics Library. London, Longmans, Green, 1965. xi, 199 pp. bibliogs.
Detailed analysis of the verb in contemporary spoken English, based mainly on British usage. Discusses the form of auxiliary and full verbs and their function in terms of a primary pattern dealing with tense (present, past, progressive and perfect) and voice, and a secondary pattern covering the modal auxiliaries. The view that English has a future tense is rejected. Sections on complex verb phrases and on phrasal and prepositional verbs. Bibliographical references after each chapter.

380 **Palmer, Harold E., and F. G. Blandford**
A grammar of spoken English. Revised and rewritten by Roger Kingdon. Cambridge, Heffer, 3rd edn. 1969. xx, 341 pp. tables. First pubd. 1924.
One of the first major attempts to construct a grammar of English based on the spoken language, now revised and rewritten to systematise the presentation of the material and incorporate new ideas. Part 1, pronunciation, including intonation. Part 2, parts of speech. Part 3, sentence structure. Many examples, given in phonetic transcription. Traditional terminology is extended by Palmer's and other additions. Designed for teachers and students of English as a foreign language.

381 **Reibel, David A., and Sanford A. Schane, eds.**
Modern studies in English: readings in transformational grammar. Englewood Cliffs, New Jersey, 1969. xiv, 481 pp. tables, diagrs. bibliogs.
Twenty-nine articles on the transformational syntax of English by N. Chomsky and other scholars in the field. Grouped under: background (which provides an introduction to the theory); conjunction; pronominalization; relativisation; other aspects of English syntax; applications and implications. Final article on the role of linguistics in the teaching of English.

382 **Roberts, Paul**
Modern Grammar. New York and Chicago, Harcourt, Brace, 1967. viii, 439 pp.
Textbook for American college students, describing the structure of English in terms of transformational grammar. Deals mainly with syntax, but includes also morphology and semantics, with some references to phonology. Plentiful examples and exercises. An abridgment of a longer course.

Scheurweghs, G., and others
See 516.

383 **Scott, F. S., and others**
English grammar: a linguistic study of its classes and structures. London and Auckland, Heinemann Educational Books, 1968. xii, 244 pp. illus. tables.
Introductory description of English designed for New Zealand students; based on the linguistic theories developed by M. A. K. Halliday. Analyses English grammar in terms of word class, group, clause, sentence; discusses these in some detail. An appendix provides an outline history of English grammar and its current developments.

384 **Strang, Barbara M. H.**
Modern English structure. London, Edward Arnold, 2nd edn. 1968. xii, 264 pp. illus. tables, bibliog. First pubd. 1962.
Descriptive analysis of present-day English, aimed to give the first-year student an awareness of the mechanisms of his own language. Uses modern linguistic techniques, though largely employing traditional terminology. Often eclectic in approach, bringing together the views of British and American linguists and grammarians. Definitions are provided and full attention is paid to the phonological bases of language. The revised edition adds an account of lexical structure and meaning. Revised bibliography.

385 **Thomas, Owen**
Transformational grammar and the teacher of English. New York and London, Holt, Rinehart & Winston, 1965. xii, 240 pp. bibliog.
Introduction to transformational grammar, written primarily for teachers of English as a mother tongue and concentrating on those aspects most relevant to their needs. Short discussion of the nature and function of grammar, exposition of the basic theories of transformational grammar as applied to English, final section on grammar and the school. Summary and points for discussion after each chapter.

386 **Whitehall, Harold**
Structural essentials of English. London, Longmans, Green, 1958. vi, 154 pp. tables. First pubd. 1951.
Aims to describe the general structural design of English, particularly in relation to the problem of writing English effectively. Deals with: word groups; sentences; modification and shift of emphasis; connectives; the verb and its helpers; word forms. Rhythm and tone patterns are briefly covered, and spoken and written usage are contrasted throughout. Written for American teachers of English as a mother tongue, but material is of application to second-language teachers.

387 **Zandvoort, R. W., and J. A. van Ek**
A handbook of English grammar. London, Longmans, Green, 5th edn. 1969. xiv, 349 pp. bibliog. First pubd. in the Netherlands, 1945; first pubd. in England, 1957.
Standard manual, originally written for Dutch students. This edition is suitable for study by any foreign student of advanced level and as a reference book for the teacher. The method is descriptive (though on conventional lines) and accidence and syntax are thoroughly illustrated by examples from current English.

PHONOLOGY AND ORTHOGRAPHY

388 **Bronstein, Arthur J.**
The pronunciation of American English: an introduction to phonetics. New York, Appleton-Century-Crofts, 1960. xvi, 320 pp. maps, tables, diagrs. bibliog.
Intended for American university students and speakers of American English, but of use to others for the descriptive methods used. Part 1 deals with basic concepts and definitions; Part 2 with the sound system; Part 3 discusses sound change, pronunciation of words and pitch and melody patterns. Pays attention to the distribution and historical development of different forms of English pronunciation, particularly American variants.

389 **Chomsky, Noam, and Morris Halle**
The sound pattern of English. Studies in Language. New York and London, Harper and Row, 1968. xiv, 470 pp. tables, bibliog.
Study of the sound structure of English based on a general theory within the framework of generative grammar. Part 1, elementary exposition of the theory. Part 2, detailed analysis of the system of rules that determines the phonetic form of the sentence in English. Part 3, the historical development of the modern English vowel system. Part 4, explicit formulation of the underlying general theory; indications of possible future developments and their consequences for the description of English and other languages.

390 **Christophersen, Paul**
An English phonetics course. London, Longmans, Green, 1956. viii, 216 pp. diagrs. bibliog.
Manual intended for university and teacher-training courses in West Africa but of value to other foreign students and teachers. Simple and practical description of English speech-elements with much practice material designed primarily for African students. Based on RP.

391 **Crystal, David**
Prosodic systems and intonation in English. Cambridge Studies in Linguistics, 1. Cambridge, Cambridge University Press, 1969. viii, 381 pp. tables, diagrs. bibliog.
Study of English intonation viewed as a complex of interacting features from different prosodic systems, e.g. tone, pitch range, loudness, rhythmicality, tempo. Reviews previous work, discusses voice quality and sound attributes in prosodic study as a whole, describes in detail the prosodic features and intonation system of English, and examines the grammar and semantics of intonation. Based on an analysis of a large sample of English. One of the aims is to provide a basis for the teaching of English intonation to foreign learners of English.

Delattre, Pierre
See 156.

392 **Dewey, Godfrey**
Relativ frequency of English speech sounds. Cambridge, Massachusetts, Harvard University Press; London, Pitman, 2nd edn. 1950. xii, 187 pp. tables. First pubd. 1923.
Pioneer frequency count, based on a sample of 100,000 words of written material. Eighteen tables analyse material into words and their frequency; syllables and their frequency; sounds and their frequency. Phonetic structure of American English indicated by relative frequency of sounds and combination of sounds. Has provided the basis for much later work.

393 **Dunstan, Elizabeth, ed.**
Twelve Nigerian languages: a handbook on their sound systems for teachers of English. London and Harlow, Longmans, Green, 1969. vi, 185 pp. diagrs. bibliog.
Simply written but authoritative guide, designed for both Nigerian and expatriate teachers. A brief account of the pronunciation and intonation of English, with advice on teaching them to Nigerian learners, is followed by a concise description of each of the twelve languages, with notes on the difficulties that speakers of each encounter in learning the sound system of English.

Fries, Charles C.
See 457.

394 **Gimson, A. C.**
An introduction to the pronunciation of English. London, Edward Arnold, 1962. xv, 294 pp. diagrs. bibliog.
Comprehensive and authoritative treatment of the phonetics of English. In three parts: speech and language (general phonetics, classification and description of speech sounds, linguistic principles); sounds of English (historical development, English vowels and consonants in detail); the word and connected speech (characteristics of connected speech, including stress, rhythm and intonation). Represents a development and expansion of many of the principles of Daniel Jones, applied especially to RP.

395 **Halliday, M. A. K.**
Intonation and grammar in British English. Janua Linguarum. Series Practica, 48. The Hague, Mouton, 1967. 61 pp. tables, diagrs. bibliog.
Reprint, in a revised and expanded form, of two papers presenting a description of English intonation from the standpoint of its function in the grammar of the spoken language. Part 1 provides an analysis according to phonological criteria, including rhythmic features, and isolates certain meaningfully contrastive patterns. A special notation is used. Part 2 demonstrates the systematic relationship of these patterns to the grammatical system of the language. Of interest to both linguistic scholars and language teachers.

Holmberg, Börje
See 355.

396 **Jones, Daniel**
An outline of English phonetics. Cambridge, Heffer, 9th edn. 1960. xx, 378 pp. illus. bibliog. First pubd. 1918.
Standard work for teachers and foreign learners; frequently revised since its first appearance. Covers the whole field of phonology and pronunciation of English, both theoretically and practically, with numerous illustrations and diagrams. The phonetic script used is that of the International Phonetic Association (1949); the norm is RP but American and other variants are commented upon.

397 **Jones, Daniel**
The pronunciation of English. Cambridge, Cambridge University Press, 4th edn. 1958. xxiv, 223 pp. illus. bibliogs. First pubd. 1909.
Simple yet comprehensive exposition for the native speaker of English, which takes into account variant and dialectical pronunciation. Part 1 covers

theory, including: organs of speech; sounds and letters; classification of sounds; syllables; duration; stress; intonation. There is a note on practical exercises and on ear training. Part 2 consists of phonetic texts in prose and verse. Material based on RP. Valuable for use with foreign learners.

Jones, Daniel
See 183.

Jones, Daniel
See 510.

398 **Kenyon, John Samuel**
American pronunciation. Ann Arbor, Michigan, George Wahr, 10th edn. 1950. xi, 265 pp. illus. bibliog. First pubd. 1924.
Standard work for American students, several times revised. Combines theory with some historical explanation and covers objectively a full range of local variations in American speech. Notes differences between British and American pronunciation.

399 **Kurath, Hans**
A phonology and prosody of modern English. Heidelberg, Winter: Universitätsverlag, 1964. 158 pp.
Detailed study of the phonology of modern American English (including regional variants) in comparison with RP. Prosodic features – intonation, stress and timing – are dealt with as patterns rather than as phonemes. Spellings of sounds are analysed.

400 **Lee, W. R.**
An English intonation reader. London, Macmillan, new edn. 1963. vii, 123 pp. bibliog.
Designed for intermediate and advanced foreign learners of English; of value also to teachers. Arranged for self-study, with many examples and practice conversations. Transcriptions in phonetic script and normal spelling with intonation shown. Includes a description of the function of intonation in conveying meaning. Refers to RP. Gramophone records available.

401 **MacCarthy, Peter A. D.**
English pronunciation: a practical handbook for the foreign learner. Cambridge, Heffer, 4th edn. 1950. viii, 179 pp. diagrs. bibliog. First pubd. 1944.

Textbook for the foreign student, based on a broad general treatment of the phonetics of English. Proceeds from elementary theory to classification of vowels, English vowels; classification of consonants, English consonants, general and particular; and intonation and stress. Many examples in phonetic script and practice exercises. Refers to RP.

402 **Mitchell, A. G.**
Spoken English. London, Macmillan, 1957. vi, 238 pp. illus. bibliog.
Introduction to English phonetics intended for Australian students, with some comparison between Australian, American and British English. Suggestions for Australian teachers. Phonetic transcriptions of prose and verse.

403 **O'Connor, J. D.**
Better English pronunciation. London, Cambridge University Press, 1967. viii, 179 pp. diagrs. bibliog.
Practical introductory handbook intended as a self-tutor for intermediate or advanced foreign learners of English but useful also to teachers. Includes general problems of pronunciation; phonetic notation; the organs of speech; an analysis of English sounds; stress and intonation; practice passages and exercises. Based on RP but takes account of other varieties and includes appendices on special difficulties of speakers of certain languages.

404 **O'Connor, J. D., and G. F. Arnold**
Intonation of colloquial English: a practical handbook. London, Longmans, Green, new edn. 1963. viii, 275 pp. tables, diagrs. First pubd. 1961.
Textbook for the advanced foreign student. Postulates ten tone-groups in association with each of four main sentence types – statement, question, command and interjection. The main part of the book consists of practice drills in association with verbal contexts. Eleven dialogues for intonation practice are appended. Based on RP. Gramophone records available.

Palmer, Harold E., and F. G. Blandford
See 380.

405 **Roberts, A. Hood**
A statistical linguistic analysis of American English. Janua Linguarum. Series Practica, 8. The Hague, London, Mouton, 1965. 437 pp. tables, diagrs.
Quantitative analysis, obtained by computer, of sequential phonemes; based on the 10,000 words of the Horn list, as spoken in the stream of speech by one informant.

Schachter, Paul
See 493.

406 **Trnka, Bohumil**
A phonological analysis of present-day standard English. Edited by Tetsuya Kanekiyo and Tamotsu Koizumi. Tokyo, Hokuou Publishing Co., new edn. 1966. ix, 155 pp. tables, bibliog. First pubd. 1935.
Analysis, based on the theories of the Prague school, of the phonological structure of English; new edition, revised and expanded. Includes a detailed statistical investigation of the phonological organisation of monomorphemic words consisting of one or two vowel phonemes.

407 **Vallins, G. H.**
Spelling. Revised by D. G. Scragg, with a chapter on American spelling by Professor John W. Clark. The Language Library. London, André Deutsch, 2nd edn. 1965. 208 pp. tables, bibliog. First pubd. 1954.
Outline, for the general reader, of English spelling conventions. Gives historical survey from the time of Caxton to the middle eighteenth century. Discusses spelling reform, dictionary makers and homonyms and synonyms. Contains useful list of variant spellings.

408 **Wijk, Axel**
Rules of pronunciation for the English language: an account of the relationship between English spelling and pronunciation. Language and Language Learning, 12. London, Oxford University Press, 1966. 160 pp. First pubd. in Sweden, 1965.
A manual for advanced students and teachers setting out the rules which govern the relationship between English spelling and pronunciation. Final chapter on proposals for spelling reform.

409 **Wise, Claude Merton**
Applied phonetics. Englewood Cliffs, New Jersey, Prentice-Hall, 1957. xii, 546 pp. diagrs. bibliogs.
Discusses extensively the pronunciation of standard, sub-standard and regional varieties of American and British spoken English. Also treats dialects of English spoken by German, Norwegian, French, French-Canadian, Spanish, Italian, Brazilian, Portuguese and Russian speakers. Intended for all who are interested in spoken English, including teachers and learners of English as a foreign language.

VOCABULARY AND USAGE

410 **Burroughs, G. E. R.**
A study of the vocabulary of young children. University of Birmingham, Institute of Education: Educational Monographs, 1. Edinburgh, Oliver & Boyd, 1957. vii, 104 pp. tables, bibliog.
Survey of the oral vocabulary of 330 English children (ages 5–6½ years) mainly in the Midlands of England, representative of children beginning to learn to read. The two main word lists show the more and the less frequently used words; further lists give comparisons with other English and American vocabularies.

Eaton, Helen S.
See 70.

411 **Flood, W. E.**
The problem of vocabulary in the popularisation of science. University of Birmingham, Institute of Education: Educational Monographs, 2. Edinburgh, Oliver & Boyd, 1957. vi, 121 pp. tables, bibliog.
Examines the nature of scientific words and their incidence in popular reading matter and suggests the compilation of a basic vocabulary. A brief note on earlier studies of science vocabularies is followed by a discussion on listing words and the criteria of selection, and an account of the evolution of the vocabulary (of 2,012 words) compiled by the author. Practical examples of the vocabulary are provided and notes on the writing of simplified texts.

412 **Flood, W. E.**
Scientific words: their structure and meaning. London, Oldbourne, 1960. xix, 220 pp. diagrs.
An explanatory glossary of about 1,150 word-elements (roots, prefixes, suffixes) which enter into the formation of scientific terms. Etymological notes are given and the use of each element in word-building is exemplified by a number of scientific terms that incorporate it. Advisedly *not* a dictionary but a useful tool for enlarging and understanding scientific vocabulary.

413 **Fries, Charles C., and A. Aileen Traver**
English word lists: a study of their adaptability for instruction. Ann Arbor, Michigan, George Wahr, 1950. ix, 107 pp. tables, diagrs. bibliog.
Monograph prepared for the Committee on Modern Languages of the

American Council on Education. Comments on aims and methods in some existing word lists compiled for various purposes, including English as a foreign language. Seven influential word lists are then discussed: Basic English; West's *Definition vocabulary*; H. E. Palmer's 1,000 word radius; the lists of Fawcett and Maki, Thorndyke, and Aiken; and the Carnegie *Interim report on vocabulary selection*. Valuable and comprehensive survey.

414 **Gowers, Sir Ernest**
The complete plain words. With amendments, London, HMSO, 1958. vi, 209 pp. bibliog. First pubd. 1954. Paper-backed edn.: Pelican, 1962.
A reconstruction of the author's *Plain words* (1948) and *The ABC of plain words* (1951), originally written to help government officials express themselves clearly. Exposition of the pitfalls of verbose, tautologous and ambiguous phraseology with constructive advice on how to avoid it.

415 **Greenbaum, Sidney**
Verb-intensifier collocations in English: an experimental approach. Janua Linguarum. Series Minor, 86. The Hague and Paris, Mouton, 1970. ii, 96 pp. tables, bibliog.
Report of research undertaken at the *Survey of English Usage*, University College London, to determine, on the basis of data obtained from informants, the verbs which collocate with certain intensifiers in pre-verb positions. Includes discussion of the general problems of investigating collocations and an evaluation of the techniques used in the present experiment.

416 **Hill, L. A.**
Prepositions and adverbial particles: an interim classification, semantic, structural, and graded. London, Oxford University Press, 1968. xxvi, 403 pp.
A practical reference book for textbook writers and teachers of English as a foreign language. Prepositions and particles, considered together, are listed alphabetically; and their uses, graded into elementary, intermediate and advanced, are analysed and illustrated. A list of sentence patterns into which they can enter is also given.

417 **Kučera, Henry, and W. Nelson Francis**
Computational analysis of present-day American English. With a foreword by W. F. Twaddell, a study by Mary Lois Marckworth and Laura M. Bell, and an analytical essay by John B. Carroll. Providence, Rhode Island, Brown University Press, 1967. xxv, 424 pp. tables, diagrs.
Presents lexical and statistical information obtained from analysis of the

Standard Corpus of Present-Day Edited American English, a corpus of language texts of over one million words, drawn from material published in 1961 and coded for computer processing. The study includes word-frequency lists of over 50,000 words (though semantic frequency ratings are not given), and analyses of word-frequency distribution, word length and sentence length, both over the corpus as a whole and in the various genres of material used. The first large-scale study of its kind to use modern data-processing methods.

418 **Meldau, Rudolf, and Ralph B. Whitling**
Synonymik der englischen Sprache. Frankfurt-am-Main, Hirschgraben-Verlag, 1964. 800 pp. bibliog.
Dictionary of English synonyms for German speakers of English arranged under 800 German headwords. Synonyms are defined in English and German and copious examples are given of their use in phrases and sentences, with German translations.

419 **Partridge, Eric**
Usage and abusage: a guide to good English. London, Hamish Hamilton, 6th edn. 1965. 392 pp. First pubd. 1947. Paper-backed edn.: Penguin Reference Books, 1963.
Compendium of information, in dictionary form, covering a wide field, including the use and misuse of words and phrases, common grammatical errors, points of style and variant spellings. Material ranges from brief notes to short and lively essays.

420 **South Africa, Republic of. Department of Education, Arts and Science**
An English word count, 1965, by C. W. Wright. Research Series, 15. Pretoria, National Bureau of Educational and Social Research, 1965. xxxii, 332 pp. tables, bibliog. mimeographed.
Word frequency lists based on a study of over one million words of written material of various genres, including religious and classical works and school textbooks. Lists the first 1,000 words in frequency of occurrence by hundreds and the first and second 10,000 words in frequency of occurrence by thousands. Frequency ratings are not given. Intended for use in teaching English in South Africa.

421 **Tennant, John**
A handbook of English usage. London, Longmans, Green, 1964. viii, 184 pp.
Based on a knowledge of the problems of foreign students, is intended as

a supplement to courses and dictionaries used at a higher secondary level. Gives, alphabetically, clear expositions of current words and phrases offering difficulty with some American equivalents and occasional indications of pronunciation and brief notes on English social customs.

422 **Thorndike, Edward L., and Irving Lorge**
The teacher's word book of 30,000 words. New York, Columbia University, Teachers College, Bureau of Publications, 1944. xiv, 274 pp.
Extension of the original *Teacher's word book* of 1921. Based on large samples of written material. Provides frequency ratings for words based on overall count and on four separate counts, including one of juvenile books. Earlier versions (1921, 1931) provided the basis for vocabulary gradings in courses of English as a second language and for the Carnegie *Interim report on vocabulary selection* (superseded) and West's *A general service list of English words* (see 424).

423 **Treble, H. A., and G. H. Vallins**
An ABC of English usage. Oxford, Clarendon Press, 1962. 192 pp. tables. First pubd. 1936.
Explanations, definitions or brief notes in dictionary form of the main grammatical elements of spoken and written English, from the standpoint of traditional analysis. Also includes pronunciation, spelling, punctuation, idiomatic usages and prosody. A useful handbook for aid in English composition, based largely on the materials and interpretations found in Fowler's *A dictionary of modern English usage* (see 506).

424 **West, Michael, ed.**
A general service list of English words: with semantic frequencies and a supplementary word-list for the writing of popular science and technology. London, Longmans, Green, 1953. xiii, 588 pp. First pubd. 1936.
A revision of the original 2,000 word list for teachers of English as a foreign language published in 1936 as the Carnegie *Interim report on vocabulary selection.* Embodies the findings of the Lorge–Thorndike semantic frequency count so that the comparative frequency values of the various meanings of each word are indicated. A standard work on which the vocabulary content and grading of many courses has been based. Of special value to writers of textbooks and simplified readers.

425 **Wood, Frederick T.**
Current English usage: a concise dictionary. London, Macmillan, 1962. vii, 273 pp.

Simple and practical guide intended to clarify debatable usage or draw attention to words and phrases commonly misused; points of syntax, punctuation, style, idiom and spelling are discussed with an occasional pointer to correct pronunciation.

426 **Wood, Frederick T.**
English prepositional idioms. London, Macmillan; New York, St Martin's Press, 1967. vii, 561 pp.
Part 1, list of prepositions with meanings and examples of use; Part 2, prepositions used idiomatically in association with other words. Each part listed alphabetically.

427 **Wood, Frederick T.**
English verbal idioms. London, Macmillan, 1964. vi, 325 pp. Paper-backed edn. 1966.
Intended as a guide for the foreign student to verbal idioms used in ordinary written and spoken English. Material is arranged alphabetically with a simple explanation of each phrase and examples of current usage, whether literary, figurative, colloquial or slang.

VARIETIES OF ENGLISH

428 **Bailey, Beryl Loftman**
Jamaican Creole syntax: a transformational approach. Cambridge, Cambridge University Press, 1966. xvi, 164 pp. illus. map, bibliog.
A detailed transformational analysis of Jamaican Creole syntax, focusing particularly on points where this differs from English. A major aim is to provide the basis for a thorough comparative study of the two languages, and then for the preparation of realistic English language textbooks for Jamaican scholars.

429 **Baker, Sidney J.**
The Australian language: an examination of the English language and English speech as used in Australia, from convict days to the present, with special reference to the growth of indigenous idiom and its use by Australian writers. Sydney, Currawong, 2nd edn. 1966. xv, 517 pp. diagrs. First pubd. 1945.
Comprehensive and well-documented survey of Australian vocabulary and idiom, with particular reference to slang and other special usages. Discusses the origin and usage of words and phrases under topic headings, e.g. the soil, the underworld, the city. Sections on overseas influences, aborigines and pidgin English. Chapter on Australian pronunciation. Rewritten and expanded since the first edition.

Bronstein, Arthur J.
See 388.

430 **Cassidy, Frederic G.**
Jamaica talk: three hundred years of the English language in Jamaica. London, Macmillan; New York, St Martin's Press, 1961. ix, 468 pp. map, diagrs. bibliog.
Detailed and authoritative account of Jamaican speech as used by Jamaicans of all ranks. Part 1 deals with history, pronunciation and grammar. Part 2, Jamaican vocabulary (defined as a type of English), gives a socio-etymological account of the development of the language from its many sources, recording *inter alia* over 4,000 Jamaicanisms. Contains a word list.

431 **Conference on Creole Language Studies**
Proceedings of the Conference on Creole Language Studies held at the University College of the West Indies, March 28–April 4, 1959. Creole Language Studies, 2. London, Macmillan; New York, St Martin's Press, 1961. vii, 130 pp. maps, tables.
Important papers on Creole language studies relevant to Sierra Leone, Jamaica, Surinam, Dominica, Haiti, and on possible affinities between Creole dialects of the Old World and the New. Attempts to relate common elements in various Creole languages.

Kenyon, John Samuel
See 398.

Kurath, Hans
See 399.

432 **Marckwardt, Albert H.**
American English. New York, Oxford University Press, 1958. xiii, 194 pp. map, diagrs.
Discusses the development of American English in its relation to the cultural life and history of America and in comparison with British English.

433 **Mitchell, A. G., and Arthur Delbridge**
The pronunciation of English in Australia. Sydney, Angus and Robertson, 2nd edn. 1965. xiv, 82 pp. diagrs. bibliog. First pubd. 1946.
Describes the varieties of Australian pronunciation and discusses their origin and distribution. Analysis of the Australian sound system, stress and intonation in comparison with RP. Contains phonetic transcriptions of Australian speech. The revised edition contains new material.

Mitchell, A. G.
See 402.

Nist, John
See 357.

Pyles, Thomas
See 359.

434 **Turner, G. W.**
The English language in Australia and New Zealand. English Language Series. London, Longmans, Green, 1966. xi, 236 pp. bibliog.
Socio-linguistic study, by a New Zealand linguist, of the characteristics and development of English in Australia and New Zealand (the two countries considered together). Discusses: semantic problems, the written language, pronunciation, colloquial language and slang, occupational and regional variations. Chapter on Pidgin.

Vallins, G. H.
See 407.

Wise, Claude Merton
See 409.

CONTRASTIVE ANALYSIS

Agard, Frederick B., and Robert J. di Pietro
See 693, 694.

Cárdenas, Daniel N.
See 818.

Delattre, Pierre
See 545.

Dunstan, Elizabeth, ed.
See 393.

Hammer, John H., and Frank A. Rice
See 157.

Stockwell, Robert P., and J. Donald Bowen
See 819.

Stockwell, Robert P., and others
See 820.

Vinay, J. P., and J. Darbelnet
See 573.

TEACHING METHODS

435 **Abercrombie, David**
Problems and principles in language study. London, Longmans, Green, 2nd edn. 1963. viii, 83 pp. First pubd. 1956.
Collection of papers (originally published between 1948 and 1954) including: linguistics and the teacher; teaching pronunciation; English accents; making conversation; gesture. Teaching problems are related to basic principles of linguistic behaviour rather than to methodology.

436 **Allen, Harold B.**
A survey of the teaching of English to non-English speakers in the United States. Champaign, Illinois, National Council of Teachers of English, 1966. 158 pp. tables.
Report of a survey based on 500 replies received to a detailed questionnaire sent to schools, colleges and institutions throughout the country. Analyses and discuss the findings under: the program in TENES; the teacher; the teaching situation; aids and materials; problems and needs. Includes the report and recommendation of a specialist conference called to discuss the findings and account of representative TENES programmes.

437 **Allen, Harold B., ed.**
Teaching English as a second language: a book of readings. New York and London, McGraw-Hill, 1965. xi, 406 pp.
Reprints of fifty articles by British and American authors, many well known, written mainly since 1950. Sections on: theories and approaches; teaching English speech; teaching English structures; teaching English vocabulary; teaching English usage and composition; teaching the printed word; reading and literature; methods and techniques; teaching with audio-visual aids; testing.

Boadi, L. A., and others
See 360.

438 **Brown, P. P., and J. Scragg**
Common errors in Gold Coast English: their cause and correction. London, Macmillan, 3rd edn. 1948. viii, 134 pp.
Careful listing and analysis of many errors commonly made in Ghana attributable to translation from or interference by Twi, Fante, Gâ and Ewe. Although arranged as a student's book, may be of use principally to teachers.

439 **Bumpass, Faye L.**
Teaching young students English as a foreign language. New York, American Book, 1963. x, 198 pp. illus. bibliog.
Based largely on experience of teaching Spanish-speaking children in the United States, provides a great deal of practical advice for the teacher of young children. Shows how activity methods, visual and audio aids, games and songs, etc., can be applied to teaching English. Discusses the advantages of beginning foreign language instruction early. Detailed descriptions of classroom procedures are included.

440 **Burgin, Trevor, and Patricia Edson**
Spring Grove: the education of immigrant children. London and New York, Oxford University Press for The Institute of Race Relations, 1967. x, 112 pp. tables, bibliog.
First-hand account of a pioneer project in English teaching to immigrant children, based on a primary school in the north of England. Describes in detail the development and work of the special department established to provide English tuition for immigrant children from schools in the area. Discusses methods of approach, materials used, testing and assessment, special problems. The experiment is seen in the wider context of integrating the children into the community.

441 **Center for Applied Linguistics of the Modern Language Association of America**
Testing the English proficiency of foreign students. Report of a conference sponsored by the Center for Applied Linguistics in co-operation with the Institute of International Education and the National Association of Foreign Student Advisers. Washington, D.C., The Center, 1961. iii, 103 pp. bibliogs.

Survey of programmes in 1961 for the testing of foreign students' proficiency in English. Conference background papers include: Fundamental considerations in testing...; English proficiency; testing in the British Commonwealth; the Michigan Overseas Testing Service, and other American programmes. Also contains a summary of conference decisions.

442 **Chapman, L. R. H.**
Teaching English to beginners. London, Longmans, Green, 1958. vii, 139 pp.
Primarily intended for young teachers in Arabic-speaking countries. A model first lesson is given. Includes explanations of the use of aids such as word and structure cards, wall charts and the blackboard. The teaching of English handwriting to Arabic-speaking pupils (and others) is described in detail.

443 **Christophersen, Paul**
Some thoughts on the study of English as a foreign language. Tiltredelses-forelesning 17. januar 1957. Oslo, Olaf Norlis, 1957. 31 pp.
Lecture on the teaching of English in Scandinavian universities with special reference to the preparation of teachers of English. Emphasises the need to study modern English.

444 **Clarkson, Marjorie**
English as a second language: a guide for primary teachers. London, Evans, 1966. 79 pp.
Simple guide designed to help African primary school teachers improve their techniques of teaching English within the framework of the syllabus and textbooks they are required to use; of value also to teachers facing similar problems in other countries. Practical advice with examples on oral work, lesson planning, activity methods, classroom techniques.

445 **Conference on the Teaching of English to Speakers of Other Languages**
On teaching English to speakers of other languages.
Series 1. Papers read at the TESOL Conference, Tucson, Arizona, May 8–9, 1964. Edited by Virginia French Allen. Champaign, Illinois, National Council of Teachers of English, 1965. xv, 158 pp. bibliogs.
Series 2. Papers read at the TESOL Conference, San Diego, California, March 12–13, 1965. Edited by Carol J. Kreidler. Champaign, Illinois, National Council of Teachers of English, 1966. viii, 167 pp. tables, bibliogs.
Series 3. Papers read at the TESOL Conference, New York City, March 17–19, 1966. Edited by Betty Wallace Robinett. Washington, Teachers of English to Speakers of Other Languages, 1967. viii, 189 pp. bibliogs.

Short practical papers intended for the non-specialist American teacher. Include general surveys, reports on programmes for particular linguistic and other groups, mainly in the USA, discussions of methods, techniques, and materials. Brief conference reports.

446 **Corder, S. Pit**
English language teaching and television. London, Longmans, Green, 1960. iv, 107 pp. tables, bibliog.
Considers the use of television as a vehicle for teaching English as a second language. Includes treatment of the psychology of learning by television; special requirements for a methodology of teaching; principles of selection and grading of material.

447 **Cutts, Warren G.**
Modern reading instruction. Library of Education. Washington, D.C., Center for Applied Research in Education, 1964. x, 118 pp. bibliog.
A review for the specialist, based on the findings of research. Includes sections on: readiness for reading at all levels; perceptual development, word recognition, and analysis; phonics – an important tool; vocabulary development; comprehension and critical reaction; motivation, interests and lifetime habits; and on the detection, correction and prevention of reading problems. Refers to reading English as a mother tongue.

Davies, Allan, ed.
See 325.

448 **Derrick, June**
Teaching English to immigrants. Education Today: Language Teaching. London, Longmans, Green, 1966. viii, 256 pp. illus. bibliog.
Practical introduction to the teaching of English as a second language to immigrant children; intended for teachers in Great Britain but of interest also to those in other countries. Discusses briefly the principles of second-language learning, then presents in some detail a scheme of work based on a structurally graded syllabus and an oral–situational approach. Chapters on: pronunciation; reading and writing; 'remedial' language teaching – West Indian and other pupils; aids and apparatus.

449 **Dixson, Robert J.**
Practical guide to the teaching of English as a foreign language. New York, Regents Publishing in association with Latin American Institute Press, 1960. 90 pp. bibliog.

Concise general guide to classroom procedures for the practical teacher without much formal training. Includes sections on the teaching of grammar, conversation, reading, vocabulary and pronunciation.

450 **Dorry, Gertrude Nye, comp.**
Games for second language learning. New York and London, McGraw-Hill, 1966. vi, 56 pp. illus.
Description of over seventy games useful in teaching English as a second language particularly to intermediate or advanced learners; a number suitable also for teaching other languages. Includes games to practise spelling, vocabulary and word-building, sentence-patterns, pronunciation. Intended for classroom use, though some games would seem more suitable for extra-classroom activities such as English groups.

Dunstan, Elizabeth, ed.
See 393.

451 **Finocchiaro, Mary**
Teaching English as a second language. New York, Harper & Row, new edn. 1969. 478 pp. bibliog. First pubd. 1958.
Practical handbook, for American teachers, which brings together theories of general education, foreign language teaching and the teaching of English. Advocates an eclectic method emphasising the importance of relating the teaching of reading, writing and speech to the general setting of school and community. Offers advice on curriculum planning, classroom management and techniques, principally at the elementary and secondary levels. Particularly useful sections on vitalising learning, contrastive analysis and materials available for teachers and teacher-trainers.

452 **Fraser, Hugh, and W. R. O'Donnell, eds.**
Applied linguistics and the teaching of English. Education Today: Language Teaching. London, Longmans, Green, 1969. xvi, 216 pp. illus. tables.
Collection of papers by specialists in applied linguistics dealing principally with problems of teaching English to native speakers. Also contains much material relevant to the teaching of English as a second or foreign language. Includes chapters on: programmed learning, linguistics and the teaching of literature; the teaching of meaning; the teaching of grammar.

453 **French, F. G.**
Common errors in English: their cause, prevention and cure. London, Oxford University Press, 1949. 132 pp. tables.

Discussion of common errors in English made by students with many different mother tongues. Indicates that interference by mother-tongue habits is not the root cause of difficulties; prevention of error depends on concentration of the patterns of English and use of structural words. Includes chapters on: causes of error; preventive measures; essential patterns; drilling-in; drilling-out.

454 **French, F. G.**
English in tables: a set of blue-prints for sentence builders. London, Oxford University Press, 1960. xii, 148 pp. tables.
A description of the form, function and use of substitution tables. Valuable guide to the construction of substitution tables with many practical suggestions for their use in the classroom. Presents fifty common constructions in current English illustrated by substitution tables with full instructions for their use. Designed to give pupils control of English structures without grammatical explanations.

455 **French, F. G.**
Teaching English as an international language. London, Oxford University Press, 1963. 112 pp.
Simply written description of teaching techniques, designed for the overseas teacher. Contains much valuable advice on the conduct of lessons, preparation of materials and the use of various types of exercise. Applies mostly to primary and secondary school class-teaching.

456 **French, F. G.**
The teaching of English abroad. A Teachers' Library. London, Oxford University Press. illus. Part 1, *Aims and methods*, 1948. Part 2, *The junior course*, 1949. Part 3, *The three senior years*, 1950.
Practical manual for teachers in schools but also adaptable to the teaching of adults. Largely based on the Oxford English courses by the same author. Part 1, introduction to oral approach through phrase- and sentence-patterns, comprising word order, structural words and inflexions. Part 2, the work of the first three years building up a vocabulary of 900 words, including a large proportion of structural words. Basic tenses presented. Use of blackboard, chorus-work, substitution tables and dramatisation discussed. Model lessons given. Part 3, expansion of vocabulary to 2,000 words. Exposition of importance of oral and written composition. Chapters on marking and specimen tests and examination papers. Written in simple language.

457 **Fries, Charles C.**
Linguistics and reading. New York, Holt, Rinehart & Winston, 1963. xxi, 265 pp. bibliog.
Survey of developments in modern linguistics in relation to the teaching of reading in English. Includes historical surveys of methods of teaching reading and the development of modern linguistics. Discusses the nature of the reading process, the place of phonics, the development of English spelling, and suggests essentials for a linguistic approach in the development of materials and methods to teach reading.

458 **Fries, Charles C.**
Teaching and learning English as a foreign language. Publications of the English Language Institute, 1. Ann Arbor, Michigan, University of Michigan Press, 1945. vii, 153 pp.
Well-known exposition of theory and techniques, based on the findings of descriptive linguistics, stressing the oral approach. Appendices include procedures for marking limited intonation and sample lesson materials from the beginners' text, *Inglés por práctica*.

459 **Fries, Charles C., and Agnes C. Fries**
Foundation for English teaching: including a corpus of materials upon which to build textbooks and teachers' guides for teaching English in Japan. Tokyo, Kenkyusha, for English Language Exploratory Committee, 1961. xiii, 378 pp. illus.
Contains the basic material for a series of textbooks through which to teach English to Japanese. Arranged in the form of a corpus of material containing the structure and vocabulary needed for the first three years of an English course. Based on contrastive structural comparisons of English and Japanese and on the structural analysis of English associated with the first author's name. Carefully worked out progression of material.

460 **Frisby, A. W.**
Teaching English: notes and comments on teaching English overseas. London, Longmans, Green, 1957. 352 pp. illus. bibliog.
Handbook primarily concerned with the teaching of English as a second language to children and based largely on experience in Malaya. The oral approach, pupil–teacher relationship, speech training, intensive and extensive reading, expression and the place of literature are discussed, and many hints for teaching techniques are given. Lists of structural words, of common errors in pronunciation and of suitable verses for children are included.

461 **Fry, Edward**
Reading faster: a drill book. London, Cambridge University Press. 1963, xi, 67 pp. tables.
See entry below.

462 **Fry, Edward**
Teaching faster reading: a manual. London, Cambridge University Press, 1963. xii, 143 pp. illus. tables.
Intended to help teachers overseas providing courses to improve reading in English at secondary school or university level. Outlines the techniques of reading skill and provides suggestions for lectures and practical work. The *Drill book* (see above) contains material for a course in reading improvement, intended for use in tropical Africa.

463 **Gatenby, E. V.**
English as a foreign language: advice to non-English teachers. London, Longmans, Green, 1944. 64 pp.
Still of value. Deals with the teacher's relations with his colleagues and his pupils, 'natural' methods, conversation, phonetics, reading, dictation, handwriting, composition, and examinations and tests.

464 **Gauntlett, J. O.**
Teaching English as a foreign language. London, Macmillan; New York, St Martin's Press, 1957. xi, 124 pp. tables, diagrs. bibliog.
Based chiefly on experience with Japanese learners and teachers of English. Examines the aims of an English language course, then surveys principles and methods. Covers psychological problems, phonetics and tonetics, and the teaching of idiomatic along with structural sentences and phrases. Includes evaluation of contributions to teaching theory by many other writers.

465 **Grieve, D. W.**
English language examining: report of an inquiry into the examining of English language at the examinations for the School Certificate and the General Certificate of Education of the West African Examinations Council. Lagos, African University Press for West African Examination Council, 1964. iv, 129 pp. tables.
Report of an inquiry into the examining of English language for secondary school certificates in West Africa. Provides critical analysis of many problems of examining English which are particularly relevant to countries where English as a second language is a medium of instruction. Contains detailed recommendations for developing objective-type tests and specimen question papers.

466 **Guénot, Jean**
Pédagogie audio-visuelle des débuts de l'anglais: une expérience d'enseignement à des adultes. Paris, S.A.B.R.I., 1964. 293 pp. illus. bibliog.
Detailed study of the construction and evaluation of an audio-visual course in English produced at Centre de Recherche et d'Etude pour la Diffusion du Français. Contains a great deal of value to those concerned with producing teaching materials for language laboratories and elaborates the underlying linguistic and pedagogical principles.

467 **Gurrey, P.**
Teaching English as a foreign language. London, Longmans, Green, 1955. 199 pp. bibliog.
Practical and detailed suggestions based partly on experience in West Africa. Stresses the need for clearly thought out particular objectives as well as broad aims. Covers most aspects of classroom work including oral work, mime and acting, grammar teaching, reading aloud and silently, composition, literature. Closely related to the practical needs of secondary schools.

468 **Gurrey, P.**
Teaching English grammar. London, Longmans, Green, 1961. ix, 154 pp. bibliogs.
A plea for a heuristic approach to grammar teaching grounded in the study of forms, grammatical functions and structures of language in close relation with the semantic or emotional meanings they express. Considers the aim of the grammar lesson should be to attain effective communication and that examples presented should be analysed with regard to the writer's intention and the reasons for the structures used. Final chapters indicate how the author's theories can be put into practice in the classroom. Refers to English as a mother tongue.

469 **Gurrey, P.**
The teaching of written English. London, Longmans, Green, 1954. vii, 238 pp. bibliog.
Addressed primarily to teachers of English in Britain but deals with many points that will help teachers of English as a second language overseas: enlargement of the pupils' vocabulary, the relation of expression to experience and interest, the aims and objectives of composition, descriptive sketches, story-telling, character-drawing and précis-writing.

Halliday, M. A. K., and others
See 221.

470 **Harris, David P.**
Testing English as a second language. New York and London, McGraw-Hill, 1969. viii, 151 pp. illus. tables, bibliog.
A short introductory work on testing for classroom teachers and teacher-trainers. Examines the purposes and methods of language testing, the characteristics of a good test, and the interpretation and use of test results. Much valuable practical advice on the construction and administration of tests. A particular feature is a chapter on basic statistical techniques in testing. Written for the non-specialist.

471 **Hill, L. A.**
Selected articles on teaching English as a foreign language. Language and Language Learning, 13. London, Oxford University Press, 1967. vii, 142 pp. illus. tables.
Fifteen articles reprinted from various journals; based on practical teaching experience in several countries. Deals with teaching at various levels; includes articles on teaching particular points of grammar and pronunciation, as well as on more general subjects such as textbooks, syllabus-writing and examinations.

472 **Hornby, A. S.**
The teaching of structural words and sentence patterns. English-Teaching Library. London, Oxford University Press. Stage 1, 1959; Stage 2, 1961; Stage 3, 1962; Stage 4, 1966.
A series of source books for teachers of English as a foreign language which aims to cover items that are normally taught during a first English course. Each book is in two parts: part 1 consists of substitution tables summarising the material presented in part 2, which gives sentence patterns and practical detailed suggestions to teachers. Stages 1 and 2 deal mainly with material which can be presented and drilled orally; Stage 3 extends the scope to material related more to written English; Stage 4 includes chapters dealing more fully with determinatives and adverbs, and contains much material that can be used orally.

473 **Kerr, J. Y. K.**
Common errors in written English: an analysis based on essays by Greek students. Harlow, Longmans, Green, 1969. x, 81 pp.
An analysis of the errors in written English of Greek students based on study of over 1,000 essays. Identifies most common mistakes. Useful as reference book for teachers.

474 **Lee, W. R.**
Language-teaching games and contests. London, Oxford University Press, 1965. viii, 167 pp. illus.
Detailed descriptions of a wide range of language games and similar activities suitable for classroom use with pupils of various ages and levels. The games are chosen for their value as language teaching aids and are grouped into: oral, pronunciation, reading and writing, spelling. Designed for teachers of English as a second language but could be useful also to teachers of other languages.

475 **Lee, W. R., ed.**
E.L.T. Selections 1 and *E.L.T. Selections 2. Articles from the journal 'English Language Teaching'.* London, Oxford University Press, 1967. 220 pp. and 242 pp.
Collections of articles, many by well-known authors, which appeared in the journal *English Language Teaching*, mostly between 1946 and 1961. Written for the practising teacher, they cover teaching at all levels, under the following headings: general theory, English language, classroom techniques, aids, the teaching of literature. Most are general in approach but some deal with particular teaching situations.

476 **Lee, W. R., and Helen Coppen**
Simple audio-visual aids to foreign language teaching. A Teachers' Library. London, Oxford University Press, 2nd edn. 1968. vii, 120 pp. illus. bibliog. First pubd. 1964.
Handbook for use in teacher-training colleges, primarily intended for teachers of English as a foreign language. Part 1 outlines the usefulness of audio-visual aids in general and discusses in detail oral work, reading and writing. Part 2 deals with the making of simple aids such as picture and reading materials, flannelboards and puppets.

477 **Lefevre, Carl A.**
Linguistics and the teaching of reading. Curriculum and Methods in Education. New York, McGraw-Hill, 1964. xxiii, 252 pp. diagrs. bibliog.
Examination of the contribution which modern linguistics can make to the teaching of reading skills in English as a mother tongue with special reference to the United States. Refers to the structure of modern American English in some detail. Useful critical bibliography.

478 **McCree, Hazel**
From controlled to creative writing. English Language Teaching Series. Lagos, African Universities Press, in association with British Council, 1969. 78 pp. bibliog.

Written principally for the four years of work leading to the West African General Certificate of Education. Contains much useful guidance to teachers on the encouragement of creative and expressive writing. Recognises that good writing often involves more than 'correct' sentences and offers practical suggestions to help in the less tangible aspects. Based on experience in Nigeria but consideration of general problems makes its appeal wider. Includes exercises for use in the classroom.

479 **Miller, D. C.**
Beginning to teach English. London, Oxford University Press, 1963. xii, 201 pp. illus.
Intended for the young teacher in training, for the untrained primary school teacher and the more experienced teacher wishing to improve his knowledge of teaching young people. Gives a simple outline of a theory of foreign language teaching and provides a set of fifty lesson plans for the first weeks of a primary school English course,

480 **Miller, D. C.**
Teaching the reading passage. London, Oxford University Press, 1966. ix, 142 pp.
Practical guide for the teacher on the effective use of the reading passage during the early and middle years of a course in English as a second language. Discusses: the function of the reading passage; the teacher's own preparation; techniques of presentation; oral questioning and drills. Many examples. Appendix listing structural words. Based on experience in West Africa and the Middle East.

481 **Morris, I.**
The art of teaching English as a living language. London, Macmillan; New York, St Martin's Press, 1954. xi, 170 pp. illus. bibliog.
Introduction to the teaching of English to foreigners, based on practical experience. The grading of vocabulary and grammar and the need for an oral approach in the early stages are stressed; reading and writing are discussed in some detail and at all levels. For oral work the value of both drills and controlled, sustained speech is discussed. Silent reading is contrasted with reading aloud. General factors such as size of classes, mental and cultural level of students, etc. are considered.

482 **Morris, Joyce M.**
Reading in the primary school: an investigation into standards of reading and their association with primary school characteristics. With a statistical ap-

pendix by P. M. Grundy. National Foundation for Educational Research in England and Wales, 12. London, Newnes Educational, for the Foundation, 1959. xviii, 179 pp. tables, bibliog.
Report of a large-scale investigation into English children's reading standards and their relation to conditions such as size of classes, types of organisation and methods of teaching. Based on enquiries in sixty schools in Kent and covering 8,000 children learning to read English as their mother tongue. Notable for thoroughness of research techniques.

483 **Murphy, M. J.**
Designing multiple-choice items for testing English language. English Language Teaching Series. Lagos, African Universities Press, in association with British Council, 1969. iv, 67 pp. tables.
Guide for teachers to the writing and compilation of multiple-choice tests in English. Contains general discussion on the advantages of multiple-choice questions and on the statistical importance of 'guessing' in the results obtained. Chapters on the preparation of items to test lexis, structure and general comprehension. Brief consideration of possibilities for testing spelling and recognition of appropriate registers.

484 **Nasr, Raja T.**
The teaching of English to Arab students. London, Longmans, Green, 1963. xv, 176 pp. illus. bibliog.
Manual, based on modern linguistic findings, for the experienced teacher. Covers both theoretically and practically the problems of teaching pronunciation, grammar, writing and vocabulary to Arabic-speaking students. Contains many examples of suitable exercises and discussions of typical linguistic difficulties and errors.

485 **Palmer, Harold E.**
The oral method of teaching languages: a monograph on conversational methods, together with a full description and abundant examples of fifty appropriate forms of work. Cambridge, Heffer, 1965. vii, 134 pp. Reprint of 1921 edn.
Practical guide to the general use of oral methods, with examples from English. Discusses advantages and techniques of oral teaching both with school pupils and adult students. Contains model dialogues for practising specific points of usage and other useful material for receptive and reproductive oral work.

486 **Palmer, Harold E.**
The teaching of oral English. London, Longmans, Green, 1940. 100 pp.
Short and still valuable manual on the oral direct method. Presents basic material for an elementary oral course by means of situational grammar; names of objects, place and position, possession, etc. Uses limited vocabulary to teach the commonest words.

487 **Palmer, Harold E., and Dorothée Palmer**
English through actions. London, Longmans, Green, 1959. x, 287 pp. table. First pubd. 1925.
Originally published in Tokyo and designed for teaching English to Japanese, edited for wider application in 1958. Contains a carefully worked out body of material on which the first years of a course or syllabus in English could be based. Together with a very full collection of teaching items (mostly oral drills) it includes an exposition of Palmer's theories and techniques of language-teaching under such headings as: technique of speech-teaching; treatment of certain difficulties in grammar and composition; imperative drill; conventional conversation; oral assimilation; action chains.

488 **Perren, G. E., ed.**
Teachers of English as a second language: their training and preparation. London, Cambridge University Press, 1968. iv, 233 pp. diagr. bibliog.
Contains original contributions by nine authors on various aspects of training teachers, based on their specialised experience in various countries over a number of years. Provides detailed information on the content of a number of successful past training programmes together with suggestions for the improvement of current practice.

489 **Pittman, G. A.**
Teaching structural English. London, Ginn, rev. edn. 1967. 211 pp. illus. bibliog. First pubd. in Australia, 1963.
An introduction to the structure of English, describing how knowledge of structure might influence the teaching of English as a second or foreign language. Intended for those teaching elementary English from a structural syllabus; emphasises the teaching of basic essentials. Some advanced structural material has also been included to help teachers see the wider significance of their work. Sections: language; the structure of English; English speech; teaching method; the 'oral–aural' approach.

490 **Press, John, ed.**
The teaching of English literature overseas: extracts from the proceedings of a conference held at King's College, Cambridge, 16–18 July, 1962, under the auspices of the British Council. London, Methuen, 1963. 181 pp. bibliog.
Includes sections dealing with the teaching of English literature in universities, schools, teacher-training colleges and adult education institutions.

491 **Quirk, Randolph, and A. H. Smith, eds.**
The teaching of English. Studies in Communication, 3. London, Secker & Warburg, 1959. 192 pp. diagrs. bibliog.
Six lectures originally delivered in 1958. Includes: English language and the structural approach, an introduction to linguistic usage; some aspects of style; the teaching of English to scientists and engineers; and the teaching of English as a foreign language, which lays down factors that must be considered in planning a course of English for foreigners.

492 **Research Club in Language Learning**
Theory and practice in English as a foreign language. Selected articles from Language Learning, 2. Ann Arbor, Michigan, The Club, 1963. vii, 258 pp.
Collection of articles by experts (mainly American) covering teacher education, techniques, pronunciation, vocabulary, grammar, reading and composition. Reflects early linguistic theories.

493 **Schachter, Paul**
Teaching English pronunciation to the Twi-speaking student. Legon, Ghana University Press, 1962. v, 60 pp. diagrs. Distributed by Oxford University Press, London.
Draws attention to the special phonetic problems of Twi-speakers when learning English pronunciation. Valuable to teachers with a basic knowledge of phonetics.

Schröter, Günter, and Hans Ladwein
See 312.

494 **Squire, James R., ed.**
A common purpose: the teaching of English in Great Britain, Canada and the United States. A report of the International Conference on the Teaching of English...Boston, Massachusetts, November 24–28, 1965. Champaign, Illinois, National Council of Teachers of English, 1966. xi, 243 pp. tables, bibliogs.
Deals with the teaching of English to native speakers; of interest however

to second-language teachers in that it reflects current thinking on mother-tongue teaching in the light of modern linguistic and educational research. Topics include: the aims of mother-tongue teaching, emphasising particularly the importance of language as a means of communication; literature teaching, examinations, teacher training and research. Of particular linguistic interest is a paper on 'Types of deviance in English sentences' by Quirk.

495 **Stevick, Earl W.**
Helping people learn English: a manual for teachers of English as a second language. New York, Abingdon Press, 1957. 138 pp. diagrs. bibliog.
Handbook intended for American newcomers to the teaching of English to foreigners, especially adults. In part 1 the oral approach and vocabulary and structure control are explained. Part 2 – teaching suggestions – gives a wealth of detailed practical hints. Part 3 – some useful information about the English language – includes notes on the sounds of English and on grammar and suggested exercises.

496 **Stevick, Earl W.**
A workbook in language teaching: with special reference to English as a foreign language. New York, Abingdon Press, 1963. 127 pp. diagrs. bibliog.
Designed for use in the initial training of new language teachers or for refresher courses, provides a great deal of practical instruction in classroom techniques. Includes sections on: the sound system of English (referring specifically to American English); the construction and use of drills; grammar. Provides many practical exercises of use to teachers of English.

497 **Stoddart, John, and Frances Stoddart**
The teaching of English to immigrant children. London, University of London Press, 1968. 120 pp. illus. bibliog.
Practical advice based on experience of teaching Indian and Pakistani immigrant children. Includes chapters on oral exercises, visual aids, ear and speech training, learning to speak through other subjects, reading and writing. Suggestions for both primary and secondary classroom work.

498 **Strang, Ruth, and others**
The improvement of reading. Curriculum and Methods in Education. New York and London, McGraw-Hill, 4th edn. 1967. viii, 564 pp. illus. tables, bibliogs. First pubd. under the title *Problems in the improvement of reading*, 1938.
Authoritative general survey based on research and practical experience of teaching reading in English as a mother tongue. New edition gives greater

prominence to the reading instruction necessary for particular specialist fields and on the reading problems of special groups such as able retarded readers, slow learners, those with severe reading disability and able learners. Also includes discussion on the reading process and methods of appraising and testing reading competence.

499 **Tiffen, Brian, ed.**
A language in common: a guide to English language teaching in schools and colleges. London and Harlow, Longmans, Green, 1969. 216 pp. bibliogs.
A guide to the teaching of English as a second language in schools and colleges, by twelve specialists from Britain, New Zealand, Nigeria and the United States. Based on the authors' teaching experience in Nigeria, but relevant to teachers in other areas. Contains sections on the language background in Africa, on the teaching of spoken English and grammatical structure, and on using and testing the language. Intended for both practising teachers and teachers in training.

500 **Tokyo University of Education. Modern Language Institute**
Report on aural-oral training in the teaching of English in primary and lower secondary schools. Tokyo, Japanese National Commission for UNESCO and The Institute, 1965. vi, 106 pp. illus. tables.
Description and results of experiments conducted with classes at three different levels, to assess the value of taped lessons in the teaching of spoken English.

Turner, John D., ed.
See 318.

501 **West, Michael**
Teaching English in difficult circumstances: teaching English as a foreign language. With notes on the technique of textbook construction. London, Longmans, Green, 1960. viii, 136 pp.
Deals with problems of teaching English, particularly to large classes, by teachers with limited resources. Based on many years' experience in India and the Middle East. Concerned to establish the best techniques and aims to ensure the greatest success under unfavourable conditions. Simply and clearly written with many practical examples. Includes sections on: useful devices in the large class; the teaching of reading; construction of reading material; speech training; lesson-forms; textbook construction; teacher training. Appendix; a minimum adequate vocabulary for speech (classified). Valuable to teachers and teacher-trainers.

502 **Wishon, George E., and Thomas J. O'Hare, eds.**
Teaching English: a collection of readings. New York, American Book, 1968. viii, 136 pp. bibliog.
Fifteen short essays by American authors on the theoretical and practical aspects of teaching English as a foreign language, written mainly over the last ten years. Intended as a textbook for teachers in training, to provide a point of view in language teaching and a foundation in techniques. Emphasis on the oral–aural approach.

DICTIONARIES

503 **Bibliographisches Institut, Mannheim, and George G. Harrap & Co. Ltd., eds.**
The English Duden: a pictorial dictionary with English and German indexes. London, Harrap, 2nd edn. 1959. 928 pp. illus. First pubd. 1937.
This revised edition is a companion volume to the 2nd revised edition of the German *Duden: Bildwörterbuch* (see 662). The illustrations and the numbers of the single items are identical, keys in English, and English and German alphabetical indexes are provided. Corresponding volumes have also been published for French, Spanish, Italian and Swedish, and a Portuguese edition is in preparation. Each volume provides an English or German index, in addition to the index in the language of the publication.

504 **Brown, A. F., ed.**
Normal and reverse English word list. 8 vols. Philadelphia, University of Pennsylvania, 1963.
354,252 entries selected from five standard dictionaries (including those of scientific terms) are recorded first in a normally alphabetised list (3 volumes) and secondly in a reverse alphabetised list (3 volumes). Two volumes are reserved for 'broken' words, in normal and reverse order.

505 **Flood, W. E., and others**
An elementary scientific and technical dictionary. London, Longmans, Green, 3rd edn. 1962. vii, 413 pp. illus. First pubd. as *An explaining and pronouncing dictionary of scientific and technical words*, 1952.
Over 10,000 words in some fifty subjects are simply explained within a defining vocabulary of about 2,000 words; sixty of these are technical terms and are defined, as are about one hundred and twenty others that might cause difficulty. Attention is given to word-elements; numerous illustrations and diagrams. Valuable handbook for the student with a limited knowledge of English and of technical and scientific subjects.

506 Fowler, H. W.

A dictionary of modern English usage. Oxford, Clarendon Press, 2nd edn. revised by Sir Ernest Gowers, 1965. xxii, 725 pp. First pubd. 1926.

Revised edition of an influential handbook, which provides numerous examples of the literary use of English words and phrases, together with much advice on style as well as clarification of meaning, pronunciation and syntax. Now pays considerably more attention to contemporary usage.

507 Hornby, A. S., and E. C. Parnwell

An English-reader's dictionary. London, Oxford University Press. 2nd edn. 1969. viii, 631 pp. illus. First pubd. 1952.

Well-established illustrated dictionary revised and enlarged in this new edition. The phonetic guide to pronunciation has been modified to conform to the broad transcription of the International Phonetic Association and additional appendices have been included on irregular verbs, British coinage (including the new decimal coinage), weights and measures and the spelling and pronunciation of important geographical names. Particularly useful for the intermediate level student.

508 Hornby, A. S., and E. C. Parnwell

The progressive English dictionary. London, Oxford University Press, 1952. vi, 313 pp. illus.

8,500 headwords, 250 illustrations. Aims to help a student who has completed an elementary course in English. Shows stress but not pronunciation.

509 Hornby, A. S., and others

The advanced learner's dictionary of current English. London, Oxford University Press, 2nd edn. 1963. xxxii, 1,200 pp. illus. First pubd. 1948.

Comprehensive illustrated dictionary with pronunciation shown in phonetic script; valuable introduction on English syntax. Compiled for advanced students.

510 Jones, Daniel

Everyman's English pronouncing dictionary: containing over 58,000 words in international phonetic transcription. Everyman's Reference Library. London, Dent, 13th edn., edited by A. C. Gimson, 1967. xliv, 544 pp. illus. bibliog. First pubd. 1917.

Standard reference work. Introduction provides a description of the criteria and characteristics of RP. The thirteenth edition contains 556 new words, reaching a total of 58,840 words. There is a glossary of phonetic terms.

Meldau, Rudolf, and Ralph B. Whitling
See 418.

511 **Ogden, C. K.**
The general Basic English Dictionary: giving more than 40,000 senses of over 20,000 words, in Basic English. London, Evans, [1940]. x, 438 pp. illus.
Applies Basic English principles to word definition, aiming to give as wide a range of words as possible without attempting to be a detailed guide to special fields. Phonetic guide to pronunciation. Contains separate lists of common short forms, and of words and word-groups taken into English from other languages.

512 **Orthological Institute**
The science dictionary in Basic English. Edited by E. C. Graham, with a foreword by Sir Solly Zuckerman. London, Evans, 1965. xvi, 568 pp.
Defines about 25,000 words and word-groups taken from both pure and applied science. Definitions are given in Basic English extended by the use of scientific terms defined elsewhere in the dictionary; non-basic words are printed in distinctive type. The level is approximately that of first-year university students.

Partridge, Eric
See 419.

Tennant, John
See 421.

Treble, H. A., and G. H. Vallins
See 423.

513 **West, Michael**
An international reader's dictionary: explaining the meaning of over 24,000 items within a vocabulary of 1,490 words. London, Longmans, Green, 1965. x, 401 pp. illus.
Over 6,000 idioms are included and examples given of their use. Pronunciation indicated in broad IPA transcription.

Wood, Frederick T.
See 425, 426, 427.

BIBLIOGRAPHIES

Hammer, John H., and Frank A. Rice
See 157.

514 **Modern Humanities Research Association**
Annual bibliography of English language and literature, 1920– , vol. 1– . Cambridge, The Association. In progress.
Coming out annually now, with a time lag of about two years. Volume 42 was published in 1969. The linguistic publications are arranged in ten main sections; there is a selective index of authors and subjects treated, and an index of contributing authors.

515 **Ohanessian, Sirarpi, and others, eds.**
Reference list of material for English as a second language. Part 1: *Texts, readers, dictionaries, tests.* Part 2: *Background materials, methodology.* Washington, D.C., Center for Applied Linguistics, 1964 and 1966.
An annotated select bibliography designed for teachers of English as a second language, covering materials published in a number of different countries. Concentrates mainly on works appearing between 1953 and 1963 but includes some important earlier works and a few later ones. Part 1 gives very full coverage of teaching materials prepared for specific language backgrounds and a section on materials for specialised fields. Part 2, which contains periodical references as well as books, covers: linguistic background, methodology, preparation of materials, teacher training, testing, programmes in particular areas.

Robinson, Janet O., comp.
See 214.

516 **Scheurweghs, G., and others**
Analytical bibliography of writings on modern English morphology and syntax, 1877–1960. 4 vols. Louvain, Belgium, Nauwelaerts for University of Louvain, 1963–68.
Extensive survey of writings on modern English morphology and syntax. Contains brief notes on a wide range of relevant articles appearing in learned journals. Vols. 1 and 2 emphasise publications in the United States and Northern and Western Europe, but both contain appendices on Japanese publications, and Vol. 2 includes works of Czechoslovak scholars published in their own country and abroad. Vol. 3 surveys publications in

Russia and contains briefer surveys of the work in Bulgaria, Poland, Rumania and Yugoslavia. Vol. 4 gives addenda for the earlier works and contains an extensive general index covering the whole series.

517 **Shen, Yao, and Ruth H. Crymes, comps.**
Teaching English as a second language: a classified bibliography. Honolulu, East–West Centre Press, 1965. xiv, 110 pp.
Covers books and articles in periodicals, arranged under the following main headings: Phonology, grammar, methodology. There is an author index, and a list of the journals consulted.

518 **Sundermann, Karl-Heinrich**
Zur Methodik und Didaktik des Englischunterrichts: eine kritische Bibliographie in- und ausländischen Schrifttums. Der Neusprachliche Unterricht in Wissenschaft und Praxis, 12. Dortmund, Lensing, 1966. 145 pp.
Select bibliography of books on language teaching, designed for German teachers of English. Critical examination with detailed summaries of forty-nine titles published between 1920 and 1965. In two parts: 1, books published in Germany; 2, books published elsewhere. Useful index.

SECTION IV

French

GENERAL

519 **Bally, Charles**

Linguistique générale et linguistique française. Bern, Francke, 4th edn. 1965. 440 pp. bibliog. First pubd. 1932.

A detailed study of linguistic methodology and of the phonological, syntactical and lexical aspects of modern French. Covers a wide variety of topics which affect French style.

520 **Brunot, Ferdinand**

La pensée et la langue: méthode, principes et plan d'une théorie nouvelle du langage appliquée au français. Paris, Masson, 3rd edn. 1953. 983 pp. tables. First pubd. 1926.

Assesses the grammatical and syntactic resources of French for their ability to express ideas, concepts and emotions. Phonology and morphology are called in aid.

521 **Ewert, Alfred**

The French language. The Great Languages. London, Faber & Faber, 2nd edn. 1966. xii, 440 pp. tables, bibliogs. First pubd. 1933.

A general description of French under the headings: history, phonology, orthography, morphology and syntax, vocabulary. Contains examples of early French literature to illustrate development. A paper-back reprint by Faber has been issued.

522 **Togeby, Knud**

Structure immanente de la langue française. Langue et Langage. Paris, Larousse, 1965. 208 pp. tables.

Detailed study of structures employing principles advocated by Hjelmslev. Phonological, syntactical and morphological elements are described by their structure, function and semantic contents.

HISTORY

523 **Cohen, Marcel**

Histoire d'une langue: le français (des lointaines origines à nos jours). Paris, Editions Sociales, 3rd edn. 1967. 516 pp. bibliog. First pubd. 1947.

A diachronic study of the language from earliest times to 1965.

Gougenheim, Georges

See 561.

Kukenheim, Louis
See 41.

Lombard, Alf
See 549.

Moignet, Gérard
See 540.

Posner, Rebecca
See 161.

524 **Wartburg, Walter von**
Evolution et structure de la langue française. Bibliotheca Romanica. Series Prima: Manualia et Commentationes, 1. Berne, Francke, 8th edn. 1967. 294 pp. bibliog. First pubd. 1946.
A diachronic study including a chapter on modern French, with helpful examples.

GRAMMAR AND STRUCTURE

525 **Blinkenberg, Andreas**
L'ordre des mots en français moderne. Two parts. Det. Kgl. Danske Videnskabernes Selskab: Historisk-filologiske Meddelelser, 17, 1 and 20, 1. Copenhagen, Munksgaard. Part 1, 2nd edn. 1958; Part 2, 2nd edn. 1950. bibliog. First pubd. 1928 and 1933.
Describes the general rules which determine order of words in French. Part 1 deals with subject and attribute, subject and verb, and verb and complement, starting from a definition of sentence structure. Part 2 deals with the determinants of the substantive, the adjective, adverb and verb, and with the negative.

526 **Blinkenberg, Andreas**
Le problème de l'accord en français moderne: essai d'une typologie. Det. Kgl. Danske Videnskabernes Selskab: Historisk-filologiske Meddelelser, 33, 1, Copenhagen, Munksgaard, 1950. 180 pp.
Examines agreements between subject and predicate and in appositive, adjectival and nominative constructions.

527 **Blinkenberg, Andreas**
Le problème de la transitivité en français moderne: essai syntactosémantique. Det. Kgl. Danske Videnskabernes Selskab: Historisk-filologiske Meddelelser, 38, 1. Copenhagen, Munksgaard, 1960. 366 pp. bibliog.
Examines structures to deduce characteristics of transitivity in verbs and of objectivity in substantives and adjectives.

528 **Chevalier, Jean-Claude, and others**
Grammaire Larousse du français contemporain. Paris, Larousse, 1964. 495 pp.
Examines in detail: constituent elements of the sentence, use of various parts of speech and rules of versification.

529 **Cohen, Marcel**
Le subjonctif en français contemporain: tableau documentaire. Paris, Société d'Edition d'Enseignement Supérieur, 2nd edn. 1965. 294 pp. bibliog.
A detailed account of the subjunctive with a summary of present trends in its use, both in speech and in writing.

Csécsy, Madeleine
See 580.

530 **Dubois, Jean**
Etude sur la dérivation suffixale en français moderne et contemporain: essai d'interprétation des mouvements observés dans le domaine de la morphologie des mots construits. Paris, Larousse, 1962. xi, 118 pp. tables, bibliog.
The definition and function of the suffix, general methodology, evolutionary changes and all aspects of suffixes are analysed in detail. A specialised study.

531 **Dubois, Jean**
Grammaire structurale du français: le verbe. Langue et Langage. Paris, Larousse, 1968. 218 pp. tables.
Examines syntagmatic features of nouns and verbs which permit transformations of verbal patterns. Sets up a hierarchy of distinctive word-endings and describes the role of adjectives and adverbs in verbal syntagms.

532 **Dubois, Jean**
Grammaire structurale du français: la phrase et les transformations. Langue et Langage. Paris, Larousse, 1969. 188 pp.
Applies generative transformational techniques to French sentence structures.

533 **Dubois, Jean**
Grammaire structurale du français: nom et pronom. Langue et Langage. Paris, Larousse, 1965. 192 pp. tables.
Describes aspects of French grammar using distributional and classificatory schemes to define the structures.

534 **Galichet, Georges**
Grammaire structurale du français moderne. Paris, Charles-Lavauzelle, 2nd edn. 1968. x, 248 pp. diagrs.
Describes an approach setting out from thought patterns to show the varied means by which the language expresses ideas. It is intended to provide native teachers with a basic pedagogical approach.

535 **Grevisse, Maurice**
Le bon usage: grammaire française avec des remarques sur la langue française d'aujourd'hui. Gembloux, Belgium, Duculot; Paris, Hatier, 9th edn. 1969. 1228 pp. tables, bibliog. First pubd. 1936.
A general reference work, with copious examples and explanations, for writers of French.

536 **Gross, Maurice**
Grammaire transformationnelle du français: syntaxe du verbe. Langue et Langage. Paris, Larousse, 1968. 181 pp. tables, bibliog.
Uses techniques developed by Chomsky and Harris to examine the role played in French sentences by verbs which they have classified as operators.

537 **Guillaume, Gustave**
Langage et science du langage. Paris, Nizet; Quebec, Presses de l'Université Laval, 1964. 286 pp. illus. tables.
Collected papers, 1933–58, by an eminent scholar, mostly referring to logical and psychological aspects of French grammar.

538 **Imbs, Paul**
L'emploi des temps verbaux en français moderne: essai de grammaire descriptive. Bibliothèque Française et Romane. Série A: Manuels et Études Linguistiques, 1. Paris, Klincksieck, 1960. viii, 272 pp. tables, diagrs. bibliog.
A detailed study of the French verb system under the categories of the indicative, the subjunctive, the imperative, infinitive and participles. Also contains discussions of the tense and mood system and attendant problems of grammar and style.

539 **Mauger, G.**
Grammaire pratique du français d'aujourd'hui: langue parlée, langue écrite. Paris, Hachette, 1968. xv, 416 pp. tables.
Directed to foreign students; distinguishes different levels of usage: popular, familiar, everyday and written French.

540 **Moignet, Gérard**
Le pronom personnel français: essai de psycho-systématique historique. Bibliothèque Française et Romane. Série A: Manuels et Études Linguistiques. Paris, Klincksieck, 1965. 178 pp. tables, bibliog.
Study of the development of the relationship between the thought and the sign-system of the personal pronoun; great overlap between the new form and the old is stressed and conclusions are drawn upon the manner in which a language evolves.

541 **Richer, Ernest**
Français parlé, français écrit: description du système de la langue française contemporaine. Essais pour Notre Temps, 1. Bruges and Paris, Desclée de Brouwer, 1964. 197 pp. tables, diagrs. bibliog.
Contrasts structures of spoken and written French in order to clarify for French secondary teachers and students the articulation of sentences.

Ruwet, Nicolas
See 169.

542 **Spang-Hanssen, Ebbe**
Les prépositions incolores du français moderne. Copenhagen, G. E. C. Gads, 1963. 256 pp. bibliog.
Classifies prepositions by criteria of meaning, function, opposition and similarity, concluding with a fundamental opposition: cohesion/dispersion.

Tesnière, Lucien
See 170.

543 **Wagner, R. L., and J. Pinchon**
Grammaire du français classique et moderne. Paris, Hachette, 2nd edn. 1968. 640 pp. bibliog. First pubd. 1962.
The first section gives a brief general summary of the evolution of French; the second defines the terminology and the analytical principles to be used. The third and principal section deals with the grammar of '*la langue correcte*' examined under the conventional headings of the major parts of speech and types of phrase and clause. The final section is a very clear thematic index.

544 **Wartburg, Walter von, and P. Zumthor**
Précis de syntaxe du français contemporain. Bibliotheca Romanica. Series Prima: Manualia et Commentationes, 2. Berne, Francke, 2nd edn. 1958. 400 pp. First pubd. 1947.
An authoritative description of the present state of French syntax, concentrating on the standard spoken language but not ignoring social registers and regional variants. Examples are drawn from modern literary texts to illustrate norms of standard speech. Each feature is numbered, which permits easy reference to it from the comprehensive index.

Wittwer, J.
See 154.

PHONOLOGY AND ORTHOGRAPHY

545 **Delattre, Pierre**
Studies in French and comparative phonetics: selected papers in French and English. Janua Linguarum. Series Maior, 18. The Hague and London, Mouton, 1966. 286 pp. tables, diagrs. bibliog.
Includes short specialised studies of liaison, accent, intonation, vowel duration and syllabication in French, originally published in various journals during the last thirty years.

Delattre, Pierre
See 156.

Falinski, Eugène
See 583.

546 **Fouché, Pierre**
Traité de prononciation française. Paris, Klincksieck, 2nd edn. 1959. lxiii, 528 pp. tables, diagr.
A detailed study in two parts, one dealing with vowels, the other with consonants. Useful to foreigners studying French and to French speakers. Proper names and deviations from normal pronunciation receive detailed treatment.

Gendron, Jean-Denis
See 572.

Kadler, Eric H.
See 225.

547 **Léon, Pierre R.**
Prononciation du français standard: aide-mémoire d'orthoépie à l'usage des étudiants étrangers. Linguistique Appliquée. Paris and Brussels, Didier, 1966. iv, 186 pp. tables, bibliog.
Includes consonants, liaison, special words, and provides supplementary exercises in phonetic transcription.

548 **Léon, Pierre R., and Monique Léon**
Introduction à la phonétique corrective à l'usage des professeurs de français à l'étranger. Collection le Français dans le Monde – B.E.L.C. Paris, Hachette et Larousse, 1964. xiii, 98 pp. illus. tables, bibliog.
Examines the sounds of French and gives detailed instructions on how they should be articulated and corrective techniques for faults in pronunciation, and for inability to discriminate between similar sounds.

549 **Lombard, Alf**
Le rôle des semi-voyelles et leur concurrence avec les voyelles correspondantes dans la prononciation parisienne. Scripta Minora Regiae Societatis Humaniorum Litterarum Lundensis, 1962–1963: 2. Lund, Gleerup, 1964. 46 pp.
Explains the phenomena of semi-vowels in modern French by referring to the evolution of the language from its origins.

550 **Malmberg, Bertil**
Phonétique française. Malmö, Hermods, 1969. 194 pp. illus. bibliog.
Provides detailed phonetic description of French sounds for the training of non-native teachers of French, concentrating on phonological aspects and using diagrams, X-ray photographs and tape-recorded voices. Assumes familiarity with basic phonetic methods and with the IPA list of phonetic signs used in the work. Accompanying tape.

551 **Salengros, R.**
Dictionnaire orthographique du vocabulaire de base. Paris, Nathan, 1965. xii, 321 pp.
A French elementary-school reference book designed to help young pupils learn rules of spelling for themselves. Six lists presenting 4,000 basic words in a variety of ways to aid memorising and to encourage systematic association of ideas on spelling.

552 **Schane, Sanford A.**
French phonology and morphology. Research Monograph, 45. Cambridge, Massachusetts, M.I.T. Press, 1968. xxi, 161 pp. bibliog.
Deals with liaison, the vowel system, verbs, using Halle's and Chomsky's model of generative phonology. Intended to be accessible to French specialists as well as to linguists.

553 **Simon, Péla**
Les consonnes françaises; mouvements et positions articulatoires à la lumière de la radiocinématographie. Bibliothèque Française et Romane. Série A: Manuels et Études Linguistiques, 14. Paris, Klincksieck, 1967. 380 pp. illus. tables, bibliogs.
Explains the techniques and reasons for new researches. Lists and describes French consonants. Comparative tables, photographs, line-drawings.

554 **Thimonnier, René**
Le système graphique du français: introduction à une pédagogie rationnelle de l'orthographie. Paris, Plon, 1967. 408 pp. bibliog.
Discusses the problems of spelling, reducing them to reasonable proportions, and suggests a means of reform. Does not take anglicisms into account.

Warnant, Léon
See 604.

555 **Zwanenburg, W.**
Recherches sur la prosodie de la phrase française. Leidse Romanistische Reeks van de Rijksuniversiteit te Leiden, 11. Leiden, Universitaire Pers, 1965. 135 pp. bibliog.
Based on seven conversations transcribed at the beginning of the book. Features of intonation and pause are examined in relation to syntax. An attempt is made to define types of sentence, and the prosodic system of the sentence is then placed in the total system of language.

VOCABULARY AND USAGE

Bailly, René
See 596.

556 **Bally, Charles**
Traité de stylistique française. 2 vols. Geneva, Georg; Paris, Klincksieck, 3rd edn. 1951. bibliog.
Volume 1 is an exploration of the expressive resources of the French language and volume 2 provides examples and extensive exercises.

Bénac, Henri
See 598.

557 **Cohen, Marcel**
Encore des regards sur la langue française. Paris, Éditions Sociales, 1966. 310 pp.
Collection of short essays on spoken and written usage. The use of various words, idioms and expressions is subjected to psychological analysis and their form commented upon. The historical evolution of words is examined.

558 **Doppagne, Albert**
Trois aspects du français contemporain. La Langue Vivante. Paris, Larousse, 1966. 215 pp.
Through an original treatment of selected words and phrases it reveals some peculiarities of French which often do not figure in more formal studies. Sections: *des signes, des mots, des tours.*

Eaton, Helen S.
See 70.

559 **France. Ministère de l'Education Nationale**
Le français fondamental. 2 vols. Paris, Institut Pédagogique Nationale. 1er degré, 2nd edn. 1959. 79 pp. First pubd. 1954. 2e degré, 1959. 64 pp.
Lists essential vocabulary, initial grammar, according to frequency and needs of self-expression on the basis of researches described in book by Gougenheim. See 562.

560 **Galliot, Marcel**
Essai sur la langue de la réclame contemporaine. Toulouse, Privat, 1955. xxxii, 578 pp. bibliog.

Examines the psychology of language in publicity and advertising. Analyses the language employed, its syntax, lexis and style, with many examples.

561 **Gougenheim, Georges**
Les mots français dans l'histoire et dans la vie. Vols. 1 (2nd edn.) and 2. Paris, Picard, 1966.
Study of the semantic development of selected words. In volume 1 the words are grouped in semantic categories such as animal and vegetable kingdom, and human activities; there is a section on grammar and pronunciation. The second volume discusses words in the categories: sensations, sentiments and actions of man; social life; space, time, light; animal life; materials and objects. Includes a section on the classics Molière and Boileau.

562 **Gougenheim, Georges, and others**
L'élaboration du français fondamental (1er degré): étude sur l'établissement d'un vocabulaire et d'une grammaire de base. Linguistique Appliquée, 1. Paris, Didier, new edn. 1964. 302 pp. illus. tables, bibliog. First pubd. 1956, entitled *L'Élaboration du français élémentaire.*
Gives the order of frequency of words regarded as basic to spoken French. Discusses methods of approach and the idea of *disponibilité.* Previous work in drawing up a basic vocabulary and grammar is analysed in detail. Psychological, geographical and sociological aspects are studied. Appendices contain transcriptions of some conversations recorded for *le français fondamental,* and specimens of teaching texts based on it.

563 **Grevisse, Maurice**
Problèmes de langage. Paris, Presses Universitaires de France, 1964. 364 pp. First pubd. 1961.
Deals with selected points where current usage does not necessarily correspond with the rules given by authoritative grammar.

Grevisse, Maurice
See 535.

564 **Levieux, Michel, and Eleanor Levieux**
Beyond the dictionary in French. London, Cassell, 1967. 156 pp.
Studies both the common and uncommon words of everyday French, explaining their particular nuances and usages often with reference to situational background. Very useful in dealing with those pitfalls into which

the English speaker can easily slip. Following the main part of the book is a series of specialised vocabularies (banking, courtesy, franglais, telephone, housing, cars, etc.). English–French cross-reference index.

565 **Nuffield Foundation. Nuffield Foreign Languages Teaching Materials Project and Centre de Recherches et d'Etudes pour la Diffusion du Français**
Enquête sur le langage de l'enfant français: document no. 1: transcriptions de conversations d'enfants de 9 ans. Nuffield Foreign Language Teaching Materials Project: Reports and Occasional Papers, 20. Leeds, The Foundation, 1966. Various pagings. mimeographed.
Transcriptions of recordings of nine-year-old French children showing idiom and centres of interest.

566 **Nuffield Foundation. Nuffield Foreign Languages Teaching Materials Project**
Enquête sur le langage de l'enfant français: document no. 2: the spoken language of nine-year-old French children: a word count based on the CREDIF transcriptions, edited by R. W. Rutherford and M. Wears. Reports and Occasional Papers, 32. York, The Foundation, 1969. iv, 95 pp. mimeographed.
An alphabetical list giving word frequencies and totals, as well as the frequency recorded in the Français Fondamental word count. Proper nouns are listed separately.

567 **Nuffield Foundation. Nuffield Foreign Languages Teaching Materials Project, and Centre de Recherches et d'Études pour la Diffusion du Français**
Enquête sur le langage de l'enfant français: document no. 2 [sic]*: transcription de conversations d'enfants de 10 ans.* Reports and Occasional Papers, 39. Saint-Cloud, CREDIF, 1968, ii, 224 pp. mimeographed.
Transcriptions of recordings of ten-year-old French children showing idiom and centres of interest.

568 **Sauvageot, Aurélien**
Français écrit, français parlé. La Langue Vivante. Paris, Larousse, 1962. 235 pp.
Reflections on many aspects of French which seek to determine those points which are most subject to change nowadays, and to show how the language is in a process of development. The emphasis is on usage rather than on linguistic classification.

569 **Sauvageot, Aurélien**
Portrait du vocabulaire français. La Langue Vivante. Paris, Larousse, 1964. 286 pp.
A discussion of present-day tendencies in functional terms. Attempts to give a picture of changes which are at present taking place in everyday French usage. Presented as a series of observations on selected topics and words.

570 **Savard, Jean-Guy, and Jack Richards**
Les indices d'utilité du vocabulaire fondamental français. Quebec, Les Presses de l'Université Laval, for the Centre International de Recherches sur le Bilinguisme, 1970. xi, 169 pp. tables, diagrs. bibliog.
A statistical analysis of the basic French vocabulary lists which sets out to verify the independence of the four criteria: frequency, combinability, availability and range.

571 **Ters, François, and others**
Programme de vocabulaire orthographique de base: cycles primaire et secondaire: répartition par centres d'étude. Neuchâtel, Messeiller, 1964. 298 pp. tables, diagr. bibliog.
Examines the frequency and distribution of written words in French in an attempt to establish a basic vocabulary. After an introductory account of the methodology employed, the findings are discussed within broad semantic categories or centres of study (animals, plants, the sciences, the arts, justice, etc.). Provides an alphabetical list of words.

VARIETIES OF FRENCH

Bélisle, Louis-Alexandre, ed.
See 597.

572 **Gendron, Jean-Denis**
Tendances phonétiques du français parlé au Canada. Bibliothèque Française et Romane. Série E: Langue et Littérature Françaises au Canada, 2. Paris, Klincksieck; Quebec, Les Presses de l'Université Laval, 1966. xx, 254 pp. illus. tables, bibliog.
A study of the pronunciation of educated Canadians against the double background of popular Canadian French and standard Parisian.

CONTRASTIVE ANALYSIS

Delattre, Pierre
See 545.

Hammer, John H., and Frank A. Rice
See 157.

573 **Vinay, J. P., and J. Darbelnet**
Stylistique comparée du français et de l'anglais: méthode de traduction. Bibliothèque de Stylistique Comparée, 1. London, Harrap, in collaboration with Didier, Paris, new edn. 1960. 331 pp. tables, diagrs. bibliog. First pubd. 1958.
Useful for advanced students in dealing with translation. Has a glossary of technical terms used in the work and several appendices, the third of which has model translations of French and English passages with fairly detailed notes. The main part of the work deals with the principles and techniques of translation and has abundant examples. There is a separate but associated workbook for students.

TEACHING METHODS

574 **Belasco, Simon, and Albert Valdman**
Applied linguistics and the teaching of French. Nittany Press, U.S.A, 1968. v, 296 pp. tables, diagrs. bibliogs. mimeographed. Obtainable from Pennsylvania State University. First pubd. 1961.
A revised version of *Manual and anthology of applied linguistics*, 1960, and *Applied linguistics*, 1961. One of a series in which the five main European languages were treated in relation to structural and transformational linguistics for teachers' refresher courses. Syntax, morphology, phonology and American students' problems.

575 **Boy, Monique**
Formes structurales du français. Collection le Français dans le Monde – B.E.L.C. Paris, Hachette et Larousse, 1969. 176 pp. bibliog.
Works from elementary spoken French towards intermediate spoken and written language by providing specimen conversations, models and suggested exercises on a structural pattern basis to construct complex expressions from simple ones.

576 **Burney, Pierre, and Robert Damoiseau**
La classe de conversation. Collection le Français dans le Monde – B.E.L.C. Paris, Hachette et Larousse, 1969. 152 pp. illus. tables, bibliog.
Deals with techniques for holding conversation classes at different levels, strategy for planning them, ways of correcting faults, and offers examples of means of exploiting a course and other stimuli.

577 **Calvert, F. I.**
French by modern methods in primary and secondary schools. Huddersfield, Schofield and Sims, 1965. 96 pp.
An introductory discussion of methods and principles, and their application to primary and secondary school language teaching.

578 **Center for Applied Linguistics**
Description of Level 1 of the self-instructional French program. Washington, D.C., The Center, 1967. 88 pp. illus.
Describes the procedures of an experimental self-instructional beginners' course.

579 **Cole, Leo R.**
Teaching French to juniors. Unibooks. London, University of London Press, 2nd edn. 1969. 128 pp. bibliogs. First pubd. 1964.
Describes the principles and techniques that underlie an audio-visual and oral approach to young children. Is concerned with effective classroom teaching procedures relevant to primary and secondary school beginners. Examples are used to illustrate techniques. Includes chapters on demonstration and imitation, visual aids, oral questioning, class activity, reading and writing.

580 **Csécsy, Madeleine**
De la linguistique à la pédagogie: le verbe français. Collection le Français dans le Monde – B.E.L.C. Paris, Hachette et Larousse, 1968. 128 pp. tables, bibliog.
Chapters on characteristics of the French verb are presented, each in two parts. In the first part is an exploration of the linguistic features of the spoken language; in the second part an examination of pedagogical questions which these features raise.

Donoghue, Mildred R.
See 220.

581 **Dunkel, Harold B., and Roger A. Pillet**
French in the elementary school: five years' experience. Chicago, University of Chicago Press, 1962. v, 150 pp. tables, diagr.
A detailed account and critical examination of the FLES programme in America. Contains explanatory tables and a diagram indicating which findings are conclusive and which are controversial.

582 **Eriksson, Marguerite, and others**
Foreign languages in the elementary school. Englewood Cliffs, New Jersey, Prentice-Hall, 1964. ix, 185 pp. illus. bibliog.
Aims to synthesise the views of specialists on the content and methodology of teaching a foreign language (primarily French) in US schools. Designed to assist teachers in training.

583 **Falinski, Eugène**
Psycho-pedagogie du langage écrit. Paris, Hermann, 1966. 99 pp. bibliog.
Chapters on pathological difficulties in writing, philological phonetics, history of writing, orthography through the ages, methodology of writing and spelling rules.

Finocchiaro, Mary
See 289.

Huebener, Theodore
See 298.

Incorporated Association of Assistant Masters in Secondary Schools
See 223.

584 **Leon, Pierre R., ed.**
Applied linguistics and the teaching of French. Linguistique appliquée et enseignement du français. Collection Éducation et Culture. Montreal, Centre Educatif et Culturel, 1967. vi, 170 pp. illus. table, bibliogs.
A collection of papers in English and French concerning various aspects of applied linguistics. Bilingualism, pronunciation, conversation, grammar, learning psychology, vocabulary and translation problems are all discussed in a practical way.

Levenson, Stanley, and William Kendrick, eds.
See 305.

585 **Marty, Fernand L.**
Linguistics applied to the beginning French course. Roanoke, Virginia, Audio-Visual Publications, 1963. xx, 271 pp. tables.
Designed as a guide for teachers using a specific course, but of value to those interested in the methods of teaching French.

586 **Marty, Fernand L.**
Programing a basic foreign language course: prospects for self-instruction. Hollins, Virginia, Hollins College, 1962. 69 pp. illus. Obtainable from Audio-Visual Publications, Box 5497, Roanoke, Virginia.
Describes in detail the programming of a basic course for teaching French. Considers the use and application of programming through audio-visual techniques, teaching machines and programmed textbooks.

587 **Marty, Fernand L.**
Teaching French. Roanoke, Virginia, Audio-Visual Publications, 1968. vi, 337 pp. illus.
A comprehensive manual consisting of an analysis of the language and a main section on methodology. Contains chapters on testing, using and maintaining audio and visual equipment.

Marty, Fernand L.
See 308.

588 **National Foundation for Educational Research in England and Wales**
French from eight: a national experiment. Occasional Publication Series, 18. Slough, The Foundation, 1968. xii, 78 pp. tables, illus.
First report on the long-term evaluation of the pilot scheme for teaching French in English primary schools. Describes the sample of pupils and the administration of tests of general attainment and of attainment in French. Provides data on test-performance (in French) of low-ability groups and analyses teachers' attitudes.

589 **Nuffield Foundation. Nuffield Foreign Languages Teaching Materials Project**
A puppet theatre for language teaching, by David Rowlands. Reports and Occasional Papers, 4. Leeds, The Foundation, 1964. 15 pp. illus. mimeographed.
Provides instructions for constructing a simple theatre and puppets for use in teaching French in the primary school.

590 **Politzer, Robert L.**
Teaching French: an introduction to applied linguistics. A Blaisdell Book in Modern Languages. London and Waltham, Massachusetts, Blaisdell, 2nd edn. 1965. xiii, 181 pp. bibliog. First pubd. 1961 by Ginn, in Boston.

Deals with the application of linguistic precepts to French teaching. Audio-lingual techniques are discussed in detail. Part 1 is concerned with the theoretical basis of audio-lingual procedures; Part 2 with French pronunciation, morphology, structures and vocabulary. Bibliography includes list of textbooks. Companion volume to Politzer's *Teaching Spanish* and *Teaching German*, q.v.

591 **Renard, Raymond**
L'enseignement des langues vivantes par la méthode audio-visuelle et structuro-globale de Saint-Cloud–Zagreb. Préface de Paul Rivenc. Paris and Brussels, Didier, [1965]. 127 pp. illus. table, bibliog.
An account of the linguistic principles underlying audio-visual language-teaching method as exemplified by the course *Voix et images de France.* Includes a description of *le français fondamental*, of classroom techniques and answers to some criticisms of *Voix et images de France.*

592 **Schools Council**
French in the primary school: the joint Schools Council Nuffield Foundation pilot scheme. Working Paper, 8. London, HMSO, 1966. vi, 84 pp.
A report on the background of the scheme and of relevant conferences. It includes implications for secondary schools.

Schröter, Günter, and Hans Ladwein
See 312.

593 **Stanford Center for Research and Development in Teaching**
Practice-centered teacher training: French: a syllabus for the training and retraining of teachers in French, by Robert L. Politzer. Technical Report, 1. Stanford, Stanford University School of Education, 1966. Various pagings. diagrs. mimeographed.
A handbook of methods and techniques suitable for the training of teachers. Includes chapters on applied linguistics, language practice, methodology and the use of video tape to record practice lessons.

Turner, John D., ed.
See 318.

594 **Valdman, Albert**
The implementation and evaluation of a multiple-credit self-instructional elementary French course. Bloomington, Indiana University, n.d. 297 pp. mimeographed.

Deals with audio-lingual techniques and the development of 'New Key' methods and materials in the United States based on an experimental course involving intensive teacher–pupil contact and allowing students to progress at optimum individual pace. All practical aspects of organisation and language laboratory procedure are dealt with.

595 **Young, Clarence W., and Charles A. Choquette**
An experimental study of the relative effectiveness of four systems of language laboratory equipment in teaching French pronunciation. Hamilton, Colgate University, 1963. iii, 110 pp. illus. tables, mimeographed.
The systems referred to are 1. inactivated headphones, 2. activated headphones, 3. playback after recording a practice session, 4. short delay playback immediately after the recording of a single utterance. Describes in detail the experiments, equipment used, the subject, materials and procedures, tests and results. Statistical data are furnished for each aspect tested.

DICTIONARIES

Only dictionaries are included which are not listed in the second edition of A. J. Walford's *A guide to foreign language grammars and dictionaries,* published by the Library Association in 1967. See 216.

596 **Bailly, René**
Dictionnaire des synonymes de la langue française. Paris, Larousse, 1966. xiii, 626 pp. First pubd. 1947.
Largely dispenses with quotations and authorities to make room for popular words and common contemporary usage.

597 **Bélisle, Louis-Alexandre, ed.**
Dictionnaire général de la langue française au Canada. Quebec, Bélisle (4 rue St Jacques), 1957. xvi, 1390 pp. illus. bibliog.
Covers the language as spoken in Canada and distinguishes Canadian words and idioms from standard French.

598 **Bénac, Henri**
Dictionnarire des synonymes, conforme au Dictionnaire de l'Académie Française. Paris, Hachette, 1956. 1025 pp.
The semantic range of each main entry is examined in depth, and where possible an example from literature is given for each nuance commented on.

599 *Dictionnaire français–français des mots rares et précieux*. Collections Seghers. Paris, Seghers, 1965. 593 pp.
Intended for the lay-reader needing guidance about artisan, technical, scientific terms, and those commonplace expressions which have their own gloss among groups of specialists.

600 **Dubois, Jean, and others, eds.**
Dictionnaire du français contemporain. Paris, Larousse, 1966. xxii, 1224 pp.
Phrases illustrate the common usage for each term. Synonyms and antonyms given for the different senses. Derivations grouped under one main entry with cross-references where needed. Tables given of certain groups of words and their use, of verbs, suffixes, prefixes and a list of common proverbs. Pronunciations presented in IPA notation.

601 **Juilland, Alphonse**
Dictionnaire inverse de la langue française. Janua Linguarum. Series Practica, 7. The Hague and London, Mouton, 1965. lx, 504 pp. diagrs.
A reverse dictionary based on the sounds of words and ignoring the spelling. There is an explanatory introduction of French phonemes and of their order and transcription in this present work. There are appendices summarising the frequencies given in the main body of the dictionary.

602 **Pradez, Elizabeth**
Dictionnaire des gallicismes les plus usités, expliqués brièvement, illustrés par des exemples et accompagnés de leurs équivalents anglais et allemands. Paris, Payot, 1965. ix, 388 pp. First pubd. 1951.
Common idiomatic expressions, set phrases and clichés succinctly explained.

603 **Sandry, Géo, and Marcel Carrère**
Dictionnaire de l'argot moderne. Paris, Dauphin, 9th edn. 1953. 430 pp. First pubd. 1922.
A general dictionary of underworld slang followed by thirty sections on specialist terms in various professions, sports, among young people, and other distinct social groups.

604 **Warnant, Léon**
Dictionnaire de la prononciation française. Gembloux, Belgium, Duculot, 3rd edn. 1968. li, 654 pp.

Introduction explains the mode of use, gives phonetic values of International Phonetic Alphabet symbols employed, equivalents in twenty-one other languages and phonetics of sentence structures. Dictionary consists of 32,000 words of normal language, four pages of vowel and consonant values as spoken by the author on an accompanying disc, and 20,000 proper names both French and non-French.

BIBLIOGRAPHIES

605 **French and European Publications, Inc.**
A comprehensive bibliography of French language & literature for schools & libraries, universities & colleges. New York, The Author, 1969. xvi, 436 pp.
In principle a bookseller's catalogue, this comprehensive list provides in its last chapter a quick guide to French works on linguistics in print in 1969. Each reference mentions the author, short title and, if the work forms part of a series, the name of that series. There are no annotations but prices are quoted in US dollars.

Goodger, B. C.
See 332.

Hammer, John H., and Frank A. Rice
See 157.

Robinson, Janet O.
See 214.

SECTION V

German

GENERAL

606 **Collinson, W. E.**

The German language today: its patterns and background. Modern Languages and Literature. London, Hutchinson University Library, 3rd edn. 1968. 186 pp. bibliog. First pubd. 1953.

The first thirteen chapters of this useful introduction to the philology of German outline the phonological and morphological systems of German and its syntactical structures. The historical aspect is included in chapters on German in relation to other languages, and its development in Germany, Switzerland and Austria. Important additions are the chapters on National Socialist and DDR German, and on English and American influences on modern German.

607 **Glinz, Hans**

Grundbegriffe und Methoden inhaltbezogener Text- und Sprachanalyse. Sprache und Gemeinschaft: Grundlegung, 3. Düsseldorf, Pädagogischer Verlag Schwann, 1965. 172 pp. tables.

The author, a leading exponent of the German school of 'meaning- and content-orientated grammar' (*inhaltbezogene Grammatik*), here develops concepts and procedures for the total analysis of German literary texts from the level of the aesthetic impact of the writer's style to that of the structural analysis of the function of paragraphs, sentences, clauses, phrases and even individual words. The intention is to propound a system of literary and linguistic analysis which will result in verifiably objective judgements.

608 **Glinz, Hans**

Die innere Form des Deutschen: eine neue deutsche Grammatik. Biblioteca Germanica, 4. Bern and Munich, Francke, 4th edn. 1965. iv, 505 pp. tables, diagr. bibliog. First pubd. 1952.

Attempts new categorisation and interpretation of grammar in relationship to new linguistic developments, with particular emphasis on sentence structure and theoretical analysis; amply supported by quotations and comparisons.

609 **Patzig, Günther, and others**

Die deutsche Sprache im 20. Jahrhundert. Kleine Vandenhoek-Reihe, 232–4. Göttingen, Vandenhoek & Ruprecht, 1966. 133 pp. bibliogs.

A symposium of six German lectures given in 1965 reviewing different aspects of the development of German in the twentieth century. The first and second lectures are of general interest. The first, *Die Sprache, philoso-*

phisch befragt (Patzig) considers the nature of language and meaning; the second, *Die Sprache als linguistisches Problem* (Hartmann) discusses the role of linguistic investigation, the variety of goals it sets itself, briefly the evolution of linguistic science, and finally the application of the techniques of linguistic analysis to stylistic studies of texts. The other papers discuss specific aspects of contemporary German.

HISTORY

610 **Bach, Adolf**

Geschichte der deutschen Sprache. Heidelberg, Quelle & Meyer, 8th edn. 1965. 495 pp. maps, bibliogs. First pubd. 1938.

A feature of this comprehensive outline of the growth of German is that it views the problems from different aspects: i.e. the language's phonetic, lexical, morphological, syntactic and stylistic evolution, its geographical spread and interrelation with other languages. It also examines contemporary political, sociological and cultural trends that have formed contemporary German.

611 **Chambers, W. Walker, and John R. Wilkie**

A short history of the German language. London, Methuen, 1970. viii, 167 pp. maps, bibliogs.

A simple, uncontroversial introduction to philology, concentrating on standard literary language. The first part deals with the development of German from Indo-European; the second with the development of German vocabulary; the third surveys changes in sounds, forms and syntax. Minimum references to dialect and colloquial language; study of phonetics and general linguistics merely mentioned in first chapter. An index, a classified bibliography and specimen texts are provided.

612 **Lockwood, W. B.**

An informal history of the German language: with chapters on Dutch and Afrikaans, Frisian and Yiddish. Cambridge, Heffer, 1965. viii, 265 pp. maps, bibliogs.

Reviews the evolution of German from primitive Germanic to the beginnings of the modern language. Followed by an account of modern standard German and regional dialects, with specimen texts. This pattern is followed in the survey of minor languages associated with German, including Pennsylvania German.

Mentrup, Wolfgang, and others

See 633.

613 **Priebsch, R., and W. E. Collinson**
The German language. The Great Languages. London, Faber & Faber, 6th edn. 1966. xx, 496 pp. map, bibliogs. First pubd. 1934.
A philological study of German tracing the origins of Germanic languages in general against their Indo-European background and in particular giving a historical survey of German phonology, morphology and syntax. Discusses influences on the development of the language at all points in its history and the evolution of its orthography and calligraphy. There are briefer sections on dialects of German. Includes a map of German dialects (showing 1939 political frontiers and pre-1944 linguistic frontiers), and a thorough index of words.

Stolte, Heinz
See 624.

GRAMMAR AND STRUCTURE

Drosdowski, Günther, and others
See 638.

614 **Erben, Johannes**
Abriß der deutschen Grammatik. Berlin, Akademie-Verlag; Munich, Max Hueber, 9th edn. 1966. xiii, 316 pp. table, diagrs. bibliogs. First pubd. 1958.
This modern description of German for teachers of the language avoids the traditional divisions into morphology, syntax, word-formation etc. in treating the two basic units of German – the word and the sentence. The work takes into account the results of research and contains word and subject indexes.

615 **Glinz, Hans**
Deutsche Syntax. Realienbücher für Germanisten. Abt. C. Stuttgart, Metzlersche Verlagsbuchhandlung, 2nd edn. 1967. xi, 112 pp. bibliog. First pubd. 1965.
Concise review of the evolution of German syntactic studies from Jacob Grimm to present day. Gives a general introduction to *inhaltbezogene Grammatik*, of which the author is a leading exponent, and discusses the application of generative grammar to the study of the syntax of German.

Glinz, Hans
See 608.

616 **Grebe, Paul, and others**
Duden: Grammatik der deutschen Gegenwartssprache. Der Große Duden, 4. Mannheim, Bibliographisches Institut, 2nd edn. 1966. 774 pp. First pubd. 1959.
Grammar of the contemporary German language, organised in two main parts. The first deals with phonetics and pronunciation, parts of speech and their morphological flexions, and the formation of compounds. The second analyses syntax and the interaction of word-order, stress, intonation and juncture in the communication of meaning. The introduction defines *Hochsprache*, *Alltagssprache*, *Umgangssprache* and *Gebietssprache*. Employs a modern approach to language analysis rather than a historical-philological approach. Includes an exhaustive index of words, discussion of problems of usage and a useful fifteen-page glossary of definitions of the grammatical terminology used in the text.

617 **Griesbach, Heinz, and Dora Schulz**
Grammatik der deutschen Sprache. Vollständiger Lehrgang der Deutschen Sprache. Munich, Max Hueber, 5th edn. 1967. xv, 445 pp. First pubd. 1960.
Reference grammar of the *Umgangssprache* of today, based on the authors' experience of teaching German to foreigners. The approach is traditional but the chapters on syntax reflect the new German approach to grammar.

Hallwass, Edith
See 644.

618 **Jørgensen, Peter**
German grammar. Translated by G. Kolisko and F. P. Pickering. 3 vols. London, Heinemann, 1959, 1963, 1966. First pubd. 1953.
A revised English edition of a standard advanced German grammar for Danish students. Essentially a compact description of the language of modern written prose, provided with a full index of words and topics covered. Phonology is not considered but there is a thorough analysis of the morphology and syntax of German. In the last, the author introduces the concepts of *parataxis* (the relation of co-ordination existing between the separate elements of compound words or compound sentences), *hypotaxis* (the relationships of subordination existing between these elements), and *nexus* (the relationship existing between fundamentally different entities which are mutually interdependent in a word group).

619 Jude, Wilhelm K.

Deutsche Grammatik. Braunschweig, Westermann, 12th edn. 1966. 320 pp. tables. First pubd. 1955 (?).

Simply written morphology and syntax of German with helpful tables and many examples. The appendix includes the German alphabet in cursive and printed forms, a list of German and foreign specialist grammatical terms, and an index.

620 Jung, Walter, and others

Grammatik der deutschen Sprache. Leipzig, VEB Bibliographisches Institut, 2nd edn. 1967. xiv, 518 pp. bibliog. First pubd. 1966.

Traditional and comprehensive treatment of German grammar which takes the needs of foreigners into account. Presented in five main sections: structure of the German sentence, syntactical relations, individual word types, word-formation, and pronunciation. There are word and subject indexes.

Mackensen, Lutz

See 645.

621 Mater, Erich

Deutsche Verben. Part 1: *Alphabetisches Gesamtverzeichnis*; Part 2: *Grundwörter und deren Zusammensetzungen*; Part 3: *Gesamtverzeichnis der Grundwörter. Stellung der Kompositionsglieder*; Part 4: *Art der Zusammensetzung*; Part 5: *Flexionsklassen.* 5 vols. Leipzig, VEB Bibliographisches Institut, 1966–8.

The first five sections of a ten-part study of the German verb. Part 1 is an alphabetical index of the verbs of contemporary German. Part 2 is a list of basic verbs and the compound verbs derived from them, selected from the global list in Part 1. Part 3 lists the basic verbs again and then the compound verbs analysed into component parts. This part also includes an analytical alphabetical index of prefixes. Part 4 lists verbs according to the grammatical nature of their prefixes, e.g. adjective, preposition, etc. Part 5 gives a list of verbs marked according to which one of five conjugation patterns they exemplify.

622 Meil, Kläre

ABC der starken Verben. Deutsche Reihe für Ausländer, C2. Munich, Max Hueber, 4th edn. 1966. 142 pp. First pubd. 1962.

A list of the major strong verbs of German giving the main forms of each and, for each basic verb and its more important compound forms, an example of a typical sentence, the meaning of which is further explained in simple German.

Priebsch, R., and W. E. Collinson
See 613.

623 **Schmitz, Werner**
Der Gebrauch der deutschen Präpositionen. Deutsche Reihe für Ausländer, C 1. Munich, Max Hueber, 4th edn. 1966. 87 pp. First pubd. 1964.
Short general study of the lexical range of forty-three German prepositions (eight using accusative alone, eight using dative alone, nine using accusative and dative and eighteen with genitive alone), with examples and short explanations of each use.

624 **Stolte, Heinz**
Kurze deutsche Grammatik: auf Grund der fünfbändigen deutschen Grammatik von Hermann Paul. Eingerichtet von Heinz Stolte. Sammlung Kurzer Grammatiken Germanischer Dialekte. A. Hauptreihe, 10. Tübingen, Max Niemeyer, 3rd edn. 1962. xvi, 522 pp. bibliogs. First pubd. 1949.
A revised and shortened version of Paul's five-volume *Deutsche Grammatik* of 1922, which covers the historical bases of New High German, phonology, morphology, syntax and word-formation.

625 **Stopp, Frederick J.**
A manual of modern German. London, University Tutorial Press, 2nd edn. 1966. xv, 619 pp. First pubd. 1957.
Combines the function of a reference grammar and a graded course for the advanced student. The first part covers all major grammatical topics except the subjunctive, which, together with certain other selected topics requiring greater detail, is dealt with in the second part. German–English and English–German translation exercises are provided, in modern language, at the end of each chapter. There are five appendices including a list of German grammatical terms, listed under their English equivalents.

PHONOLOGY AND ORTHOGRAPHY

626 **Berger, Dieter**
Duden: Komma, Punkt und alle anderen Satzzeichen: mit ausführlicher Beispielsammlung. Duden-Taschenbücher. Sonderreihe zum Großen Duden, 1. Mannheim and Zurich, Bibliographisches Institut, 1968, 208 pp.

Comprehensive manual on punctuation with copious examples and brief historical notes.

627 **Bithell, Jethro**
German pronunciation and phonology. London, Methuen, 1952. xx, 415 pp. map, table, diagrs. bibliog.
Gives an outline of general and historical phonetics, discusses standard German speech and gives a diachronic study of German phonology, paying considerable attention to the effect of syllabication, pitch, stress and rhythm on pronunciation and the spelling conventions of the written language. The work leans heavily on German scholarship and consistently gives German equivalents for all technical terminology employed in English.

628 **Boor, Helmut de, and others, eds.**
Siebs deutsche Aussprache: reine und gemäßigte Hochlautung mit Aussprachewörterbuch. Berlin, De Gruyter, 19th edn. 1969. x, 494 pp. tables, diagrs. bibliog. First pubd. 1898.
This standard work on the pronunciation and intonation of modern educated German has been extensively revised to include regional, Austrian and Swiss variations. Examples have been recorded on three discs. The pronunciation of words and names was indicated in two separate lists in the eighteenth edition. These have been conflated in the new edition and occupy 324 pages.

Delattre, Pierre
See 156.

Drosdowski, Günther, and others
See 638.

629 **Grebe, Paul**
Duden: Rechtschreibung der deutschen Sprache und der Fremdwörter. Der Große Duden, 1. Mannheim, Bibliographisches Institut, 16th edn. 1967. 800 pp.
Standard reference book for the rules of punctuation, orthography and the formation of compound forms. Includes an exhaustive word list showing the correct spelling for each main entry and of its variants and compounds.

Hallwass, Edith
See 644.

Helmers, Hermann
See 658.

Jung, Walter, and others
See 620.

Kadler, Eric H.
See 225.

Mackensen, Lutz, ed.
See 645.

630 **Mangold, Max, and others**
Duden: Ausspracheworterbuch. Der Große Duden, 6. Mannheim, Bibliographisches Institut, 1962. 827 pp. diagrs. bibliog.
Pronouncing word-list of more than 100,000 entries, giving in the International Phonetic Alphabet the pronunciation and stress not only of the major part of the vocabulary of German, but also of a large selection of the foreign words and names met in German. An introduction of some 100 pages explains the system of IPA and gives a summary of the workings of the vocalic, consonantal, syllabication, stress and intonational systems of German. There is also a brief summary of the phonetic characteristics of twenty-six other major languages and a bibliography of pronouncing dictionaries for most of these.

631 **Martens, Carl, and Peter Martens**
Phonetik der deutschen Sprache: praktische Aussprachelehre; mit 136 Abbildungen in gesondertem Kunstdruckteil. Munich, Max Hueber, 2nd edn. 1965. 294 pp. bibliog.
Detailed study of pronunciation of standard German speech, with examples, tongue-twisters and poetical quotations; also text of LP record. The illustrations are published in a separate leaflet, *Abbildungen zu den deutschen Lauten*, 2nd edn. 1966, 32 pp.

632 **Mentrup, Wolfgang**
Duden: die Regeln der deutschen Rechtschreibung: an zahlreichen Beispielen erläutert. Duden-Taschenbücher. Sonderreihe zum Großen Duden, 3. Mannheim and Zurich, Bibliographisches Institut, 1968. 232 pp.
Standard reference book for rules of punctuation, orthography and the formation of compound forms in German. An exhaustive word-list refers back to the appropriate section.

633 **Mentrup, Wolfgang, and others**
Duden: Wann schreibt man groß, wann schreibt man klein? Regeln und ausführliches Wörterverzeichnis. Duden-Taschenbücher. Sonderreihe zum Großen Duden, 6. Mannheim and Zurich, Bibliographisches Institut, 1969, 256 pp.
Reference book on the use of majuscules and minuscules at the beginning of words, in titles, abbreviations, and variants. Pages 33–244 give an alphabetical list of words affected by these rules. Book ends with brief survey of historical development in the use of capitals.

Priebsch, R., and W. E. Collinson
See 613.

Stolte, Heinz
See 624.

634 **Wängler, Hans-Heinrich**
Grundriß einer Phonetik des Deutschen: mit einer allgemeinen Einführung in die Phonetik. Marburg, N. G. Elwert, 2nd edn. 1967. viii, 250 pp. illus. bibliog. First pubd. 1960.
This authoritative survey of German phonetics includes material on language and speech, general and applied phonetics and the evolution of phonetics and phonology. Deals with anatomical, physiological and neurological bases of speech production and perception. The sounds of German are classified and an account is given of syllabication, stress and intonation. Includes copious references and a combined subject and author index. An English translation has been published by EMC-Corporation, St Paul, Minnesota.

VOCABULARY AND USAGE

635 **Agricola, Erhard, and others, eds.**
Wörter und Wendungen: Wörterbuch zum deutschen Sprachgebrauch. Leipzig, VEB Bibliographisches Institut, 3rd edn. 1968. xxxii, 792 pp. First pubd. 1962.
A list of approximately 8,000 words, most of which have more than one meaning. The meanings of these words are illustrated by 150,000 constructions in which they typically occur. Certain aspects of the language, e.g. use of prepositions, receive special attention, since they present particular difficulty to non-native speakers of German.

636 **Carstensen, Broder**
Englische Einflüsse auf die deutsche Sprache nach 1945. Beihefte zum Jahrbuch für Amerikastudien, 13. Heidelberg, Carl Winter, Universitätsverlag, 1965. 296 pp. bibliog.
Study of the influence of British and American English on the German language since 1945. The greatest impact is on vocabulary rather than on syntax. Analyses in detail the extent to which modifications have taken place in orthography, pronunciation, morphology and syntax. Language discussed is that of the press. The influence of the weekly *Der Spiegel* is described. Examines other sources of anglicisms (e.g. advertising, *Fachsprache*, NATO) and the stages in Germany's post-war history at which they started to become evident.

637 **Dornseiff, Franz**
Der deutsche Wortschatz nach Sachgruppen. Berlin, De Gruyter, 6th edn. 1965. iv, 166, 922 pp. bibliogs. First pubd. 1933.
A classic lexicographic study of synonyms and associated expressions in German, classified in twenty major categories and under a very large number of individual key subheadings according to theme or concept. Its organisation was influenced by the classification of Roget's *Thesaurus of English words and phrases*. The prefaces to the successive editions and the introduction together form an interesting survey of the evolution of lexicography and its problems. Includes exhaustive bibliographies and a general alphabetical index.

638 **Drosdowski, Günther, and others**
Duden: Hauptschwierigkeiten der deutschen Sprache. Der Große Duden, 9. Mannheim, Bibliographisches Institut, 1965. 759 pp. bibliog.
Lists alphabetically a comprehensive selection of the most frequent orthographical, lexical, grammatical and stylistic difficulties in German usage, and offers a picture of current developmental tendencies in the written and spoken educated language. Gives a complete list of the sources of all illustrative quotations.

Eaton, Helen S.
See 70.

639 **Eggeling, H. F.**
A dictionary of modern German prose usage. Oxford, Clarendon Press, 1961. xii, 418 pp.

A guide to modern German standard usage written in English, not dissimilar in the way it presents information to the monolingual *Duden: vergleichendes Synonymwörterbuch*. The entries here, however, are both English and German words which commonly present translation difficulties to the English-speaking advanced student. For all entries – which are listed alphabetically, not according to grammatical function – there is a full discussion of the syntactic problems involved, an examination of the semantic range of the items in question and of related synonyms. All statements are illustrated by examples.

640 **Farrell, R. B.**
Dictionary of German synonyms. London, Cambridge University Press, 1966. viii, 429 pp. First pubd. 1953.
A study of some aspects of the translation into German of about 700 common English words which present special problems for the English student. Under English head-words different shades of meaning and German translations are discussed with examples. Separate English and German indexes of words treated are provided.

641 **Friederich, Wolf**
Moderne deutsche Idiomatik: systematisches Wörterbuch mit Definitionen und Beispielen. Munich, Max Hueber, 1966. 824 pp. bibliog.
More than 7,000 idioms are listed, grouped by theme, in thirty sections. Within each section entries are made in the alphabetical order of the keywords. The meaning of each entry and an example of its use are given. The book contains a short introduction and an index of the keywords and some other important words.

642 **Grebe, Paul, and Wolfgang Müller**
Duden: vergleichendes Synonymwörterbuch: sinnverwandte Wörter und Wendungen. Der Große Duden, 8. Mannheim, Bibliographisches Institut, 1964. 792 pp. bibliog.
Dictionary of German synonyms. Where necessary, there is an indication of the stylistic level and emotional overtones of each word in question, and its place in current usage is illustrated by quotations from writings published in the previous decade. An appendix synthesises, under 316 thematic headings, the wider semantic categories into which the total vocabulary can be classified. An index of authors quoted is included.

643 **Grebe, Paul, and Gerhart Streitberg**
Duden: Stilwörterbuch der deutschen Sprache: das Wort in seiner Verwendung. Der Große Duden, 2. Mannheim, Bibliographisches Institut, 5th edn. 1963. 800 pp.
A standard reference book of acceptable stylistic usage in educated German. Each entry has a number of examples showing the permissible range of its various meanings, applications and dependent structures. The introduction by Ludwig Reiners is a discussion of the major pitfalls of German style.

644 **Hallwass, Edith**
Gutes Deutsch in allen Lebenslagen. Düsseldorf and Vienna, Econ-Verlag, 1967. 454, lxxxvi pp. tables, bibliog.
Popular but exhaustive guide to style, vocabulary, grammar and usage, with sections on loan words, proper names, punctuation, and a grammatical appendix.

645 **Mackensen, Lutz, ed.**
Gutes Deutsch in Schrift und Rede. Rororo Taschenbuch Ausgabe. Gütersloh, Bertelsmann Ratgeberverlag Reinhard Mohn, 1968. 446 pp. illus.
Informal popular guide to style, spelling and grammar, the proper use of language in speeches, correspondence, reports and minutes, with hints on reading for pleasure and information.

646 **Oehler, Heinz, ed.**
Grundwortschatz Deutsch: essential German. London, Harrap, in association with Ernst Klett, Stuttgart, 1968. 184 pp. bibliog.
Presents a basic vocabulary of about 2,000 items and some 3,000 words drawn from the contemporary spoken and written German language. The criterion for selection of items is not only statistical frequency but also the known practical utility of the items in terms of expressive value and range of meaning and application. Gives English equivalents for each German entry, has also short separate sections for structural words, cardinal and ordinal numerals, days of the week and months of the year. Contains a useful short bibliography on frequency analyses and basic language studies of German and English.

647 **Pfeffer, J. Alan**
Basic (spoken) German idiom list. Grunddeutsch. Grundstufe. Publications of the Institute for Basic German, University of Pittsburgh, 3. Englewood Cliffs, New Jersey, Prentice-Hall, 1968. xi, 91 pp. table, diagr.
Third in a series of related studies to establish the core elements of spoken German. The first in the series represents statistically 85 per cent of the free forms and semantic fields of any ordinary conversation, and this study adduces a proportionately equal segment of the restricted forms and related patterns of everyday German speech.

648 **Pfeffer, J. Alan**
Basic (spoken) German word list. Grunddeutsch. Grundstufe. Publications of the Institute for Basic German, University of Pittsburgh, 1. Englewood Cliffs, New Jersey, Prentice-Hall, 1964. ix, 79 pp. diagr. bibliog.
The first of four lexical and semantic studies intended to provide source material for the teaching of elementary spoken German. The source material, recorded in fifty-five localities in all parts of Germany, Austria and German-speaking Switzerland, was analysed by computer to yield a total basic vocabulary of 1,269 words. These are tabulated: 1. in alphabetical order; 2. by parts of speech; 3. in order of frequency and origin. A short appendix gives topical terms – i.e. commonly used specific names of varieties of animal and plant life, etc., and regional parallels. The introduction summarises the development of modern research in establishing the basic cores of the major European languages and gives a brief account of the procedures adopted in establishing the Basic German word list.

649 **Pfeffer, J. Alan**
Index of English equivalents for the basic (spoken) German word list. Grunddeutsch. Grundstufe. Publications of the Institute for Basic German, University of Pittsburgh, 2. Englewood Cliffs, New Jersey, Prentice-Hall, 1965. vii, 107 pp.
Gives English equivalents of the 1,269-word basic spoken German vocabulary described in the author's *Basic (spoken) German word list* (see above). All entries are given in alphabetical order according to the German word list. These equivalents are claimed to cover at least 75 per cent of the semantic fields for each German item listed. Meanings for each item are given in order of descending frequency to show respective weight and relative importance of each. Introduction gives a brief account of procedures used to establish the semantic scope of each word and the frequency of its use in its different meanings.

650 **Taylor, Ronald, and Walter Gottschalk**
A German–English dictionary of idioms: idiomatic and figurative German expressions with English translations. Munich, Max Hueber, 2nd edn. 1966. 598 pp. First pubd. 1960.
A dictionary of idioms, where possible listed alphabetically according to the principal noun of the example quoted, or, failing that, according to the other most significant part of speech present. For each item, quotations in both English and German show the different meanings given. The authors' short introduction warns the user that he must not assume a total correspondence in range of application in English and German for apparently identical idioms and even less for approximate equivalents.

651 **Wängler, Hans-Heinrich**
Rangwörterbuch hochdeutscher Umgangssprache. Marburg, N. G. Elwert, 1963. 67 pp.
Word frequency list of 1,022 items based on an analysis of a total corpus of 160,532 words. Exactly one half of this was taken from popular magazines, etc., the other half from recordings made of conversations between Germans of various ages in North Germany. Four lists are offered. The first is an alphabetical list showing the number of occurrences of each word in analyses of the written, the spoken and the combined corpora. The second shows, in order of frequency, the number of occurrences in the spoken and written corpora combined. The third shows, in order of frequency, the number of occurrences in the spoken corpus. The fourth shows, in order of frequency, the number of occurrences in the written corpus.

652 **Wustmann, Gustav**
Sprachdummheiten. Revised by Werner Schulze. Berlin, De Gruyter, 14th edn. 1966. xiv, 391 pp. First pubd. 1891.
Clear, informal discussion of common errors in German intended for German native speakers. Contains a wealth of information on common problems of morphology, word-formation, syntax, vocabulary and semantics.

VARIETIES OF GERMAN

Boor, Helmut de, and others, eds.
See 628.

Collinson, W. E.
See 606.

653 **Hard, Gerhard**
Zur Mundartgeographie: Ergebnisse, Methoden, Perspektiven. Beihefte zur Zeitschrift 'Wirkendes Wort', 17. Düsseldorf, Pädagogischer Verlag Schwann, 1966. 75 pp. illus. bibliog.
Short but authoritative account of the current position of German dialect geography studies. Eight chapters deal with the growth of the geographical approach to dialect study in Germany and the evolution of its techniques of investigation, endogenous phonetic change, social and regional divergences in pronunciation and vocabulary, variation in speech styles as a function of social role, socio-psychological attitudes to dialect speech, content and concept formation in dialect speech and the relationship in research techniques of dialectology to those of other socio-geographic studies. Bibliography includes recent and current work largely but not entirely in the field of German.

Lockwood, W. B.
See 612.

CONTRASTIVE ANALYSIS

Hammer, John H., and Frank A. Rice
See 157.

654 **Kufner, Herbert L.**
The grammatical structure of English and German: a contrastive sketch. Contrastive Structure Series. Chicago, University of Chicago Press, 1962. xi, 95 pp.
Companion volume to Moulton's *The sounds of English and German* (see below) aiming to be not a full description of the whole of German syntax but a contrastive study of the points at which the syntax of English and German clearly diverge. Main stress is on speech, though problems of written style are not neglected. Demonstrates the inadequacy of older definitions of the sentence when applied to German. Proposes a broad classification into normal and subnormal sentence types based on terminal intonation pattern, and within the normal sentence type further distinguishes the subgroups of major sentences – containing a finite verb in an independent clause, and minor sentences – from all other utterances. Also analyses all main types of German clause and demonstrates the differences in the phrase structure, the use of the different parts of speech and the compulsory grammatical and semantic categories of both languages.

655 Leisi, Ernst
Der Wortinhalt: seine Struktur im Deutschen und Englischen. Heidelberg, Quelle & Meyer, 3rd edn. 1967. 136 pp. bibliog. First pubd. 1952.
Presents an analysis and categorisation of English and German words and, in doing so, takes up a position between two schools of linguistic thought. Attempts to give words a sociological definition and to indicate the connection between the word and concept. Aims to provide practical help for English speakers to use German words correctly and vice versa.

656 Moulton, William G.
The sounds of English and German. Contrastive Structure Series. Chicago, University of Chicago Press, 1962. ix, 145 pp. tables, diagr.
Companion volume to Herbert L. Kufner (see above), provides a systematic contrastive analysis of the sound systems of German and American English. Examines the consonants, vowels and characteristic patterns of stress, intonation and juncture of each language, and attempts to identify and explain sources of interference and suggest the lines along which corrective drills might be designed. Aimed at the student who already has an established command of the language and, particularly, at teachers and writers of teaching materials. Although chiefly concerned with the phonetic difficulties of the American speaker of English learning German, is very valuable for preparing course materials, planning courses and developing special classroom techniques for the teaching of German in Britain.

TEACHING METHODS

657 Aberystwyth. University College of Wales. Faculty of Education
Foreign and second language learning in the primary school, by C. J. Dodson. Pamphlet 14 (1966). Aberystwyth, The College, 1966. 47 pp. diagrs.
Describes experimental teaching of German to a class of children bilingual in Welsh and English at eight years of age.

658 Helmers, Hermann
Didaktik der deutschen Sprache: Einführung in die Theorie der muttersprachlichen und literarischen Bildung. Stuttgart, Ernst Klett, 1966. 340 pp. tables, diagrs. bibliogs.
Manual on the theory and practice of teaching the mother tongue and German literature in German primary and secondary schools. The sections on orthography, the teaching of reading and corrective phonetics and speech training contain much that is relevant to teachers of German as a foreign language. The section entitled *Ringen um eine neue deutsche Grammatik*

offers a succinct account of some of the proposals for a new *inhaltbezogene Grammatik* by the modern indigenous school of German linguistics, and gives a clear and simple explanation of its terminology.

Huebener, Theodore
See 298.

Incorporated Association of Assistant Masters in Secondary Schools
See 223.

Levenson, Stanley, and William Kendrick, eds.
See 305.

659 **Politzer, Robert L.**
Teaching German: a linguistic orientation. A Blaisdell Book in the Modern Languages. Waltham, Massachusetts, and London, Blaisdell, 1968. vii, 178 pp. tables, diagrs. bibliog.
Companion volume to author's *Teaching French* and *Teaching Spanish.* An account of the contribution that applied linguistics can make to the teaching of German. There is an acceptance of audio-lingual habit-forming learning procedures but there is also an awareness of the insights offered by the cognitive code theory where mastery of a highly inflected language is dependent on conscious control of certain structural patterns to an even greater degree than with French or Spanish.

660 **Schulz, Dora, and Heinz Griesbach**
Lehrerhandbuch: eine Gemeinschaftsarbeit der Goethe-Institute im Inland. Deutsche Sprachlehre für Ausländer. Grundstufe 1. Teil. Munich, Max Hueber, 2nd edn. 1965. xii, 235 pp. First pubd. 1963.
Manual on the teaching of German as a foreign language with suggestions as to visual and other aids to classroom procedures.

661 **Triesch, M., ed.**
Probleme des Deutschen als Fremdsprache: Forschungsberichte und Diskussionen. Bericht von der 1. Internationalen Deutschlehrertagung 1967 in München. Munich, Max Hueber, 1969. 216 pp. illus. bibliogs.
Collection of conference papers dealing with various aspects of learning, teaching and testing German as a foreign language, but there are also papers on general methodology, evolutionary trends in the contemporary language and literature, and reports on current research.

Turner, John D., ed.
See 318.

DICTIONARIES

The following is a selection of a small number of up-to-date general dictionaries; dictionaries of predominantly etymological or historical content are excluded. Specialised dictionaries such as technical dictionaries or *Fremdwörterbücher* have not been considered for inclusion.

Agricola, Erhard, and others
See 635.

662 **Bibliographisches Institut, Mannheim, and Dudenredaktion, eds.**
Duden: Bildwörterbuch der deutschen Sprache. Der Große Duden, 3. Mannheim, The Institute; London, Harrap, 2nd edn. 1958. 672, D 112, 2 pp. illus. First pubd. 1936.

Illustrated dictionary of the concrete vocabulary of German. The material world is classified in fifteen major categories, each of which is broken down into a series of individual topics and activities, illustrated by 360 pages of line drawings and eight colour plates in which each item is numbered; the key to each illustration provides the corresponding German terminology. An alphabetic index of the 25,000 items is provided.

A companion volume, *The English Duden,* is available with identical illustrations, keys in English, and both English and German indexes. See 503

Eggeling, H. F.
See 639.

Farrell, R. B.
See 640.

Friederich, Wolf
See 641.

Grebe, Paul, and Wolfgang Müller
See 642.

Grebe, Paul, and Gerhart Streitberg
See 643.

663 **Jones, Trevor, ed.**
Harrap's standard German and English dictionary. Part 1: *German–English*: vol. 1: *A–E*; vol. 2: *F–K*. London, Harrap, 1963; 1967.
The first two volumes of Part 1 of the dictionary, which will comprise four volumes. Part 2, also to follow, will be English–German. Treats the language fully and includes both general vocabulary and specialised terms. Stylistic level, field of knowledge and dialect are indicated; fixed and frequent collocations are given and numerous other examples of German usage. Proverbial sayings and idiomatic uses are illustrated. Austrian and Swiss German are recorded. Where required, English translations are provided for the North American user. Necessary grammatical information is provided and phonetic transcriptions are given for *Fremdwörter* and for German words with peculiarities of pronunciation. An essential work of reference.

664 **Mater, Erich**
Rückläufiges Wörterbuch der deutschen Gegenwartssprache. Leipzig. Bibliographisches Institut, 1965. viii, 695 pp. bibliog.
A list of about 140,000 words (no meanings or grammatical explanations are offered), arranged in reverse alphabetical order, i.e. the first word listed is *Saba*, the last *Negerjazz*. Its main use for teachers is to provide a source of German words with the same final element.

665 **Messinger, Heinz, and Werner Rüdenberg**
Langenscheidt's concise German dictionary. 2 vols. *English–German*, by Heinz Messinger and Werner Rüdenberg, 1964. *German–English*, by Heinz Messinger, 6th edn. 1965. First pubd. 1959. Berlin and Munich, Langenscheidt; London, Hodder & Stoughton.
A medium-sized dictionary which, though useful, is necessarily restricted in range and treatment. The selection of items is, however, reasonable and the layout fairly helpful.

666 *Der Sprach-Brockhaus: Deutsches Bildwörterbuch für jedermann*. Wiesbaden, Brockhaus, 7th edn. 1966. 800 pp. illus.
A monolingual dictionary providing brief definitions with some grammatical information and useful illustrations.

667 **Springer, Otto, ed.**
Langenscheidt's encyclopaedic dictionary of the English and German languages. Based on the original work by E. Muret and D. Sanders. Part 1: *English–*

German: vol. 1: *A–M*; vol. 2: *N–Z*. Berlin–Schöneberg, Langenscheidt; London, Hodder & Stoughton, 1962; 1963. First pubd. 1891–1901.
Contains 180,000 main entries. Extensive in coverage, it gives some examples of usage and collocations. North American and British entries are given. Phonetic transcriptions are provided. Part 2, German–English, is expected to follow.

Taylor, Ronald, and Walter Gottschalk
See 650.

668 **Wahrig, Gerhard**
Das große deutsche Wörterbuch: mit einem 'Lexikon der deutschen Sprachlehre'. Die Große Bertelsmann Lexikon-Bibliothek. Gütersloh, Bertelsmann, 1967. 1,437 pp.
A defining dictionary with good coverage. Indicates stress and fields of knowledge, shows division of words, gives many derivations and some antonyms. Examples of usage are given. The initial section 'Lexikon der deutschen Sprachlehre' includes useful grammatical and other linguistic information. There are also tables of declensions and conjugations.

BIBLIOGRAPHIES

669 **Goethe Institut München. Wissenschaftliche Arbeitsstelle**
Arbeitsmittel für den Deutschunterricht an Ausländer. Munich, The Institute, 5th edn. 1967. 44 pp.
Though concerned mainly with teaching materials, there are five sections (of the thirteen in the bibliography) which deal respectively with grammar, orthography, phonetics, dictionaries and vocabulary.

Goodger, B. C.
See 332.

Hammer, John H., and Frank A. Rice
See 157.

670 **Hansel, Johannes**
Bücherkunde für Germanisten: Studienausgabe. Berlin, Erich Schmidt, 1961. 132 pp.
Bibliography dealing with German language, literature, phonology and linguistics. Includes a section on periodicals, a combined index of authors' names and titles, and a subject index.

671 **London University. Institute of Germanic Studies**
German language and literature: select bibliography, by L. M. Newman. London, The Institute, 1966. 60 pp.

Bibliography in seven sections covering research method, German language and literature and other related topics. There are name, title and subject indexes.

Robinson, Janet O.
See 214.

SECTION VI

Italian

GENERAL

672 **Gabrielli, Aldo**
Dizionario linguistico moderno: guida pratica per scrivere e parlar bene. Verona, Mondadori, 5th edn. 1969. 1189 pp. tables. First pubd. 1956.
Part 1: Alphabetical list of rules of grammar, unusual words, guidance on usage. Part 2: Guide to spelling and pronunciation, irregular verbs and difficult constructions.

673 **Migliorini, Bruno**
The Italian language. Abridged and recast by T. Gwynfor Griffith. The Great Languages. London, Faber & Faber, 1966. 533 pp. bibliog.
Fully revised edition, recast in English, of Migliorini's *Storia della lingua italiana.* The chapters on Latin were considerably abbreviated and an additional chapter was added by T. G. Griffith to cover the developments in the period 1915–65. Language is studied almost exclusively in the context of literary culture. An Italian paperback version of Migliorini's original, up-dated by I. Baldelli, was published by Sansoni in 1964. 372 pp. with bibliog.

674 **Migliorini, Bruno**
Lingua contemporanea. Biblioteca di Lingua Nostra, 4. Florence, Sansoni, 4th edn. 1966. vi, 280 pp.
Discusses a number of developments in modern Italian and then continues with essays on such subjects as purism, the relationship of language and dialect, taste as a linguistic norm.

HISTORY

675 **Mauro, Tullio de**
Storia linguistica dell'Italia unita. Biblioteca di Cultura Moderna, 585. Bari, Laterza, 1963. 521 pp. tables, bibliog.
Describes the effects of social, political and economic changes on the language from 1861 to 1961. The four chapters of the main part trace the effect of political writing on Italian; particular attention is paid to the results of emigration, industrialisation and the growth of literacy. Followed by seventy-six pages of notes and a 158 page appendix which reproduces documents and discusses marginal problems.

Posner, Rebecca
See 161.

676 **Rohlfs, Gerhard**
Grammatica storica della lingua italiana e dei suoi dialetti. Manuali di Letteratura, Filologia e Linguistica. 3 vols. Torino, Einaudi. Vol. 1, translated by Salvatore Persichino: *Fonetica.* 1966. xxvi, 520 pp. bibliog. Vol. 2, translated by Temistocle Franceschi: *Morfologia.* 1968. xxxii, 401 pp. bibliog. Vol. 3, translated by Temistocle Franceschi and Maria Caciagli Fancelli: *Sintassi e formazione delle parole.* 1969. xl, 576 pp. bibliog.
First published by A. Francke, Berne, as *Historische Grammatik der italienischen Sprache und ihrer Mundarten*, 3 vols., in 1949. The Italian edition has been completely revised by the author prior to and after translation. A comprehensive survey of the development of the Italian language which also furnishes considerable information about the contemporary standard language as well as about the dialects.

GRAMMAR AND STRUCTURE

Agard, Frederick B., and Robert J. di Pietro
See 693.

677 **Battaglia, Salvatore, and Vincenzo Pernicone**
Grammatica italiana. Turin, Loescher-Chiantore, 2nd edn. 1968. viii, 628 pp. First pubd. 1951.
Traditional grammar which embodies some new material and allows a fairly comprehensive treatment of morphology. Intended for teachers and secondary school pupils. Includes a short appendix on Italian prosody.

678 **Costabile, Norma**
Le strutture della lingua italiana: grammatica generativo-trasformativa. Bologna, Ricardo Patron, 1967. vii, 211 pp. bibliog.
Explains the theory of transformational grammar and applies the method to the Italian language.

679 **Regula, M., and J. Jernej**
Grammatica italiana descrittiva: su basi storiche e psicologiche. Berne and Munich, A. Francke, 1965. 296 pp.
Based on the contemporary language, and written with foreign students of Italian in mind. Includes copious examples in a traditional presentation. Attempts to combine historical insights into the reasons for the present state of the language with psychological criteria for the definition of syntactic categories.

Rohlfs, Gerhard
See 676.

PHONOLOGY AND ORTHOGRAPHY

Agard, Frederick B., and Robert J. di Pietro
See 694.

680 **Camilli, Amerindo**
Pronuncia e grafia dell'italiano. Terza edizione riveduta a cura di Piero Fiorelli. Biblioteca di Lingua Nostra, 2. Florence, Sansoni, 1965. viii, 338 pp.
Detailed account of pronunciation and orthography. Includes passages from literary texts in a script designed to provide pronunciation practice. It takes Florentine as a norm.

681 **Castiglione, Pierina Borrani**
Italian phonetics, diction and intonation. New York, Vanni, 1957. vi, 104 pp. diagrs.
Accompanied by tapes and exercises (including intonation patterns). There is a section on 'Difficulties for American students' and an appendix on open and closed *e* and *o* and voiced and voiceless *s* and *z*.

682 **Migliorini, Bruno, and others, eds.**
Dizionario d'ortografia e di pronunzia. Turin, ERI – Edizioni RAI Radiotelevisione Italiana, 1969. cviii, 1344 pp.
A detailed and thorough introduction precedes a list of about 100,000 words. Treated solely to resolve doubts concerning pronunciation and spelling. Most words are Italian, space is found for some non-Italian expressions; a very large number of proper names (family and place names) is included.

683 **Muljačić, Žarko**
Fonologia generale e fonologia della lingua italiana. Bologna, Il Mulino, 1969. viii, 596 pp. tables, diagrs. bibliog.
Up to page 374 an account in Italian of Roman Jakobson's general theory of phonology; from page 375 to the end a classification by acoustic and logical criteria of Italian phoneme patterns after Jakobson's method.

Rohlfs, Gerhard
See 676.

VOCABULARY AND USAGE

684 **Bascetta, Carlo**
Il linguaggio sportivo contemporaneo. Biblioteca di Lingua Nostra, 12. Florence, Sansoni, 1962. 280 pp. bibliog.
Sections discuss: I, Development of sporting terminology in the press, loan-words, outdated terms; II, Sources of special sporting vocabulary; III, Grammar and style, devoted chiefly to recurring stylistic forms; IV, eleven pages of bibliographical references – the latest being dated 1961; V, a sixty-six page glossary of technical terms used in sport.

685 **Cesana, Gianni**
La parola giusta al momento giusto: dizionario ragionato dei sinonimi e dei contrari. Milan, De Vecchi, 1967. vii, 662 pp.
A dictionary of synonyms and antonyms with explanations of their uses. There is an alphabetical index to all terms quoted.

686 **Fucci, Franco**
Dizionario del linguaggio giornalistico. Biblioteca Italiana di Opere di Consultazione. Milan, Ceschina, 1962. 529 pp.
Lists words, phrases and acronyms commonly used in newspapers and not listed in standard dictionaries, with short explanations of derivations and Italian usage.

Gabrielli, Aldo
See 672.

687 **Giovanelli, Paolo, ed.**
Grund- und Aufbauwortschatz: Italienisch. Stuttgart, Ernst Klett, 1961. 212 pp.
Lists grammatical words and commonly recurring vocabulary from non-technical Italian texts as an aid to Germans when reading Italian. No criteria are described for arriving at the selection; the foreword claims that a knowledge of 2,000 Italian words will render 85 per cent of a normal text intelligible. In the absence of other frequency lists the classification here by alphabetical order and by centres of interest could help teachers.

688 **Junker, Albert**
Wachstum und Wandlungen im neuesten italienischen Wortschatz. Erlanger Forschungen. Reihe A: Geisteswissenschaften, 2. Erlangen, Universitätsbund Erlangen, 1955. 230 pp. bibliog.

Chapters on new words in administration, the armed forces, technology, radio, the arts and sport, followed by chapters on the morphology of new nouns, adjectives, verbs and prefixes. An examination of the origins (such as foreign loans) of new vocabulary, a bibliography of authorities consulted, a list of sources and an alphabetical list of words quoted.

689 **Provenzal, Dino**
Perché si dice così? Origine dei modi di dire, delle locuzioni proverbiali, di tante frasi dell'uso comune. Milan, Hoepli, 1966. vi, 247 pp.
Explanations of proverbs and sayings, providing information on their origins, evolution and correct interpretation.

VARIETIES OF ITALIAN

690 **Barbagallo, Renato**
Panorama delle parlate dialettali italiane: con appendice sul sardo e il ladino. Florence, Vallacchi, 1965. 60 pp.
A very brief account of the Italian dialects.

691 **Gregor, D. B.**
Friulan: the language of Friuli. Northampton (34, Watersmeet), The Author, 1965. 24 pp. bibliog.
Preface on Italian dialects, historical introduction, phonetics, accidence, pronouns, demonstratives, numerals, proverbs, a sketch of literary history, an anthology of prose and poetry and a glossary of words not recognisable from Italian.

692 **Gregor, D. B.**
Romagnol: the dialect of Romagna. Northampton (34, Watersmeet), The Author, n.d. 23 pp. bibliog.
Consonant with the same author's *Friulan*, q.v.

Rohlfs, Gerhard
See 676.

CONTRASTIVE ANALYSIS

693 **Agard, Frederick B., and Robert J. di Pietro**
The grammatical structures of English and Italian. Contrastive Structure Series. Chicago and London, University of Chicago Press, 1965. vii, 91 pp. tables.

Makes use of Hall's descriptive Italian grammar to deal with a selected group of significant grammatical and syntactical contrasts to clarify problems of interference between American English and Italian.

694 **Agard, Frederick B., and Robert J. di Pietro**
The sounds of English and Italian. Contrastive Structure Series. Chicago and London. University of Chicago Press, 1965. vii, 76 pp. tables.
Gives a fairly comprehensive survey of the comparative sound systems of American English and Italian.

Hammer, John H., and Frank A. Rice
See 157.

TEACHING METHODS

695 **Amorini, Enzo**
Esercizi e conversazioni di lingua viva (ad uso degli stranieri). Perugia, Università Italiana per Stranieri, new edn. 1966. 180 pp. illus.
A series of lessons complementing and amplifying the Guarnieri *Metodo di lingua italiana per gli stranieri* (q.v.) and constituting a valuable guide to method. See also 696.

696 **Amorini, Enzo**
La tecnica del far parlare (con il 'Metodo Guarnieri'). Perugia, Università Italiana per Stranieri, 1967. v, 97 pp. bibliog.
Designed to accompany and explicate the Guarnieri *Metodo di lingua italiana per gli stranieri* (q.v.) it goes step by step through a series of specimen lessons, alerting the novice teacher to signs of progress, suggesting 'ploys' to overcome silence among students, cautioning against unwise assumptions and too great haste.

697 **Busnelli, M. D., and U. Pittola**
Guida per l'insegnamento pratico della fonetica italiana. Perugia, Università Italiana per Stranieri, 3rd edn. 1960. 159 pp.
Using educated Italian usage as a norm the booklet describes ways of teaching all the sounds required in Italian and offers graded practice sequences and groups of words accompanied by reading passages to train diction.

698 **Esposito, Giovanni**
Per un nuovo insegnamento della grammatica italiana. I Rubini, 8. Torino, Società Editrice Internazionale, 1969. 126 pp. bibliog.

Considers the new aims which the classroom teacher of Italian (mostly at the secondary level) might have for his pupils' performance after examining the concepts of structural linguistics as applied to the Italian language. Describes clearly the kind of awareness of language-structure, by reference to examples, required of the pupil; a final chapter sketches the overall teaching process.

699 **Guarnieri, Romano**
Metodo di lingua italiana per gli stranieri. Nuova edizione, ampliata dell'autore in collaborazione con...Enzo Amorini... Perugia, Università Italiana per Stranieri, 1966. xxxiii, 112 pp.
Should be read in conjunction with books by Enzo Amorini (q.v.) for the fullest understanding of the method. The introduction by Amorini explains the implications for the teacher behind the outlines of lesson content which comprise the text proper.

Huebener, Theodore
See 298.

Incorporated Association of Assistant Masters in Secondary Schools
See 223.

DICTIONARIES

Only dictionaries are included which are not listed in the second edition of A. J. Walford's *A guide to foreign language grammars and dictionaries*, published 1967 by the Library Association, London. See 216.

700 **Alinei, Mario L.**
Dizionario inverso italiano: con indici e liste di frequenza delle terminazioni. A reverse index of the Italian language with frequency count and frequency lists of terminations. Ricerche Linguistiche e Lessicografiche dell'Istituto di Lingua e Letteratura Italiane dell'Università di Utrecht, 1. The Hague, Mouton, 1962. 607 pp.
43,506 words drawn from the *Prontuario etimologico della lingua italiana* (Migliorini-Duro, Turin, 1958) listed in reverse order of spelling (last letters first, then penultimates and so on), followed by frequency lists of final letters.

701 **Cantamessa, Giuseppe, and Giuseppe L. Messina**
Dizionario della lingua italiana. Milan, Signorelli, 1966. 1,423 pp. tables, illus.

Monolingual. Stress indicated for every word, pronunciation of *e*, *o*, *s* and *z* distinguished by accent or typography, gender of all nouns, auxiliaries for intransitive verbs. Twenty-six plates showing simple expressions concerning industrial, engineering and technical concepts, lists of chemical symbols, world currencies, Italian acronyms, vehicle registrations. Whole-page tables outline grammatical uses of the main parts of speech.

Gabrielli, Aldo
See 672.

702 **Macchi, Vladimiro, ed.**
Sansoni–Harrap standard Italian and English dictionary. Part 1: *Italian–English* vol. 1: *A–L*. London, Harrap; Florence–Rome, Sansoni, 1970: xxiv, 759 pp.
The two volumes of the Italian–English section will include about 150,000 headwords, not only words of everyday use, but also regionalisms and neologisms, words from classical and modern literature and some technical vocabulary. An English–Italian section of 2 volumes, containing about 170,000 headwords, is to follow within the next three years.

Migliorini, Bruno, and others, eds.
See 682.

703 **Zanco, Aurelio, and Grazia Caliumi**
Nuovissimo dizionario italiano–inglese, inglese–italiano. Milan, Ceschina, 1967. xi, 2,388 pp.
The Italian headwords are all accented, pronunciation of English headwords is given in the IPA script. Many examples of idiomatic usage. Appendices of irregular English verbs, of symbols, acronyms.

BIBLIOGRAPHIES

Goodger, B. C.
See 332.

704 **Hall, Robert A., jr.**
Bibliografia della linguistica italiana. 3 vols. Biblioteca Bibliografica Italica, 13–15. Florence, Sansoni Antiquariato, 2nd edn. 1958. With: *Primo supplemento decennale (1956–1966)*. Biblioteca Bibliografica Italica, 35. 1969. 524 pp.
Part 1 in the first volume deals with the history of Italian; Part 2, in the

same volume, with the description of the language in four sections, divided into centuries from the thirteenth to the twentieth. Part 3, in the second volume, is concerned with dialectology in general, followed by sections on each dialect. Part 4, in the third volume, is the history of Italian linguistics, with entries under three main headings: general aspects; by century from the thirteenth century to 1860; the modern period. This volume also contains the appendix of new items coming to the knowledge of the compiler during the production of the bibliography. Besides the general index, separate indexes by author and title, locality and dialect, Italian and dialect words, root words are given.
The first ten-yearly supplement (1956–66) has appeared, comprising additions and corrections to the 1958 edition. It continues the same classificatory system.

Hammer, John H., and Frank A. Rice
See 157.

Robinson, Janet O.
See 214.

SECTION VII

Russian

GENERAL

705 **Galkina-Fedoruk, E. M., ed.**

Современный русский язык. Часть 1: *Лексикология, фонетика, словообразование.* Часть 2: *Морфология, синтаксис.* 2 vols. Moscow, Izdatel'stvo Moskovskogo Universiteta, 1962; 1964. bibliog.

A comprehensive study of the Russian language intended as a textbook for Russian university students. Vol. 1 deals at length with lexicology, phonetics and word formation. Vol. 2 deals in similar fashion with morphology and syntax.

706 **Sebeok, Thomas A., and others, eds.**

Current trends in linguistics. Vol. 1: *Soviet and East European linguistics.* The Hague, Mouton, 1963. xii, 606 pp. bibliogs.

Designed to review linguistic activity in the USSR and East Europe. Part 1 contains authoritative essays on selected topics in Soviet linguistics, general (including phonemics, morphemics, syntax, lexicography) and applied: mathematical linguistics, machine translation, and a review of foreign language teaching by Jacob Ornstein. Language families and areal groupings are discussed. Part 2 covers, in less detail, Bulgaria, Czechoslovakia, Hungary, Poland and Yugoslavia.

707 **Vinogradov, V. V., and others, eds.**

Грамматика русского языка. Vol. 1: *Фонетика и морфология.* Vol. 2 (in 2 parts): *Синтаксис.* 3 vols. Moscow, Akademiya Nauk SSSR, 1960. First pubd. 1952–4.

Authoritative comprehensive grammar of the Russian language covering phonetics, morphology and syntax. Contains some corrections to the text of the 1952–4 edition.

HISTORY

708 **Borkovskiĭ, V. I., and P. S. Kuznetsov**

Историческая грамматика русского языка. Moscow, Nauka, 2nd edn. 1965. 555 pp. First pubd. 1963.

Historical Russian grammar organised in three main sections: phonetics, morphology and syntax. The section on phonetics includes notes on the orthography of Old Russian and changes in vowels and consonants. The main parts of speech and categories like voice and aspect are discussed under 'morphology'. 'Syntax' deals with developments in simple and complex sentences.

709 **Entwistle, William J., and W. A. Morison**
Russian and the Slavonic languages. The Great Languages. London, Faber & Faber, 2nd edn. 1964. 407 pp. maps, bibliog. First pubd. 1949.
Examines the development of Russian from its origins to the twentieth century. Contains chapters on Common Slavonic and Old Bulgarian, West Slavonic and South Slavonic. There are suggestions for further study and a list of Slavonic words with page references.

710 **Ivanov, V. V.**
Историческая грамматика русского языка. Moscow, Prosveshchenie, 1964. 452 pp. illus. tables.
This historical grammar of Russian deals thoroughly with developments in the phonetic and morphological systems of the language and in rather less detail with syntax. The first few sections contain a number of photographs of ancient manuscripts.

711 **Matthews, W. K.**
Russian historical grammar. London East European Series, 45. London, University of London; Athlone Press, 1967. xiv, 362 pp. bibliog. First pubd. 1960.
Part 1 deals with Indo-European and Common Slavonic, with chapters on the historical background, the alphabet and spelling etc. It also examines the characteristics of Old Russian, which is taken as a starting point for the consideration in Part 2 of the phonological, morphological and other changes in Russian. Part 3 consists entirely of appendices, which include excerpts from the historical records of the language, a history of Russian historical grammar, and a classified and annotated bibliography. Besides the general index, there is a Russian word index.

712 **Matthews, W. K.**
The structure and development of Russian. London, Cambridge University Press, 1953. x, 225 pp. tables, diagrs. bibliog.
Part 1 deals with the structure of Russian. Part 2, the development of Russian, includes chapters on the Kiev and Tartar periods, the Moscow period, the eighteenth century, the nineteenth century and after, and the post-revolutionary period. Part 3 comprises specimens taken from Russian literature from the eleventh to the twentieth century.

Unbegaun, B. O., and J. S. G. Simmons
See 768.

GRAMMAR AND STRUCTURE

Benson, Morton, ed.
See 728.

Borkovskiĭ, V. I., and P. S. Kuznetsov
See 708.

713 **Borras, F. M., and R. F. Christian**
Russian syntax: aspects of modern Russian syntax and vocabulary. Oxford, Clarendon Press, 1963. xi, 404 pp. First pubd. 1959.
Reference book on certain aspects of Russian syntax and vocabulary. While not aiming at comprehensive coverage of these fields, contains much invaluable information. Discusses the parts of speech fully and comments briefly on word order. Has an English and a Russian index. Each chapter contains copious illustrations drawn from Soviet literature and the Soviet press as well as from nineteenth-century Russian authors. Does not deal with the theory of syntax or sentence classification.

714 **Daum, Edmund, and Werner Schenk**
Die russischen Verben: Grundformen, Aspekte, Rektion, Betonung, deutsche Bedeutung. Mit einer Einführung in die Flexion und Aspektbildung des russischen Verbs, by Rudolf Ružička. Leipzig, Verlag Enzyklopädie, 6th edn. 1968. viii, 798 pp. First pubd. 1954.
Lists more than 14,000 Russian verbs with notes on their forms, conjugations, aspects, government, stress and meanings (given in German).

Federov, M. Ya., and I. P. Kryukova
See 738.

715 **Foote, I. P., and R. M. Davison**
Verbs of motion, by I. P. Foote, and *The use of the genitive in negative constructions*, by R. M. Davison. Studies in the Modern Russian Language, 1 and 2. London, Cambridge University Press, 1967. 64 pp. bibliogs. Also available as paperbacks.
First essay provides a systematic discussion of the determinate and indeterminate verbs of motion; a definition of the functions of these types of verbs follows. Examples are drawn from nineteenth and twentieth century authors. The second essay tries to indicate the criteria which operate when the choice between the genitive and accusative cases has to be made in negative constructions. Treats the formulation of rules and provides a summary of indications for case choice.

716 **Forbes, Nevill**
Russian grammar. Revised and enlarged by J. C. Dumbreck. Oxford, Clarendon Press, 3rd edn. 1964. xii, 438 pp. First pubd. 1914.
One hundred and twenty-two paragraphs deal with pronunciation and the parts of speech. Each aspect of Russian grammar is given thorough treatment. Many paragraphs have been substantially revised and extended, and the section on pronunciation has been entirely rewritten in the light of advances made in phonetics since the first edition.

717 **Forsyth, James**
A grammar of aspect: usage and meaning in the Russian verb. Studies in the Modern Russian Language. Extra Volume. London, Cambridge University Press, 1970. xiii, 386 pp. bibliog.
Comprehensive and copiously illustrated description of the aspects of the Russian verb, intended also as a contribution to the theoretical study of the category of aspect in Russian. Contains sections on aspect and form, aspectual pairs, past tense, present and future tenses, multiple action, modals, gerunds and participles, and verbs of motion. Contains Russian and English indexes.

Galkina-Fedoruk, E. M., ed.
See 705.

718 **Harrison, W., and J. Mullen**
The expression of the passive voice, by W. Harrison, and *Agreement of the verb-predicate with a collective subject*, by J. Mullen. Studies in the Modern Russian Language, 4 and 5. London, Cambridge University Press, 1967. 59 pp. bibliogs.
First essay describes the three main ways of expressing the passive voice in Russian, i.e. by using active constructions, passive participles and reflexive verbs. Shows how emphasis is changed by the choice of one or other of these constructions where more than one is possible. In an analysis of examples, drawn from literature and newspapers, the author of the second essay shows which factors influence the choice of agreement of the verb predicate with a collective subject.

Ivanov, V. V.
See 710.

Matthews, W. K.
See 711, 712.

719 **Morison, Walter Angus**
Studies in Russian forms and uses: the present gerund and active participle. London, Faber & Faber, 1959. 75 pp.
Deals with the various forms of the gerund, the gerund of perfective verbs, etc. Includes sections on the present participle active, the participle formed from perfective verbs, adjectival forms and the use of the past participle active of imperfective verbs. These sections are copiously illustrated with examples drawn largely from literature and for which translations are given. Word stress is indicated throughout and there is some guidance on sentence stress and pronunciation. Intended to be a practical work; the illustrative sentences are envisaged as tests in comprehension.

720 **Murphy, A. B.**
Aspectival usage in Russian. Pergamon Oxford Russian Series. Teaching Aids, 7. Oxford and London, Pergamon Press, 1965. xvi, 158 pp. bibliog.
Whilst not attempting a complete description of aspects in the Russian verb, the author provides guidance in the choice of aspects in the past tenses, future tense, the imperative and infinitive. There is also a brief chapter on the present tense, since its usage in Russian overlaps with concepts belonging to the past and future. The examples, which are drawn from Soviet authors and conversation, are translated into English.

721 **Pirogova, L. I., and S. I. Makarova**
Conjugation of Russian verbs: reference book for foreigners. Introduction translated by V. Korotky. Moscow, Progress Publishers, [between 1964 and 1967]. 312 pp. Provides complete conjugation patterns of common Russian verbs. Discusses a classification of verbs in seven groups, based on an analysis of all the verbs (excluding special or obsolete verbs), in the *Словарь русского языка*, by S. I. Ozhegov. (See 762.) In addition provides notes on the rules according to which various verb forms are obtained, and on reflexive and impersonal verbs. Second part comprises 100 tables showing verb conjugations which indicate how all the verb forms are obtained, with any peculiarities of stress, etc. The third part is an alphabetical list of approximately 12,000 common verbs, each followed by a number showing the relevant type-table in the preceding part.

722 **Pulkina, I. M.**
A short Russian reference grammar: with a chapter on pronunciation. Edited by P. S. Kuznetsov. Translated by V. Korotky. Moscow, Progress Publishers, 3rd edn. [196–]. 351 pp. tables. First pubd. 1960.

Systematic exposition of Russian spelling, pronunciation and morphology in which syntax is dealt with only in so far as it affects morphology. Genders of nouns and agreements of adjectives, meanings and uses of cases with and without prepositions, aspects of the verb and the classification of the verb into productive and non-productive type verbs and word building receive special attention. No definitions of grammatical categories are given; where possible, grammatical material is set out in tables. Many examples taken from contemporary colloquial Russian.

723 **Rassudova, O. P.**
Употребление видов глагола в русском языке. Moscow, Izdatel'stvo Moskovskogo Universiteta, 1968. 140 pp.
Practical discussion of the problem of aspect in verbs of high frequency in modern Russian. Concentrates on the use of aspects in the past tense and the infinitive. Less space is given to less problematical areas, e.g. the future tense and the imperative. Illustrations are drawn mainly from dialogue. Some exercises are included.

Rozental', D. E.
See 743.

724 **Unbegaun, B. O.**
Russian grammar. London, Oxford, Clarendon Press, 1962. xxx, 319 pp. bibliog. First pubd. 1951.
This edition differs from the original French edition (volume 5 of *Les Langues du Monde*), in that it has been adapted to the requirements of English students and has been improved in other respects. After a brief introduction, which discusses some of the influences at work in contemporary Russian, the main grammatical categories are dealt with systematically and clearly under sixteen broad headings.

Vinogradov, V. V., and others, eds.
See 707.

PHONOLOGY AND ORTHOGRAPHY

725 **Avanesov, R. I.**
Русское литературное произношение: учебное пособие для студентов педагогических институтов. Moscow, Prosveshchenie, 4th edn. 1968. 287 pp. First pubd. 1950.
This revision of Avanesov's standard work on the pronunciation of Russian

has been substantially expanded by the addition of five new sections on the pronunciation of names and patronymics and thirty more pages of text transcribed into phonetic script.

726 **Avanesov, R. I., and S. I. Ozhegov, eds.**
Русское литературное произношение и ударение: словарь-справочник. Moscow, Gosudarstvennoe Izdatel'stvo Inostrannykh i Natsional'nykh Slovareĭ, 1959. 709 pp.
Contains approximately 52,000 entries in which correct stress is indicated, with notes on pronunciation. Meanings of words are not given.

727 **Barkhudarov, S. G., and others, eds.**
Орфографический словарь русского языка. Moscow, Sovetskaya Entsiklopediya, 8th edn. 1968. 612 pp.
Reliable orthographical dictionary of Russian containing about 104,000 words listed in three columns per page. Meanings of words are not given and the notes which appear (for example on verb-conjugations) are only those required for establishing the correct spelling of words.

728 **Benson, Morton, ed.**
Dictionary of Russian personal names: with a guide to stress and morphology. University of Pennsylvania Studies in East European Languages and Literatures. Philadelphia, University of Pennsylvania Press, 2nd edn. 1967. viii, 175 pp. bibliog. First pubd. 1964.
Contains approximately 23,000 surnames and a list of Russian given names with their diminutives. Chapter 1 provides a guide to reconstruction of the original Cyrillic from the English transliteration. Chapter 2 contains notes on the declension of surnames and stress in them, the list of surnames itself and a list of individual pronunciations of famous surnames. Chapter 3 contains a general description of Russian given names, a list of most frequently used names with their diminutives, an alphabetical list of diminutive forms, and a list of less frequently used names.

Borkovskiĭ, V. I., and P. S. Kuznetsov
See 708.

729 **Boyanus, Simon Charles**
Russian pronunciation and Russian phonetic reader. Vol. 1: *Russian pronunciation: The Russian system of speech habits in sounds, stress, rhythm and intonation.* London, Lund Humphries, 1965. xl, 122 pp. tables, diagrs. bibliog. First pubd. 1955.

Although somewhat dated, this is a clear and simple guide to Russian pronunciation. Includes chapters on consonants, vowels, glides, some exercises on the palatalised consonants, stress and rhythm and the main types of intonation. The accompanying volume 2 is a phonetic reader.

730 **Bryzgunova, E. A.**
Практическая фонетика и интонация русского языка. Moscow, Izdatel'stvo Moskovskogo Universiteta, 1963. 306 pp. diagrs.
Description of the phonetics and intonation of Russian intended for teachers of Russian as a foreign language; based on material used by the author in lectures given to the International Seminars for Teachers of Russian between 1957 and 1962. The book is divided into three parts: phonetics, the phonetic structure of the word, and intonation.

Bryzgunova, E. A., ed.
See 756.

731 **Bylinskiĭ, K. I., and N. N. Nikol'skiĭ**
Справочник по орфографии и пунктуации для работников печати. 4th edn. Moscow, Izdatel'stvo Moskovskogo Universiteta, 1970. 344 pp.
Part 1 of this reference work contains the rules governing orthography and punctuation in modern Russian. Part 2 is an orthographical dictionary containing more than 30,000 words.

732 **Cheshko, L. A., ed.**
Russian orthography. Translated by T. J. Binyon; edited by C. V. James. Pergamon Oxford Russian Series. Teaching Aids, 4. Oxford and London, Pergamon Press; New York, Macmillan, 1963. xv, 147 pp.
A translation of the first part of *Правила русской орфографии и пунктуации.* Includes chapters on the correct use of vowels and consonants in spelling, the use of hard and soft signs, the hyphen, capital letters, and initial, compound and graphic abbreviations. Some rules are also given for the division of words, and the book contains a combined vocabulary and index.

733 **Cheshko, L. A., ed.**
Russian punctuation. Translated by T. J. Binyon; edited by C. V. James. Pergamon Oxford Russian Series. Teaching Aids, 1. Oxford and London, Pergamon Press, 1962. viii, 54 pp.
A translation of the second part of *Правила русской орфографии и пунктуации*, published in 1957. Use of punctuation marks in Russian is closely bound up with grammar and is therefore very different from their

use in English. Contains the rules of punctuation confirmed by the Academy of Sciences of the USSR in 1956.

Forbes, Nevill
See 716.

734 **Forsyth, James**
A practical guide to Russian stress. Edinburgh and London, Oliver & Boyd, 1963. ix, 150 pp. bibliog.
The main purpose of Part 1 is to give rules determining whether a word has fixed or mobile stress and provide patterns of mobile stress with lists of examples. Part 2 deals with word-formation alone and particularly those suffixes which may be stressed or unstressed, and with certain special classes of words – proper names, diminutives, etc. Index gives clear guidance on whether the stress in the 2,500 words given is fixed or mobile.

Galkina-Fedoruk, E. M., ed.
See 705.

735 **Jones, Daniel, and Dennis Ward**
The phonetics of Russian. London, Cambridge University Press, 1969. xi, 308 pp. illus. tables.
Part 1 describes the necessary general phonetic theory. Part 2 provides a description of the sounds and intonation patterns of modern Russian. There is a chapter containing passages in which both tone and stress are marked for practising pronunciation. An appendix deals with the principles of Russian orthography.

Kadler, Eric H.
See 225.

Matthews, W. K.
See 711.

Pulkina, I. M.
See 722.

Rozental', D. E.
See 743.

736 **Shapiro, A. B.**
Современный русский язык: пунктуация. Moscow, Prosveshchenie, 1966. 296 pp. bibliog.

After a short history of Russian punctuation the author gives a detailed exposition of the rules governing it. These are illustrated by examples from classical Russian and Soviet literature. A supplement provides passages for practice in inserting the correct punctuation.

737 **Strichek, A.**
Руководство по русскому ударению: склонение и спряжение. Paris, Pyat' Kontinentov, 1966. 296 pp.
Clear exposition of the problem of mobile stress in flexion; deals with nouns, adjectives, pronouns and verbs. For nouns, which are classified according to declension type and subdivided where necessary according to gender, stress patterns are represented schematically. This is followed by lists of nouns grouped according to morphological features, stress type etc. There are four indexes of 1. morphological items, of 2. word-endings, of 3. semantic groups and 4. of words – those with fixed stress appearing in italics.

Unbegaun, B. O.
See 724.

Vinogradov, V. V., and others, eds.
See 707.

VOCABULARY AND USAGE

738 **Federov, M. Ya., and I. P. Kryukova**
Handbook of Russian verbs. Edited by C. V. James. Pergamon Oxford Russian Series. Teaching Aids, 6. Oxford and London, Pergamon Press; New York, Macmillan, 1963. vi, 261 pp.
A list of approximately 1,000 Russian verbs in alphabetical order, showing imperfective and perfective aspects, their conjugations, and constructions used with them. Meanings of the verbs are given in English with a varying number of illustrations of some of the constructions used with each verb. Some verbs are included because English-speaking students find difficulty in using them without specific knowledge of the construction used with them, and others because of irregularities in the formation of aspects. Introduction contains some notes on the government of cases by verbs, basic meanings of cases and prepositions and aspects.

739 **Gvozdev, A. N.**
Очерки по стилистике русского языка. 3rd edn. Moscow, Prosveshchenie, 1965. 408 pp. First pubd. 1959.

In his consideration of stylistics, the author sets out to make some contribution to the establishment of a standard literary usage of Russian. The book contains sections on lexis, morphology and syntax, and a supplement which comprises three articles on stylistics which were published in journals after the second edition of this book. Some dated references and quotations in the second edition have been replaced or deleted.

740 **Jaszczun, Wasyl, and Szyman Krynski**
A dictionary of Russian idioms and colloquialisms: 2,200 expressions with examples. Pittsburgh, University of Pittsburgh Press, 1967. xvi, 102 pp. bibliog.
Contains the following types of expression: phraseological fusions, units and combinations, single words used figuratively, and colloquialisms. Regional and dialectal expressions and proverbs are excluded. About twenty per cent of the illustrations are taken from literary works, the remainder are provided by the authors. Entries are made according to a system of key-words, which depends on the structure of individual phrases and is fully explained in the notes.

741 **Mordvilko, A.P.**
Очерки по русской фразеологии: именные и глагольные фразеологические обороты. Moscow, Prosveshchenie, 1964. 132 pp.
Brief survey of the types of phraseological constructions in modern Russian, in three sections. The first deals, inter alia, with the classification of phrases, their relation to individual words and to the parts of speech, the second with nominal phrases, the third with verbal phrases.

742 **Palevskaya, M. F.**
Синонимы в русском языке. Moscow, Prosveshchenie, 1964. 128 pp.
First part deals broadly with synonymy in vocabulary. After briefly introducing the history of the problems of the classification of synonyms, discusses them under various headings: semantic, stylistic, etc. A second, shorter part deals with synonymy in grammar and concludes with a brief chapter on the study of synonyms in schools.

743 **Rozental', D. E.**
Modern Russian usage. Translated by M. A. Green; edited by C. V. James. Pergamon Oxford Russian Series. Teaching Aids, 3. Oxford and London, Pergamon Press, 1963. x, 131 pp. First pubd. 1959.
First published in Moscow as *Культура речи*. In four parts, with a brief

chapter on the special features of the pronunciation of names and patronymics. Part 1 deals with choice of words and contains a useful survey of Russian dictionaries. Part 2, which gives guidance on difficult points of grammar and contemporary usage under seventy-four headings, is the largest part of the book and has a valuable index. Part 3 contains rules of pronunciation, with particular reference to foreign borrowings in contemporary Russian. Part 4, on stress, includes a list of commonly misstressed words.

744 **Sazonova, I. K.**
Лексика и фразеология современного русского литературного языка. Edited by S. I. Ozhegov, Moscow, Izdatel'stvo Literatury na Inostrannykh Yazykakh, 1963. 136 pp. bibliog.
Deals with the vocabulary and phraseology of Russian under various headings; vocabulary from the point of view of its structural features, synonyms, homonyms and the constant change in vocabulary and phraseology. Covers the structural semantic features of contemporary Russian vocabulary and phraseology, and recent and current changes in them.

745 **Shanskiĭ, N. M.**
Фразеология современного русского языка. Moscow, Vysshaya Shkola, 2nd edn. 1969. 231 pp. bibliog. First pubd. 1964.
Considers, inter alia, phrases as linguistic units, their lexical composition, structure and derivation, the relation between the meanings of their individual parts and the meanings of whole phrases. Other topics considered are changes in the meanings, composition and structure of phrases, phraseology and word-formation. Contains an alphabetic list of phrases discussed in the book.

746 **Shanskiĭ, N. M.**
Russian lexicology. Translated by B. S. Johnson; edited by J. E. S. Cooper. Pergamon Oxford Russian Series. Oxford and London, Pergamon Press, 1969. 130 pp. bibliog.
Includes material on varieties of lexical meaning, the history of Russian lexis, lexis and register, and the means by which the vocabulary of a language is increased. See also 747.

747 **Shanskiĭ, N. M.**
Russian word formation. Translated by B. S. Johnson; edited by J. E. S. Cooper. Pergamon Oxford Russian Series. Oxford and London, Pergamon Press, 1968, vii, 174 pp. bibliogs.

Begins with an examination of the principles of word-formation analysis. Other chapters include discussions of etymological analysis of words, the word as a fundamental unit of language, the Russian word as a structural whole, morphemes as meaningful units of language, and changes in the morphological structure of the word. The book concludes with a chapter on the role of word formation in the enrichment of the Russian vocabulary. This book is an edited version of Part 1 of *Очерки по русскому словообразованию и лексикологии*, first published by Uchpedgiz, Moscow, 1959. Part 2 was published in 1969 in the same series, under the title: *Russian lexicology*. See 746.

748 **Steinfeldt, E.**
Russian word count: 2,500 words most commonly used in modern literary Russian: guide for teachers of Russian. Translated by V. Korotky. Moscow, Progress Publishers, [1965]. 228 pp. tables.
Based on samples drawn almost exclusively from reading matter: articles from periodicals, fiction and radio broadcasts for young people; fiction in Soviet magazines and plays for adults. The first three chapters discuss Russian word frequency dictionaries and the sources and structure of the present one. Words selected as the most commonly used in modern literary Russian are arranged in three lists: general word frequency list, lists arranged according to parts of speech, and alphabetical word frequency list. There is also a list of verbs indicating which grammatical forms are most frequently used.

749 **Townsend, Charles E.**
Russian word-formation. London and New York, McGraw-Hill, 1968. xviii, 270 pp.
Practical description of Russian derivational morphology, divided into four sections. The first provides a working theory of Russian word structure. The other three deal with verbs, in which conjugation is presented as a one-stem system, nouns and adjectives. The book contains a combined subject index and glossary and three appendices. These contain a list of roots, an index of nominal suffixes and an index of adjectival suffixes.

750 **Universitet Druzhby Narodov Imeni Patrisa Lumumby. Kafedra Russkogo Yazyka**
2380 наиболее употребительных слов русской разговорной речи. Moscow, The University, 1968. 78 pp.

Word-frequency count of conversational Russian based on an analysis of a corpus of 400,000 words. The corpus is comprised of conversations recorded on tape between 1964 and 1966 in a variety of situations, conversations taken down in shorthand, where tape-recording was not feasible, and material supplied by the Institute of Russian Language of the Academy of Sciences. The 2,380 most frequent words appear in an alphabetical list and in a list arranged according to their number of occurrences. Introduction gives information about numbers, education and sex of informants, and a list of topics.

751 **Vogt, Helger Oleg**
Grund- und Aufbauwortschatz Russisch. Stuttgart, Ernst Klett, 1967. 329 pp. diagr. bibliog.
4,600 words selected on the basis of the results of word frequency investigations. A list of about 100 structure-words is followed by 2,000 items comprising the 'basic' vocabulary, given in alphabetical order. The next 2,500 most frequent items are listed in seventy-three sections, thematically grouped under thirteen general headings, e.g. sport, travel. Meanings are given in German. Other lists include numerals, personal pronouns and verbs in both aspects.

VARIETIES OF RUSSIAN

752 **Avanesov, R. I., and V. G. Orlova, eds.**
Русская диалектология. Moscow, Nauka, 2nd edn. 1965. 304 pp. tables, diagrs. maps.
The first part defines the place of dialectology within Russian language studies, and deals with the structure of Russian dialect language in four chapters, i.e. under 'phonetics', 'morphology', 'syntax' and 'lexis'. The second part is concerned with the distribution of dialects within the European part of the Soviet Union.

753 **Filin, F. P., ed.**
Лексика русских народных говоров. Moscow and Leningrad, Nauka, 1966. 223 pp.
Collection of twelve essays on the vocabulary of Russian dialects, most of which are based on work done on the *Словарь русских народных говоров.* One deals with sources of dialect vocabulary, another attempts a definition of dialect vocabulary and the vocabulary of slang. Five others deal with word formation in dialects of Russian. Others are concerned with the history of dialect words etc. The volume contains a review of three recent dictionaries.

CONTRASTIVE ANALYSIS

Hammer, John H., and Frank A. Rice
See 157.

TEACHING METHODS

754 **Barkhudarov, S. G., ed.**
Методика преподавания русского языка иностранцам. Moscow, Izdatel'stvo Moskovskogo Universiteta, 1967. 302 pp.
Presented in three sections: the linguistic basis of methodology, procedures to be employed, and the teaching of Russian in specific registers. A full description of Russian is not attempted but the implications of its morphological and syntactical features for methodology are considered. Central to the second chapter is oral mastery of the language, and separate sections deal with teaching at an elementary level and audio-visual aids. The third section considers the teaching of scientific Russian to foreigners in view of its particular lexical and structural features.

755 **Bazilevich, L. I., and others, eds.**
Русский язык для студентов-иностранцев. Сборник методических статей, 9. Moscow, Vysshaya Shkola, 1969. 272 pp. tables.
This collection of articles on methodology is divided into two parts. The first (thirteen articles) gives a brief history of Soviet methodology, a brief account of the activities of Soviet organisations concerned with the methodology of teaching Russian as a foreign language, the international seminars for teachers etc. The second part contains twelve articles concerned mainly with the teaching of pronunciation and the teaching of Russian in special registers.

756 **Bryzgunova, E. A., ed.**
Работа по фонетике и интонации при обучении русскому языку иностранцев: сборник методичечких статей... Moscow, Izdatel'stvo Moskovskogo Universiteta, 1967. 90 pp.
Collection of eleven articles on those aspects of the phonetics and intonation of modern Russian most closely connected with the practical command of the spoken language and aural comprehension. The articles on intonation are based on five intonation patterns described in the first article.

757 **Great Britain. Ministry of Education and Scottish Education Department**
The teaching of Russian [the Annan report]. London, HMSO, 1962. v, 55 pp.
Gives a comprehensive account of the state of the teaching of Russian in

Britain in 1961. Deals with the need to expand Russian studies and the feasibility of that expansion, and includes a chapter on methods of teaching, examinations and aids to study.

Incorporated Association of Assistant Masters in Secondary Schools
See 223.

758 **Turkevich, Ludmilla B., ed.**
Methods of teaching Russian. Princeton, New Jersey, Van Nostrand, 1967. viii, 216 pp. illus. bibliog.
A collection of twelve articles written by ten different authors. First two articles deal with the need for more Russian teaching in American schools and its introduction into the curriculum; remainder mainly with classroom techniques. All stages of teaching Russian, from the first lesson and teaching handwriting to teaching language through literature, are dealt with. Contains articles on programmed instruction and its application to the teaching of Russian, and on automated techniques and teaching Russian by television.

Turner, John D., ed.
See 318.

DICTIONARIES

Only the most important dictionaries which might find a place in the personal libraries of teachers of Russian are included. Technical dictionaries and those of predominantly etymological or historical content are excluded. A wider selection of Russian dictionaries may be found in the 2nd edition of A. J. Walford's *A guide to foreign language grammars and dictionaries*, published by the Library Association, London, in 1967.

Avanesov, R. I., and S. I. Ozhegov, eds.
See 726.

Barkhudarov, S. G., and others, eds.
See 727.

Benson, Morton, ed.
See 728.

759 **Bielfeldt, Hans Holm, ed.**
Rückläufiges Wörterbuch der russischen Sprache der Gegenwart. Veröffentlichungen des Instituts für Slawistik der Deutschen Akademie der Wissen

schaften zu Berlin, Sonderreihe Wörterbücher. Berlin, Akademie-Verlag, 2nd edn. 1965. iv, 392 pp. First pubd. 1958.
A list of approximately 80,000 words (no meanings or grammatical explanations are offered though words of more than one syllable are stressed), arranged in reverse alphabetical order, i.e. the first word listed is *a*, followed by *ба*, the last is *малолетняя*. Its main use for teachers is to provide a source of Russian words with the same final element.

Bylinskiĭ, K. I., and N. N. Nikol'skiĭ
See 731.

760 **Koritskiĭ, B. F., ed.**
Словарь сокращений русского языка. Moscow, Gosudarstvennoe Izdatel'stvo Inostrannykh i Natsional'nykh Slovareĭ, 1963. 486 pp.
Contains approximately 12,500 abbreviations, which are in wide and current usage. The dictionary has been compiled from abbreviations found in current periodicals and other publications. After each entry a guide to its pronunciation is given and the full word from which the abbreviation has been formed. Where an abbreviation has a gender of its own, this is indicated.

761 **Müller, V. K., ed.**
English–Russian dictionary. Moscow, Sovetskaya Entsiklopediya, 13th edn. 1967. 912 pp. First pubd. 1945.
Considerably expanded since it was first published, contains approximately 70,000 words and fixed collocations. Under each entry the various meanings of each English word are listed separately, and relevant English idioms and sayings follow; these are translated into Russian. Includes lists of English names which are transliterated, geographical names, and the most common English abbreviations for which English meanings are given, followed by a translation into Russian.

762 **Ozhegov, S. I.**
Словарь русского языка. Moscow, Sovetskaya Entsiklopediya, 7th edn. 1968. 900 pp. First pubd. 1949.
Monolingual dictionary containing approximately 53,000 entries with examples of usage. Concise notes on Russian grammar are given in the guide to the use of the dictionary.

763 **Smirnitskiĭ, A. I., and others, eds.**
Russian–English dictionary. Moscow, Sovetskaya Entsiklopediya, 8th edn. 1969. 766 pp. First pubd. 1948.
Approximately 50,000 entries. The various meanings of each Russian word are listed separately. Examples of usage and fixed collocations are given, with translations. Includes brief series of notes on some aspects of Russian grammar, and a list of geographical names.

764 **Ushakov, D. N., ed.**
Толковый словарь русского языка. Moscow, Sovetskaya Entsiklopediya, 4 vols. 1935–40.
Monolingual dictionary containing more than 85,000 entries drawn from spoken Russian and the written literary language. Nuances of meaning, stylistic notes and examples are given systematically. The notes on the use of the dictionary contain some information on Russian grammar.

BIBLIOGRAPHIES

Goodger, B. C.
See 332.

Hammer, John H., and Frank A. Rice
See 157.

765 **Horecky, Paul L., ed.**
Basic Russian publications: an annotated bibliography on Russia and the Soviet Union. Chicago, University of Chicago Press, 1962. xxvi, 313 pp.
1,396 entries including general reference aids, bibliographies, and other books under the following general headings: the land, the people, history, the state, economic and social structure, society and intellectual life. The section on language contains seventy-two entries. There is also an author, title and subject index in one alphabetical sequence.

766 **Neiswender, Rosemary**
Guide to Russian reference and language aids. SLA Bibliography, 4. New York, Special Libraries Association, 1962. iv, 92 pp.
Working guide to Russian linguistic and reference works. Only the sections on textbooks, dictionaries and teaching aids aim at being comprehensive, though the areas of Russian science and technology have been stressed. Very little attempt made to cover the social sciences or the humanities, and entries have in the main been confined to post World War II publications. Some items included are now out of print. Appendices deal with Russian

transliteration systems, retail sources for Russian publications, abbreviations of Soviet publishing houses and Russian bibliographic and book-trade terminology.

Robinson, Janet O.
See 214.

767 **SSSR. Akademiya Nauk. Institut Russkogo Yazyka**
Словари, изданные в СССР: библиографический указатель, 1918–62. Edited by V. V. Veselitskiĭ and N. P. Debets. Moscow, Nauka, 1966. 232 pp.
Very comprehensive bibliography of dictionaries published between 1918 and 1962 in the USSR. Dialect, etymological, orthographical, phraseological, bilingual, terminological and defining dictionaries are included. In languages where there is a long lexicographical tradition, only those with more than 7,000 entries are listed. Those dealing with Russian appear as a subsection of 'Slavonic Languages'. As the bibliography as a whole is arranged according to language families, the section dealing with Slavonic languages appears under Indo-European languages. Within sections, dictionaries are listed in order of date of publication. There are indexes of compilers' names and languages.

768 **Unbegaun, B. O., and J. S. G. Simmons**
A bibliographical guide to the Russian language. Oxford, Clarendon Press, 1953. xi, 174 pp.
Lists publications which deal with the Russian language and its history. Systematically arranged with full cross-references, annotations and occasional hints on the best procedure for investigating specific problems. Selective in that only works of genuine scholarship are included. Deals in ten chapters with books on the history of Russian philology, the history of the Russian language, modern literary Russian, etc.

SECTION VIII

Spanish

GENERAL

769 Alonso, Amado

Estudios lingüísticos: Temas españoles. Biblioteca Románica Hispánica. II. Estudios y Ensayos. Madrid, Gredos, 3rd edn. 1967. 286 pp.

Contains studies on geographical linguistics, the interaction of Spanish and Arabic, the article, the diminutives, verbs of movement and phonemics.

770 Alonso, Martín

Ciencia del lenguaje y arto del estilo. Madrid, Aguilar, 5th edn. 1960. xxxi, 1619 pp. illus. First pubd. 1947.

A manual which covers a vast field of style and language. Chapters on philology, methodology, genesis and evolution of Spanish; phraseology; vocabulary; semantics; etymology; neologisms; aesthetics; textual criticism. Gives practical exercises in editing reviews of the best prose-writers and poets, an ideological dictionary and sections on idioms, linguistic and literary terms, foreign phrases, abbreviations.

771 Alvar, M., and others, eds.

Enciclopedia lingüística hispánica. Madrid, Consejo Superior de Investigaciones Científicas, 1960– .

Major reference work on all aspects of the Spanish language. The first two volumes of a projected six-volume collection include sections on Castilian, Catalan and Portuguese philology.

772 Congreso de Instituciones Hispánicas 1963

Presente y futuro de la lengua española: actas de la Asamblea de Filología del I Congreso de Instituciones Hispánicas. 2 vols. Publicación de la Oficina Internacional de Información y Observación del Español, Ofines. Madrid, Cultura Hispánica, 1964. maps.

Collection of papers embracing world-wide descriptions of the language, including toponymy, literary Spanish and influence between Spanish and other languages; unity of certain aspects of the language; methods of teaching it.

Sebeok, Thomas A., and others, eds.

See 140.

773 Seco, Manuel

Diccionario de dudas y dificultades de la lengua española. Madrid, Aguilar, 4th edn. 1966. xx, 516 pp. illus. bibliog. First pubd. 1961.

A reference work, alphabetically arranged, which gives explanation and examples of usage for those words which can offer difficulties. Encompasses syntax, phonology, the use of tenses, American-Spanish, and other aspects of language. Includes a synopsis of Spanish grammar, an alphabetical list of all words whose spelling can prove difficult, a list of abbreviations, a section on matters related to punctuation and Royal Academy rulings on prosody and spelling.

HISTORY

Alonso, Amado
See 791.

774 **Alonso, Martín**
Evolución sintáctica del español: sintaxis histórica del español desde el iberorromano hasta nuestros días. Madrid, Aguilar, 2nd edn. 1964. xxiv, 495 pp. maps, illus.
A full historical account of the development of Spanish style with analysis of many examples from literature and everyday speech.

775 **Entwistle, William J.**
The Spanish language together with Portuguese, Catalan and Basque. The Great Languages. London, Faber & Faber, 2nd edn. 1962. xiii, 367 pp. maps. First pubd. 1936.
Traces the development of Spanish from pre-Roman times and gives an abundance of examples to illustrate the phonetic and morphological changes that have taken place. Contains chapters on the Latin of Spain, Catalan, the rise of Castilian amidst the various dialects, standard Spanish, American Spanish, and Portuguese. Includes comparative tables of phonetics and phonology.

776 **Lapesa, Rafael**
Historia de la lengua española. Madrid, Escelicer, 6th edn. 1965. 421 pp. maps. First pubd. 1942.
Covers the evolution of forms from pre-Roman times. The influences of other languages, dialect forms within Spain and American-Spanish receive treatment. Maps are included to illustrate phonetic changes in relation to regional location. Provides a thorough scientific study of philological change and describes broad movements of language development always with reference to concrete examples.

777 **Menéndez Pidal, Ramón**
Manual de gramática histórica española. Madrid, Espasa-Calpe, 12th edn. 1966. vii, 367 pp. First pubd. 1904.
A standard textbook of Spanish philology. Traces the sources from which the language has grown and provides many examples to show the evolution of words. Vowels and consonants are studied in detail and their relation to the original Latin forms is described. The work is divided into sections dealing with nouns, adjectives, pronouns, verbs and other parts of speech.

Posner, Rebecca
See 161.

778 **Spaulding, Robert K.**
How Spanish grew. Berkeley and Los Angeles, University of California Press, 1967. xvii, 259 pp. bibliogs. First pubd. 1943.
A philological study, illustrated by examples of phonetic and morphological changes. Covers pre-Roman, Roman, Germanic and Arabic influence, the rise and evolution of Castilian, the period of Spanish ascendancy from 1500 to 1700, the period of French prestige from 1700 to 1808, and the modern period, in which there is included a study of the various dialects.

GRAMMAR AND STRUCTURE

779 **Bello, Andrés, and Rufino José Cuervo**
Gramática de la lengua castellana. Buenos Aires, Editorial Sopena Argentina, 6th edn. 1960. 541 pp.
An examination and discussion of grammar and usage particularly useful for its thorough treatment of nice distinctions. Detailed comment is given for each point and reference is made to the writings of poets, dramatists, and novelists. Attention is also paid to differences in American-Spanish speech.

780 **Bull, William E.**
Time, tense and the verb: a study in theoretical and applied linguistics, with particular attention to Spanish. University of California Publications in Linguistics, 19. Berkeley and Los Angeles, University of California Press, 1963. viii, 120 pp. First pubd. 1960.
A very detailed and specialised analysis. Much of the theoretical discussion of time concepts is philosophical in character but examples of everyday language are given to justify the principles advocated. Terminology is

defined and tenses and adverbial phrases of time are analysed in detail at a conceptual rather than a formal level.

781 **Gili y Gaya, Samuel**
Curso superior de sintaxis española. Barcelona, Bibliograf, 9th edn. 1964. 347 pp. First pubd. 1943.
Divided into three parts: 1. simple sentence; 2. function of parts of the sentence; 3. compound sentence. A descriptive treatise on structure for pedagogical purposes, which takes into account diachronic as well as synchronic aspects, while psychological factors are given some attention.

782 **Goldin, Mark G.**
Spanish case and function. Washington, D.C., Georgetown University Press, 1968. iv, 83 pp. diagrs. bibliog.
A transformational study of the relationship between meaning and the notions of subject, object and the pronoun system.

783 **Harmer, L. C., and F. J. Norton**
A manual of modern Spanish. London, University Tutorial Press, 2nd edn. 1957. xii, 623 pp. First pubd. 1935.
A comprehensive grammar of modern Spanish for the English learner. Points are illustrated by ample examples from specified literary sources. There are forty-four lessons, each of which has two-way translation exercises with the Spanish sentences taken from various authors. Full treatment of verb conjugations, vocabularies in English and Spanish, and an index, are provided.

784 **Keniston, Hayward**
Spanish syntax list. Publications of the Committee on Modern Languages. New York, Holt, 1937. xi, 278 pp. bibliog.
A statistical study of grammatical usage based on extensive research. Gives an account of the commonest syntactic phenomena, illustrating the function of each construction by a sentence from a specified source. Figures indicating range and frequency are given for each construction and the sections of the study are grouped according to parts of speech. An introduction describes the methods used in the compilation of the list.

785 **Lloyd, Paul M.**
Verb-complement compounds in Spanish. Beihefte zur Zeitschrift für Romanische Philologie, 116. Tübingen, Max Niemeyer, 1968. v, 100 pp. bibliog.

A study of verb-complement nouns demonstrating their contribution to the creative power of the language.

786 **Lorenzo, Emilio**
El español de hoy, lengua en ebullición. Biblioteca Románica Hispánica. II. Estudios y Ensayos. Madrid, Gredos, 1966. 179 pp.
Eight studies of various aspects of contemporary spoken Spanish with special emphasis on the verb and a chapter on the influence of other languages.

787 **Pottier, Bernard**
Introduction à l'étude de la morphosyntaxe espagnole. Paris, Ediciones Hispano Américanas, 4th edn. 1966. 123 pp. First pubd. 1959.
A synchronic and diachronic structural study of modern Spanish.

788 **Ramsey, Marathon Montrose, and Robert K. Spaulding**
A textbook of modern Spanish as now written and spoken in Castile and the Spanish American Republics. New York, Holt, Rinehart & Winston, 1966. xix, 692, xvii pp. First pubd. 1894.
A standard reference work for English students and teachers which provides thorough treatment of all aspects of grammar. The first part covers orthography and pronunciation and the second, longer part covers forms and uses. Each point has examples and the English translation is given. Includes a careful study of agreement, word formation and word order. Appendices on forms of address, social and epistolary usage and geographical adjectives.

789 **Saporta, Sol, and others**
Structural studies on Spanish themes. Urbana, University of Illinois Press, 1959. 414 pp.
Studies of morpheme alternants, taxemic redundancy, function classes and a structural analysis of the epic style of the *Cid.* Linguistic descriptions are treated from a structuralist point of view.

Stockwell, Robert P., and others
See 820.

PHONOLOGY AND ORTHOGRAPHY

790 **Alarcos Llorach, Emilio**
Fonología española. Biblioteca Románica Hispánica. Madrid, Gredos, 4th edn. 1965. 290 pp. bibliog.

The subject is divided into general phonology and the phonology of Spanish. Part 1 is further subdivided to distinguish between synchronic and diachronic phonology. Part 2 reflects a similar subdivision with a detailed study of Spanish phonemes.

791 **Alonso, Amado**
De la pronunciación medieval a la moderna en español. Ultimado y dispuesto para la imprenta por Rafael Lapesa. 2 vols. Biblioteca Románica Hispánica. I. Tratados y Monografías, 5. Madrid, Gredos. Vol. 1, 2nd edn. 1967; first pubd. 1955. vol. 2, 1969.
A highly detailed study of the history of Spanish pronunciation with special reference to the problem of *ç* and *z*.

Cárdenas, Daniel N.
See 818.

Delattre, Pierre
See 156.

792 **Harris, James W.**
Spanish phonology. Research Monograph, 54. Cambridge, Massachusetts, M.I.T. Press, 1969. xv, 218 pp. bibliog.
Presents a theory of the facts of Spanish phonology in the form of a generative grammar against the background of the phonological theories of Halle and Chomsky.

Kadler, Eric H.
See 225.

793 **Malmberg, Bertil**
Estudios de fonética hispánica. Traducción de Edgardo R. Palavecino. Collectanea Phonetica, 1. Madrid, Consejo Superior de Investigaciones Cientificas. Instituto 'Miguel de Cervantes', 1965. xv, 154 pp. diagrs. bibliog.
A collection of papers, many published between 1948 and 1964. First four deal with Spanish phonetics and phonology from a diachronic and synchronic viewpoint. Four more deal with American Spanish and with syllabic structural developments from Latin.

794 **Navarro Tomás, T.**
Estudios de fonología española. New York, Las Americas Publishing Co., 1966. 217 pp. First pubd. 1946.
Phonemes, syllables, intensity, intonation and accent are studied, with frequency tables. The second part of the book applies this knowledge to particular examples in literature.

795 **Navarro Tomás, T.**
Manual de entonación española. Biblioteca del Estudiante. New York, Hispanic Institute, 1944. 306 pp. diagrs.
A study of intonation in the speech of educated Spaniards, including regional and American-Spanish patterns. Rhythms that characterise declarative, interrogative, imperative and emotive utterances are examined. Includes exercises for practice.

796 **Navarro Tomás, T.**
Manual de pronunciación española. Publicaciones de la Revista de Filología Española, 3. Madrid, Consejo Superior de Investigaciones Científicas. Instituto 'Miguel de Cervantes', 13th edn. 1967. 326 pp. illus. tables, bibliogs.
A description of Spanish pronunciation intended for teaching purposes. Covers prosodic features of stress, intonation, and duration as well as phonetic aspects. Includes diagrams to illustrate articulatory positions and intonation patterns. Numerous passages are given for intonation practice and exercises for all the vowels and consonants. Includes passages with phonetic transcription.

797 **Quilis, Antonio, and Joseph A. Fernández**
Curso de fonética y fonología españolas: para estudiantes angloamericanos. Collectanea Phonetica, 2. Madrid, Consejo Superior de Investigaciones Científicas. Instituto 'Miguel de Cervantes', 2nd edn. 1966. xxxi, 203 pp. tables, illus. First pubd. 1964.
A detailed study with many exercises for practice in transcription and pronunciation. Includes chapters on the syllable, accentuation and intonation and is illustrated with clear diagrams.

Ramsey, Marathon Montrose, and Robert K. Spaulding
See 788.

798 **Saporta, Sol, and Heles Contreras**
A phonological grammar of Spanish. Seattle, University of Washington Press, 1962. iii, 43 pp.
Discusses finite-state, phrase structure and transformational models of phonological descriptions of Spanish. Phonemic contrast and distribution are illustrated schematically and rules for generating phonologically grammatical sequences are set out. A specialist work for those acquainted with basic procedures of linguistic analysis.

Stockwell, Robert P., and J. Donald Bowen
See 819.

VOCABULARY AND USAGE

799 **Beinhauer, Werner**
El español coloquial. Biblioteca Románica Hispánica. II. Estudios y Ensayos. Madrid, Gredos, 1963. 445 pp. bibliog.
Translated from the second edition of *Spanische Umgangsprache* (Bonn, Dümmlers, 1958) by Fernando Huarte Morton. A detailed study divided into chapters from a psychological viewpoint. Contains chapters on ways of introducing and closing conversation, and expressions of politeness and the whole range of emotions.

Eaton, Helen S.
See 70.

800 **Folley, T.**
A dictionary of Spanish idioms and colloquialisms. London and Glasgow, Blackie, 1965. 68 pp.
Gives a representative selection of the most current idioms and colloquialisms in modern Spanish, as found in everyday speech and the works of contemporary writers. Often more than one equivalent is given in English to make the meaning clear.

801 **Gerrard, A. Bryson, and José de Heras Heras**
Beyond the dictionary in Spanish: a handbook of colloquial usage. London, Cassell, 4th edn. 1968. 160 pp. First pubd. 1953.
A Spanish–English dictionary which comments upon the use and meaning of words, and also contains vocabularies on specialised subjects. There is an English index referring to the Spanish key words in the main section.

802 **Gooch, Anthony**
Diminutive, augmentative and pejorative suffixes in modern Spanish: a guide to their use and meaning. Pergamon Oxford Spanish Series. Oxford, Pergamon Press, 1967. xii, 304 pp. bibliogs.
A systematic presentation of suffixes and their meanings, with numerous examples. Separate chapters are devoted to each of the three main types of suffix, and within these chapters there are subgroupings according to the base word of which they are a part.

803 **Heupel, Carl**
Grund- und Aufbauwortschatz: Spanisch. Stuttgart, Klett, 1966. 188 pp. diagr.
Some 4,600 words selected on the basis of the results of word frequency studies. A list of 116 structure words is followed by 2,000 items comprising the basic vocabulary, in alphabetical order. The next 2,500 most frequent items are listed in seventy-three sections, thematically grouped under general headings, e.g. sport, travel. Meanings are given in German.

804 **Instituto de Lengua y Cultura Españolas para Extranjeros**
Textos para el estudio del español coloquial. Introducción y selección de F. Gonzales Ollé. Pamplona, Ediciones Universidad de Navarra, 1967. 117 pp.
A collection of extracts from modern plays and novels selected to demonstrate colloquial usage and intended to aid the teaching of Spanish conversation to non-Spanish speakers.

805 **Juilland, Alphonse, and E. Chang-Rodriguez**
Frequency dictionary of Spanish words. The Romance Languages and Their Structure. First Series, 51. The Hague and London, Mouton, 1964. lxxviii, 500 pp. diagrs.
An investigation of word frequency and dispersion prepared with the help of computers. The counts are based on the vocabulary of plays, novels, essays, periodicals, and technical literature. In the first part words and their variants are listed in alphabetical order. In the second part words are listed in three parallel columns, in decreasing order of their coefficients of usage, frequency and dispersion. The three lists are divided into ten groups of 500 words in rank order. An extensive introduction discusses the sample in terms of the lexical worlds of the different types of literature, how the sample is processed and the results obtained.

806 **Keniston, Hayward**
A standard list of Spanish words and idioms. Boston, Heath, 1941. xiv, 108 pp. bibliog.
Lists of the most common 2,000 words, divided into four groups of 500; a thorough revision of the earlier *Basic list of Spanish words and idioms* (based mainly on three major word-counts of the 1920s). Also over 1,000 derivatives and 575 idioms are listed. The basic 2,000 words are given in alphabetical order with their English meaning and sometimes their Latin source and the group to which they belong. As a guide for students, teachers, and course-makers, the four groups are printed again separately without

definitions. Following these are studies on word-formation (noun endings, adjectives, diminutives, augmentatives, prefixes, verb endings), cognates (including deceptive cognates), and sound changes from the original Latin. Includes a bibliography of word-count studies in the main European languages.

807 **Lyon, J. E.**
Pitfalls of Spanish vocabulary. London, Harrap, 1961. 120 pp.
A glossary, listing in alphabetical order Spanish words which vary in usage from their apparent English equivalents. Each word's meaning is explained, precise translations are offered, and sentences illustrating uses are given. The Spanish meaning of the English word with which it can mistakenly be equated is stated with authentic examples. Includes an index to English words and a list of authors quoted in the text.

808 **Nuffield Foundation. Foreign Languages Teaching Materials Project**
Child language survey: the language of twelve-year-old Spanish children. Transcript No. 1. Recorded by Matilde Lazcano, transcribed by Rafael Sala. Reports and Occasional Papers, 36. York, The Foundation, 1969. vi, 133 pp.
Conversations between boys and girls from two schools in Madrid. A source for the study of structures and children's interests.

809 **Rodríguez Bou, Ismael, and others**
Recuento de vocabulario español. Vols. 1 and 2 (in 2 parts). Trabajos de Investigación Auspiciados por el Consejo Superior de Enseñanza. Publicaciones Pedagógicas, Serie 2, Núm. 12. Puerto Rico, Universidad de Puerto Rico, 1952.
Based on a word-frequency count of more than seven million words, taking into account the vocabulary of press and radio, language of children, literary and technical material. Designed to serve as a basis for the preparation of Spanish teaching materials and the result of extensive research. Introduction gives an account of previous work in this field.

810 **Smith, C. Colin**
An English–Spanish word list. London, Harrap, 1964. 109 pp.
Covers a basic working vocabulary divided into forty sections (animal kingdom, food, the arts, sports, transport, etc.) clearly headed and indexed. Words are set out in groups of ten for the easier organisation of teaching and learning. The gender of nouns is given and indicated where it differs from the general rule. Includes sections on idioms and verb constructions.

811 **Toscano, Humberto**
Hablemos del lenguaje. Palabras liminares por Fernando Villaverde. Compilación, introducción, ordenamiento e índices de César García-Pons. New York, Powers, 1965. xxi, 457 pp. illus.
A collection of linguistic comments on some 2,000 words, originally published in the review 'Hablemos'. The first three chapters cover the origins, development and contemporary use of the language, the fourth deals with the etymology of names. There is some speculation on the future of the language, and a useful index.

VARIETIES OF SPANISH

812 **Alcalá Venceslada, Antonio**
Vocabulario andaluz. Madrid, Real Academia Española, 1951. 676 pp.
An extensive dictionary of those words characteristic of the regions of Andalusia. A definition in Spanish, for each entry, is followed by one or more sentences showing how the word is used and in what context. Single words with several meanings are listed as separate entries.

Alonso, Amado
See 791.

Alvar, M., and others, eds.
See 771.

Congreso de Instituciones Hispánicas 1963
See 772.

Entwistle, William J.
See 775.

813 **García de Diego, Vicente**
Manual de dialectología española. Madrid, Cultura Hispánica, 2nd edn. 1959. 374 pp. bibliogs. First pubd. 1946.
Asturian, Leonese, Basque, Aragonese, Navarrese are examined from a philological viewpoint which stresses the historical development of forms, their geographical distribution and their evolution from Vulgar Latin. Minor as well as major dialects are dealt with. Includes a bibliography for each dialect. Phonetic and morphological features are taken into account.

814 **Kany, Charles E.**
American-Spanish euphemisms. Berkeley and Los Angeles, University of California Press, 1960. xi, 249 pp. illus. bibliog.
A useful introductory study, classified under the headings of superstition, delicacy, mental and moral defects, financial status, offences and consequences, decency (the body); decency (love). There are appendices on local taboos and gestures, and indexes of subject and word.

815 **Kany, Charles E.**
American-Spanish semantics. Berkeley and Los Angeles, University of California Press, 1960. viii, 352 pp. bibliog.
A large collection of material from South America arranged according to a new classification which is based on those of Ullmann and Stern, and which concentrates upon the different types of metaphorical change using standard peninsular speech as a norm.

816 **Kany, Charles E.**
American-Spanish syntax. Chicago, University of Chicago Press, 2nd edn. 1951. xii, 467 pp. bibliog.
A compendium of the chief syntactical peculiarities diverging from standard Spanish usage. Geographical distribution is indicated where known. The approach is basically through the parts of speech.

Lapesa, Rafael
See 776.

Malmberg, Bertil
See 793.

Santamaría, Francisco J.
See 831, 832.

817 **Zamora Vicente, Alonso**
Dialectología española. Biblioteca Románica Hispánica. III. Manuales. Madrid, Gredos, 2nd edn. 1967. 587 pp. maps, bibliog.
Contains chapters on four main dialects and four minor ones; on American and Philipino Spanish and on particular accents. Has useful maps, three specialised indexes and one general index.

CONTRASTIVE ANALYSIS

Alvar, M., and others, eds.
See 771.

818 **Cárdenas, Daniel N.**
Introducción a una comparación fonológica del español y del inglés. Washington, Center for Applied Linguistics of the Modern Language Association of America, 1960. x, 68 pp. illus.
A systematic study of the problems of pronunciation which confront the student of Spanish, based on a contrastive analysis of English and Spanish speech. Phonemic differences are emphasised, and the pedagogical implications are discussed in detail. Covers syllabic patterns, stress, *sinalefa* and intonation as well as main phonetic aspects. Includes glossary of special terms which occur in the text.

Delattre, Pierre
See 545.

Hammer, John H., and Frank A. Rice
See 157.

819 **Stockwell, Robert P., and J. Donald Bowen**
The sounds of English and Spanish. Contrastive Structure Series. Chicago and London, University of Chicago Press, 1965. xi, 168 pp.
Very useful for pedagogical implications which are fully discussed in the appendix. The structure of the sound systems is described with explanations of the main linguistic terms involved in this analysis. A hierarchy of difficulty for the English-speaking learner is drawn up based on points of interference and phonemic differences. Stress, rhythm and intonation are examined. See also 820.

820 **Stockwell, Robert P., and others**
The grammatical structures of English and Spanish. Contrastive Structure Series. Chicago and London, University of Chicago Press, 1965. ix, 328 pp. diagrs. bibliog.
A theoretical approach mainly based on transformational-generative grammar. Emphasises interference expected from English structures when the student learns Spanish. Pedagogical implications are stressed and a separate appendix deals specifically with problems of teaching Spanish grammar. See also 819.

TEACHING METHODS

821 **Bull, William E.**
Spanish for teachers: applied linguistics. New York, Ronald Press, 1965. vii, 306 pp. illus.
All aspects of lexis and syntax are studied from the viewpoint of the pedagogical implications of linguistic analysis. Review questions provided at the end of each chapter.

Donoghue, Mildred R.
See 220.

822 **Feldman, David M., and Walter D. Kline**
Spanish: contemporary methodology. A Blaisdell Book in the Modern Languages. Waltham, Massachusetts, and London, Blaisdell, 1969. ix, 191 pp. tables, diagrs. bibliogs.
A comprehensive coverage of all aspects of teaching Spanish. Contains chapters on linguistics, pronunciation, syntactic drills, the laboratory, reading and writing, testing and evaluation, adaptation of textbooks, meaning and vocabulary building.

Finocchiaro, Mary
See 289.

823 **Hansen, Carl F.**
A guide for the teaching of Spanish in the elementary schools. Washington, D.C., Government Printing Office, 1954. xviii, 87 pp.
A suggested syllabus of structures, vocabulary, questions, games and songs for the elementary school teacher.

824 **Harter, Hugh A., and Rupert Allen, jr.**
A first Spanish handbook for teachers in elementary schools. Modern Language Handbooks. Pittsburgh, University of Pittsburgh Press, 1961. xi, 129 pp.
Contains clear explanations of the sounds and spellings of Spanish and a programme of material for each of the first thirty lessons of an elementary course, plus material to be taught in additional weeks. Programme designed with aural–oral objectives in mind.

825 **Harter, Hugh A., and Rupert Allen, jr.**
A second Spanish handbook for teachers in elementary schools. Modern Language Handbooks. Pittsburgh, University of Pittsburg Press, 1963. viii, 120 pp.
Continuation of above publication. Emphasis on the teaching of verbs and adjectives. Word-games, riddles and songs are included. Programme of teaching material is divided into twelve units, the last of which contains three short tales.

Huebener, Theodore
See 298.

Incorporated Association of Assistant Masters in Secondary Schools
See 223.

Levenson, Stanley, and William Kendrick, eds.
See 305.

826 **MacRae, Margit W.**
Teaching Spanish in the grades. Boston, Houghton Mifflin, 1957. xi, 408 pp. illus. bibliog.
A comprehensive handbook of techniques and approaches to beginners' Spanish. Includes theory, classroom oral work, games, songs, riddles, dramatisations, records, tapes, television, reading, testing and specimen playlets.

827 **Politzer, Robert L., and Charles N. Staubach**
Teaching Spanish: a linguistic orientation. A Blaisdell Book in the Modern Languages. Waltham, Massachusetts, Blaisdell, 2nd edn. 1965. x, 198 pp. bibliog. First pubd. 1961.
A study of the application of linguistics to the materials and techniques of teaching Spanish. Linguistic justification of pattern practice is given considerable discussion. All the main categories of Spanish phonology and grammar are treated and pedagogical procedures are explained in detail. Bibliography includes modern Spanish courses published in United States. Companion volume to Politzer's *Teaching French* and *Teaching German*, See 590 and 659.

828 **Stanford Center for Research and Development in Teaching**
Practice-centered teacher training: Spanish. A syllabus for the training or retraining of teachers of Spanish, by Robert L. Politzer and Diana E.

Bartley. Technical Report, 2. Stanford, California, Stanford University School of Education, 1967. ix, 238 pp. bibliogs.
A syllabus handbook for the training of teachers, divided into four main sections: applied linguistics, language practice, performance criteria and micro-lesson plans. Notes are given on such topics as testing, setting homework and using laboratories.

Turner, John D., ed.
See 318.

829 **Walsh, Donald Devenish, ed.**
A handbook for teachers of Spanish and Portuguese. Lexington, Massachusetts, Heath, 1969. xi, 338 pp. bibliog.
A practical guide to many aspects of interest to teachers, including chapters on methods, materials, linguistics, teacher training, the laboratory, testing, bilingualism, the history of the teaching of Spanish and Portuguese and background philosophy.

DICTIONARIES

Only dictionaries are included which are not listed in the second edition of A. J. Walford's *A guide to foreign language grammars and dictionaries,* published 1967 by the Library Association, London.

830 **Moliner, María**
Diccionario de uso del español. 2 vols. Biblioteca Románica Hispánica. V. Diccionarios. Madrid, Gredos, 1966.
A valuable monolingual dictionary designed for the use of non-Spanish speaking students of the language. A sign system and layout are used which aid the comprehension of usage range and of the relationships between similar and contrasting words and idioms.

831 **Santamaría, Francisco J.**
Diccionario de Mejicanismos. Mexico, Porrua, 1959. xxiv, 1197 pp. bibliog.
A comprehensive monolingual dictionary giving definitions and quotations to demonstrate meaning. Comparison is made with usage in other American countries.

832 **Santamaría, Francisco J.**
Diccionario general de Americanismos. 3 vols. Mexico, Pedro Robredo, 1942. bibliog.
A monolingual dictionary of words originating in America and accepted

as part of the American Spanish language, and those from the peninsular having special meanings in the American countries. Geographical distribution is given. There is an appendix giving popular forms of flora and fauna.

833 **Toro y Gisbert, Miguel de**
Larousse Universal: diccionario enciclopédico en seis volúmenes; adaptación hispanoamericana del Nouveau Larousse Universel... Paris and Buenos Aires, Larousse, 1968. maps, illus.
A monolingual dictionary of peninsular and American Spanish, attractively illustrated with photographs and colourful maps. Quotations are given for rarer words and idioms. Technical and scientific data have been revised.

BIBLIOGRAPHIES

834 **Arnaud, E., and V. Tusón**
Guide de bibliographie hispanique. Toulouse, Privat-Didier, 1967. 353 pp.
Covers civilisation, language and literature. Part 2, on language, is subdivided into sections on general, specialised, and bilingual dictionaries; modern Spanish, again subdivided into grammar and syntax, phonetics and orthography, semantics and lexicography; varieties of Spanish, subdivided under dialectology, American Spanish and slang; history of the language and style.

Goodger, B. C.
See 332.

Hammer, John H., and Frank A. Rice
See 157.

835 **Nuffield Foundation. Nuffield Foreign Languages Teaching Materials Project**
A bibliography of Spanish teaching materials. Compiled by H. Sharples. Reports and Occasional Papers, 34. Leeds, Nuffield Foundation, 1968. 97 pp.
Covers audio-visual, audio-lingual, textbook courses; drills for laboratory and classroom use; reference grammars; translation; linguistic aspects; readers of various types; periodicals; dictionaries and vocabularies; filmstrips, films, slides, and background materials; books for children. Full details and prices are given.

Robinson, Janet O.
See 214.

836 **Serís, Homero**
Bibliografia de la lingüística española. Publicaciones del Instituto Caro y Cuervo, 19. Bogotá, The Institute, 1964. lix, 981 pp.
A comprehensive review divided into seven main sections: general, romance and Spanish linguistics; peninsular languages and dialects; extra peninsular dialects; American-, African- and Philipino-Spanish; the teaching of Spanish. Each section is further subdivided, becoming progressively more detailed.

837 **Solé, Carlos A.**
Bibliografía sobre el español en América, 1920–1967. Washington, D.C., Georgetown University Press, 1970. vi, 175 pp.
Part 1 contains general works on the language of Spanish America. Part 2 is divided into sections for each country. These are again subdivided into sections on books or articles on phonology, morphology, toponymy etc. A list of abbreviations and an index of authors are provided.

Author Index

References are to entry numbers